CU00922343

HUMAN RESOURCES

HUMAN RESOURCES

Slavery and the Making of Modern Britain
in 39 Institutions, People, Places and Things

RENAY RICHARDSON
with
ARISA LOOMBA

Profile Books

First published in Great Britain in 2025 by
Profile Books Ltd
29 Cloth Fair
London
ECIA 7JQ

www.profilebooks.com

1 3 5 7 9 10 8 6 4 2

Typeset in Sabon by MacGuru Ltd
Printed and bound in Great Britain by
CPI Group (UK) Ltd, Croydon CRO 4YY

The moral right of the author has been asserted.

A CIP catalogue record for this book is available from the British Library.

We make every effort to make sure our products are safe for the purpose
for which they are intended. For more information check our website
or contact Authorised Rep Compliance Ltd., Ground Floor, 71 Lower
Baggot Street, Dublin, D02 P593, Ireland, www.arccompliance.com

ISBN 978 1 80081 622 0
eISBN 978 1 80081 624 4
Audio 978 1 80522 513 3

For Auguste and Sage, the air I breath and the star that guides me.

RR

For my four grandparents, whose strength, inspiration and sacrifices have allowed me to be who I am.

AL

Contents

Contents

Introduction

At some point during our school education, we, like many others, came to the realisation that, in the classroom, all the bad things that had happened in the past – the so-called 'lessons of history' – always seemed to have happened elsewhere. Fascism, eugenics and genocide in Germany; authoritarianism in Russia and China; slavery and racism in America, to name a few. But these things had never been done in, or perpetrated by, Britain. Britain was always a powerhouse of democracy, progress, industry and modernity.

This might help explain our surprising inability as a society to reckon with the legacy of the transatlantic slave trade. We might see it as a definitive historical atrocity, or as a sad fact about a more brutal period in human existence. We might even feel some pride that Britain had a role in bringing about its abolition. But overall, we tend to think of slavery as done with – a grim chapter that no longer needs to be revisited, and that mostly occurred elsewhere. Nothing could be further from the truth.

The transatlantic slave trade began in the sixteenth century and lasted until the early nineteenth century, a period when Europeans forcibly captured people from West and central Africa and transported them to the Americas and the Caribbean to be sold for profit. Throughout history, and even as historians work to uncover their stories, these people's identities have mostly been lost. Often, all we know about them are the unbelievably brutal conditions in which they lived, worked and died. Before they were enslaved, these people were musicians, farmers, religious leaders, teachers, merchants and healers. They were mothers, fathers, brothers and sisters. They were in the middle of these lives when they were taken.

Between 1501 and 1867 it is estimated that nearly 13 million African men, women and children were abducted from their homes and forced into slavery.[1] Regrettably, around 2 million of the kidnapped and enslaved perished during the torturous voyage across the Atlantic, what is now known as the 'Middle Passage'.[2] And while slavery has been a fact of human existence for millennia, Britain's crucial role in the transatlantic slave trade over centuries is something that many of us were barely taught about in schools.

As European countries sought to expand and colonise the world in the early modern period, the transatlantic slave trade expanded with them, as demand rose for labour in the new territories of the Americas. The Portuguese were the first to ship enslaved Africans to work in Europe, from the early 1440s.[3] The Portuguese initially traded with African merchants and kings for enslaved people. Instead of performing the kidnapping themselves, the Portuguese encouraged African leaders to supply enslaved people as a trade commodity, in the same way they would supply goods such as ivory and gold.

In Africa, slavery had existed for centuries before Europeans arrived. Slavery was a recognised institution within African societies, and one could be enslaved for a number of reasons: as punishment for a crime, as a prisoner of war, or simply for being an outsider in the wrong place. There were also occasions where people would sell themselves into slavery or servitude to pay off outstanding debts.[4] Unlike the slave trade that Europe and America engaged in across the Atlantic, this earlier form of slavery was not simply based on race. Anyone could be enslaved, and the practice was very much part of economic structures, with established networks of slave trading that transported people to regions like the Middle East and, in earlier times, the Roman Empire. African societies were initially enticed by trade with Portugal for access to European goods such as guns, alcohol, textiles and metalware. Access to these goods made slave societies rich, enhancing their economies and strengthening their militaries while simultaneously gaining the wealth and prestige that made the trade so attractive to Europe's elite.

In 1492, under the guidance of the Spanish Crown, Christopher Columbus was credited with 'discovering' the Americas.[5] He made his first voyage across the Atlantic and landed in the Bahamas, specifically on an island he named San Salvador on 12 October 1492.[6] This event marked the start of European expansion and the colonisation of the Americas. Initially, European powers, led by Spain and Portugal, sought to enslave local indigenous communities to meet their demand for labour, but the colonisers brought new diseases to which the indigenous people had no natural immunity and, in a matter of decades, a combination of disease, warfare and the migration of indigenous people away from the east coast left the European colonisers in need of a new workforce. As a result, they turned to African slave societies to supply labour for their plantations and mines, believing that darker-skinned people were more suited to working long hours in hotter climates.[7] The first enslaved Africans were brought to the Americas not long after Columbus's voyages, and demand for enslaved workers grew with the advent of plantations and the profitable cash crops they produced.

Britain's involvement began in the 1560s, as English

merchants traded enslaved Africans captured on the west coast of Africa with the Spanish Americas.[8] Sir John Hawkins was an English naval commander and the first known British slave trader, and he played a pivotal role in bringing England into the transatlantic slave trade.[9] Hawkins's voyages to the west coast of Africa to capture and trade enslaved Africans were supported by Queen Elizabeth I, who provided him with ships and guns for his expeditions. Once England began to establish colonies in the New World the country's participation in the slave trade expanded significantly. The first successful English colony was Jamestown, Virginia, in 1607, and the English had settled in St Christopher (now known as St Kitts) by 1624 and in Barbados by 1627.[10]

By the 1700s, after the acts of union that joined England (together with Wales) and Scotland into the Kingdom of Great Britain, the British had established a significant number of colonies in the New World, including an unbroken strip of land along America's east coast that stretched from Maine down to South Carolina. These colonies helped Britain become a major player in the 'Triangular Trade', which saw merchants ship manufactured goods from Britain to the west coast of Africa to be traded for enslaved Africans and African goods, which were then sailed along the Middle Passage to the Americas to be sold to European plantation owners. They returned from the Americas to Britain loaded with commodities produced on the plantations, which were then sold for more manufactured goods – beginning the cycle once more.

Olaudah Equiano, also known as Gustavas Vassa, was born around 1745. He was kidnapped as a child in West Africa and eventually sold into slavery. Equiano was forced to travel the Middle Passage, and his first-person account of it has been integral to our understanding.[11] In 1766, Equiano was able to buy his freedom for between forty and seventy pounds, and he then made his way to Britain where he became a prominent abolitionist.[12] He wrote about his experiences in his auto-biography, *The Interesting Narrative of the life of Olaudah Equiano*, which was published in 1789 and detailed the horror of the Middle Passage:

> I was soon put down under the decks, and there I received such a salutation in my nostrils as I had never experienced in my life; so that, with the loathsomeness of the stench, and crying together, I became so sick and low that I was not able to eat, nor had I the least desire to taste anything. I now wished for the last friend, death, to relieve me.[13]

Many of the enslaved would become sick from the cramped, stuffed conditions of travelling the eighty-odd days in the ship's hold, body to body, stacked as you would an overfilled suitcase, trying to fit as much as possible into the space. It's estimated that between 12 to 15 per cent of enslaved people would die on each leg of the Middle Passage voyage.

The legacy of slavery continues to have a significant impact on the Caribbean. On many of the islands, sugar was the dominant cash crop for centuries, and through its production European owners and traders were able to generate life-changing amounts of wealth. For a time, the Caribbean plantations and colonies were more lucrative than those on mainland America. Slavery, and the diseases that colonisers brought, permanently altered the demographics of the Caribbean, with indigenous people being all but wiped out during the initial waves of exploration. By the eighteenth century, enslaved Africans and their descendants had become the majority population on many Caribbean islands.[14]

The transatlantic slave system also introduced a hierarchical system where those with lighter skin were seen to be in closer proximity to whiteness. Being white put you at the top of the scale – white people were always the owners, overseers and in positions of power over Black people, even if they themselves were poor. Those with lighter skin had more chance of gaining a position within the house, whereas the darker-skinned were virtually guaranteed to be doing the most physically punishing jobs outside. This colourism persists today within the Caribbean, and across the Black diaspora globally.

In Africa, the displacement of nearly 13 million Africans forced into slavery had a devastating effect on the millions more back home.[15] Families were torn apart, and whole societies were disrupted. The demand for enslaved labour, which grew as Europe expanded in the Americas, led many African leaders to engage in wars and raids to capture their own people to sell to European traders. These betrayals weakened political structures and bred distrust among those in power. While there were some African leaders and merchants who profited from the trade, the overall economic impact of slavery on Africa was devastating. As the slave trade became an ever more profitable business, local industries and agriculture suffered and declined. The removal of significant numbers of the young and able also reduced the number of people left behind who could lead and innovate. The story of the slave trade is so vast, and affected so many places and people around the world, that we have to ask: why don't we hear more about it in classrooms and the media?

This book was inspired by a podcast, also called *Human Resources*. We wanted to create an accessible entry point into this history, and we thought the best way would be to show people the links between their own lives and the (not so) distant past. So we took modern (or familiar) people, items and companies and explored their direct – or indirect – links to the slave trade. We soon discovered that, far from being a closed historical chapter, the slave trade continues to shape our lives: from the food we eat to the clothes we wear; from the way our workplaces are structured to the financial products we use; from the statues we put up in our towns and museums to the gyms and holiday resorts of our leisure time, the transatlantic slave trade is completely enmeshed with modern life.

However, it still often seems that the subject of slavery is regarded as a Black issue. You can anticipate the familiar eye roll when Britain's history of slavery is brought up – and those of us who are descendants of slaves are often made to feel as if it's something we should just move on from and forget. It's not a history we tell, or which is taught, in any detail in school; knowledge is either assumed or you must seek it out yourself. The nuances of this history are rarely explored in a way that considers the narratives of the enslaved themselves, as opposed to those who bought, sold and exploited them. It's also a history that is completely divorced from the lives we currently live. This separation comes from the difficulty in acknowledging that many of us now benefit from systems developed within the slave trade – and that slavery still exists today.

Why is this, then? Two things we noticed during our research might provide part of the answer.

There is a lack of Black British historians in the formal academic world, especially among experts in this field, although there have been some positive developments in recent years. Systemic problems in education and academia have a lot to answer for. Black children, particularly those of Caribbean heritage, often find themselves punished and discouraged – and eventually written off – for even minor acts of misconduct such as talking in class, when their white counterparts are given opportunity after opportunity to turn around bad behaviour. An exclusive analysis by the *Guardian* found 'exclusion rates for Black Caribbean students in English schools are up to six times higher than those of their white peers in some local authorities'.[16] A report into the underachievement of Black Caribbean students in English schools found that poor leadership on equality issues, a low expectation of Black students and a lack of a diverse workforce were just some of the factors that contributed to poor outcomes for Black Caribbean students.[17] We can't ignore the fact that Black Caribbean children in the UK may be disconnected from their history, which is why we believe that this book is important as an entry point to the complexities of the past. Systemic biases that see Black students excluded from lessons where they might learn more about their past, and that doubtlessly contribute to fewer of them entering higher education, have certainly played a big part in preventing more of us from knowing about the legacy of slavery. Following the shocking case of 'Child Q', a Black child who was strip-searched by police at a Hackney secondary school in 2020, the Children's Commissioner released a report that found 'Black children are now four times more likely to be strip-searched compared to the national population figures'.[18] Statistics like these recall the stereotypes used to justify slavery and racial inequality, and the fact that, in the eyes of the authorities, Black people are somehow more violent and less trustworthy than the white population.

For Arisa, being a British Indian historian of race, empire and migration is political, and stakes a claim on a subject that people like her were told was not for them. But the aim of this book is not the uncovering of contentious information. Rather, it hopes to enrich the story of Britain, bringing the whole country, including Scotland, Wales and the North of England, as well as Ireland, into the narrative of how the modern UK was made. The podcast gave us a chance to work with scholars who are women, people of colour and early career researchers from Britain and the US, but also, importantly, from Africa

8

and the Caribbean. A focus of the project was also to speak to community workers, activists and local historians, to diversify the types of historical research typically considered reliable and valid. It has been an honour to highlight such new and innovative research and the fresh stories uncovered by all the incredible people involved.

The other thing we noticed was a squeamishness around how organisations describe their links with the trade, if they disclose them at all. An imaginary border seems to have been established, between indirect and direct involvement in slavery. A direct link would mean that a company or organisation actually owned enslaved people, whereas an indirect one would involve more general financial entanglement – trading merchandise that was produced on plantations, for example. This is frustrating, because it suggests that profiting from slavery at one remove is somehow more acceptable than, say, owning a plantation, and because it seems to gloss over one of the most important reasons why Europe grew vastly richer and more developed in the eighteenth and nineteenth centuries – its trade in human beings. In fact, slavery was so fundamental to the way British society then worked that, in many cases, it simply wasn't possible to separate yourself from it. From factory workers in remote Scottish villages to the politicians, scientists and religious leaders of the time, everyone was involved (and often benefited) in one way or another from slavery. An analogy might be the internet today: you might not work for Apple, Meta or Google, but you wouldn't be able to get through your day without using their services, and they make life easier, simpler and cheaper than if you were to cut them out entirely. It's all too easy to ignore the hidden costs of modern life to the environment, to global democracy, or simply to the person who made your smartphone or mined the minerals in your laptop. We have no idea what our luxuries rely on, just as those during slavery pleaded ignorance to the realities of what happened on plantations.

Leaving aside distinctions between direct and indirect involvement, however, we can understand why many people today feel more comfortable speaking about their connections to the trade as long as they are situated firmly in the past. It's a history that no one wants to be associated with – but it's one that we have to reckon with. We need to find a way to deal with the discomfort, so that we can truly understand what these traumatic histories represent, and perhaps then begin to dismantle their toxic legacies in the modern day. If we do not, we continue the harm to those whose lives the slave trade destroyed, and we fail to recognise the true consequences of this history for present-day Britain. We are not here to reprimand or condemn companies for their pasts. We're here to reveal our shared history so that we can properly understand our present and future.

In 1807, the British government passed the Slave Trade Act, which began the process of ending slavery, though the use of indentured Indian and South-east Asian servitude continued long after slavery was eventually abolished. While the 1807 law did have some impact on British merchants' ability to bring newly kidnapped Africans into enslavement, it didn't stop them from being able to trade enslaved people among other European colonies across the Caribbean, and it didn't free enslaved people or forced labourers working on plantations. Emancipation did not come until the passing of the 1833 Slavery Abolition Act, which came into force in 1834. This Act banned slavery across the British Empire and made enslaved people 'free'. The British government was only able to pass the Act by promising to pay a combined sum of £20 million as compensation – not to the enslaved people but to their 'owners' for the loss of income. Abolitionists also had to lobby hard to convince slave owners and politicians that other commercial opportunities existed that could bring in as much money as enslaved labour.

Although many humanitarians and religious groups such as the Quakers were firm campaigners against slavery, the idea that the British state championed abolition as a positive, humanitarian cause obscures the fact that by the 1800s slavery was already losing its lustre for investors and traders.[19] The speed and efficiency of mechanised labour in the Industrial Revolution meant that forced labour was no longer the most efficient way to run plantations. Many plantations had already exhausted their fertile land, which was needed to grow crops like sugar and tobacco.[20] Newer plantations in other European colonies were also beginning to supply UK sugar refineries and tobacco plants, which added to the pressure on existing plantation owners.[21]

Abolition was far from a 'full stop' to slavery, though it is sometimes presented as such. As a crucial part of Britain's economic development, it has left a long shadow across the modern nation. To take just two examples, we still use scientific principles today developed during the era of transatlantic slavery that would have been impossible to establish without the global networks that it maintained. We still use medical procedures based on experiments carried out on non-consenting enslaved women. We cannot, as Professor Kathleen S. Murphy of California's Polytechnic University says, just 'throw it out'.[22] We have to find a way to honour and acknowledge those whose bodies were made use of in order to secure these advancements, and to show how enslaved people contributed in myriad ways to the advances that have made our modern lives possible. Their labour, knowledge and creativity, and their bodies, are all part of the story; a story that has been, until now, mostly hidden or folded into that of the 'great white men' who get most of the credit.

Working on this book, Renay definitely had moments of realisation that have helped her understand why certain things within her Jamaican and Trinidadian heritage were normalised. Why Caribbean people favour European names, for example, which was a way for enslaved people in the Caribbean to distance themselves from their enslaved pasts upon emancipation, and why wedding and funeral traditions in her communities are embedded in European Christian traditions rather than African ones – a legacy of cultural erasure and forced assimilation. There remains, as we will see, a clear divide in Caribbean culture between those who acknowledge African origins and those who historically favoured assimilation into European culture.

This is by no means an exhaustive history of the exploitation of enslaved Africans within the transatlantic slave trade, but it is a starting point, linking modern Britain with its foundational past, and casting light on our society today. We hope that this book helps more people to question what they were taught at school. As we travel through history, we can link the past to contemporary questions around race, equity, climate and justice. We are constantly dealing with the same problems in new forms. Injustices are often not overcome, but simply reshaped into different, if perhaps less overt, injustices, a fact that becomes clearer the deeper you dive into the histories of empire and slavery.

We hope that adults and children alike will read the stories we've put together and will feel a sense of peace, closure and belonging. And we hope, too, that everyone will walk away with a better understanding of how history has empowered some and disempowered others, as well as a new appreciation for the importance of history in understanding ourselves.

1

Accounting

However brutal slavery was, however much enslavers tried to justify their actions through a perceived racial hierarchy, the slave trade was always, at its heart, about profit. It turned individual human beings, each with a unique and personal experience of the world, into entries in a ledger book, examples of profit and loss – literal human resources. As historian Trevor Bernard put it, 'they commodified everything, including people'.[1] He is, of course, talking about how capitalism evolved over time. And while slavery was eventually abolished in the British empire, the conceptual links established between the commodification of humans in this way and in our own society still exist, especially in our businesses and workplaces.

So, is the accountancy we all rely on today rooted in practices that were developed during the shameful era of enslavement? And, if the answer is yes, does this mean that those of us who engage in management and profit-making have inadvertently developed the same viewpoint as a plantation owner? We might instinctively feel that the answer is no, that there's a huge difference between modern working practices – however unpleasant and impersonal – and the violence and exploitation of plantation slavery. But if the value we place on people, and the way we measure their worth, is based on processes developed during the transatlantic slave trade, then the answer may not be that simple.

I spoke to Caitlin Rosenthal, a historian and author of *Accounting for Slavery*, who explained that accounting practices were essential for keeping the entire infrastructure of slavery running smoothly, as well as a way for enslavers to mentally separate themselves from the realities of their work. Accountancy, she said, was what made 'all of these long-distance and financial relationships work.'[2] Reducing the image of enslaved people toiling on a plantation to a profit and loss column, Rosenthal argues, 'let people, from a distance, not have to deal with the moral repugnance of slavery, [while still] funding it and profiting from it at the same time'.[3]

To take Jamaica and Barbados as two examples, many of the plantations there were owned by absentee enslavers, who ran the plantation business from Britain and transferred their Caribbean profits abroad. Overseers on the plantations sent monthly reports to the owners in Britain, tallying the number of slaves they had working, what these individuals generated in labour and ultimately how much profit they were making. If it was a cotton plantation, how many bags of cotton have been packed for export? How many slaves were bought or traded each month? How many were sick, unable to work, or had died or been born? The bureaucracy may have obscured the reality of life on a plantation, but, looking at these inventories today, it's impossible to ignore the barbarity inflicted upon enslaved people, and how their humanity had been stolen from them.

Detailed records were essential for absentee owners. Labour logs were common, detailing the tasks that individuals performed and the amount of goods produced, as well as the health of enslaved people and the total number of workers. An example of this record-keeping can be taken from 'Daily Record of cotton picking' taken from Thomas Affleck's 'Cotton

Plantation record and Account Book'.[4] Thomas Affleck was a planter, writer and agricultural reformer, originally from Scotland, who had moved to the southern states of America in the early 1800s. Affleck soon became a significant figure in banking, and had associations with the South Sea Company and the management of the Queen Anne's Bounty trust (see chapter 4, 'The Church of England').[5] Here's an example from the 'daily record of cotton picked', this one from the week commencing 28 October 1861 (errors from the original manuscript are reproduced here):[6]

TABLE 1

Name	No.	Mon.	Tues.	Wed.	Thurs.	Fri.	Sat.	Week
Lewis	41	255	245	265	266		270	1296
Tad	42	56	45	66	60		67	288
Levy	43	105	100	115	105		100	526

From this table, we can infer that Lewis was an adult man, Tad the youngest child, and Levy slightly older, but also a child. All three were likely beholden to their quotas, and records like these functioned as a kind of surveillance – carefully monitoring their productivity and ensuring that any inability to meet targets could be addressed by overseers.

Another accounting practice common on plantations was valuations. Plantation owners developed various ways to calculate the value of enslaved people, who were not only regarded as plantation labourers but also as capital assets that could be bought or sold, taking into account appreciation and depreciation. Children were valued according to age, with their value rising annually. When an enslaved person reached their peak efficiency as a worker, their value would then depreciate each year.

Seeing babies listed on property valuations as 'unnamed infants' is hard to forget, and we might struggle to understand how the enslaved were viewed by people for whom the birth of a baby was a financial event. But that is to look at those lists from a modern perspective. For an absentee owner, someone who was tallying up their finances, it may have been easier to see everything in the abstract, in a simple spreadsheet. They might have seen 'unnamed infant' as a bonus, an asset that would grow in value with each passing year.

Caitlin Rosenthal told me that while it's hard to trace the specific origins of accounting, there are features of plantation slavery that accelerated its development as a business practice. In labour terms, plantations were some of the largest organisations in Britain and its colonies in the early 1700s, with the biggest workforces and operations. During this period, while British factories tended to be larger, most factories were reliant on sub-contractors, whereas plantations had direct responsibility for hundreds of workers. The sheer scale of slavery, along with the slave owners' ability to control their workers, made it especially easy to, in Rosenthal's words, 'treat people as if they were just an input to production'.[7]

The complex management structures that slave owners developed to oversee their operations required detailed record-keeping in order to monitor productivity and output, a practice that is used throughout modern business management today. The amount of work an enslaved person could perform during a set window was calculated so as to push them to their maximum output. Standardised records were also trialled in plantation society, with overseers using preprinted forms to execute record-keeping across multiple plantations.

According to Rosenthal, when we think about slavery as a kind of unfree labour, it's easy to reduce our understanding of what it means to be a slave to a condition of 'not being paid'. For Rosenthal, 'the more important dimension to me is people not being able to quit'.[8] Being enslaved was physical, and just as often included sexual abuse as it did mental degradation. It was the erasure of culture, individuality and autonomy. It's an example of the complete degradation of an entire race. But how does this relate to modern working?

Rosenthal points to undocumented workers, especially in the US. 'I think some businesses prefer to have undocumented workers because it gives them a lot of power and it gives them the ability to be coercive in a way that they couldn't be otherwise.'[9] In 2014, 22 per cent of undocumented workers in the United States worked in private residences.[10] The majority of these workers were female, and reported not only unregulated pay but physical and sexual abuse including rape, and frequently being forced to work twelve-hour days with little to no breaks and no paid overtime.[11] The abuse of undocumented workers is, sadly, not uncommon, but people are reluctant to report their experiences due to a fear of deportation. This is just another way in which these workers can be exploited, treated badly, and coerced into staying in an environment.

Thinking of slavery in this way, as a condition where people are unable to quit or say no to their bosses, makes it easier to understand its toxic legacy in the modern world of work. There are many people in jobs they feel cannot leave, and countless reasons why they might feel trapped. The cost of living crisis, economic downturns, interest rate hikes – all these things can lead to a feeling of insecurity and to holding out in a negative environment for fear of unemployment.

There are so many ways that accounting and slavery are intertwined, from the meticulous scrutiny of workers' productivity to the exploitation of undocumented workers. Taking humanity out of any decision-making process is likely to create inhumane standards – whether that's employment prospects or credit scores being determined by algorithms, or slave owners treating newborn infants like assets awaiting maturity. We are still grappling with the legacy of slavery and the toxic forms of accountability in the workplace that it gave rise to. With the rise of corporate capitalism, these links seem only more entrenched.

But the detailed records and accounts kept by slave plantations do have one benefit – for historians. In them, we can find what Rosenthal calls 'the stories that we don't have the sources for', the traces of lives that would otherwise have entirely disappeared. When we look at the 'inventory of people' that a slave owner produced, historians can often use them to find living descendants today and connect them with their lost ancestry. Although she allowed that 'it's a trickier genealogical task than for a free white person', Rosenthal assured us that 'it's doable in many cases'.[12]

For decades race inequality in the workplace, in workers' incomes and in generational wealth has been laid at the feet of Black people who, it is insinuated, don't or can't work as hard as their white counterparts. But in these account books and balance sheets lies a different story – one that connects the plantations of the past with the workplaces of the present day. If you look beyond the violence and past the numbers, you begin to see the infrastructure that benefited those in power, and helps keep them there today.

RR

2

Gunpowder

All of us 'remember, remember the fifth of November, gunpowder treason and plot'. Guy Fawkes (1570–1606), centuries-long enemy of our nation, the man burned at the stake in gardens and parks up and down the country every year on Bonfire Night, hatched a plot to blow up the Houses of Parliament and kill the king using thirty-six kegs of gunpowder in 1605. In punishment, he was sentenced to be hung, drawn and quartered, executed for his betrayal of the state. This is one of the earliest stories drummed into us all at school, but have you ever learned of the deeper, darker history of Guy Fawkes's weapon, the gunpowder itself?

I spoke to the historian of Atlantic slavery, Nicholas Radburn at the University of Lancaster, who has researched its entanglements with the history of gunpower, and he explained how gunpowder technology originating in China in 800 AD spread to India, eventually making its way to Europe from Bihar in the fourteenth and fifteenth centuries. Later, it was taken on to the Americas, where it was used by both Europeans and the indigenous people. But its largest market was the coast of West Africa, where it was sold in exchange for slaves.[1] Made up of saltpetre, charcoal and sulphur ground together into a fine-grained powder, gunpowder was then dried out in dedicated rooms, and shovelled into barrels to be exported and sold.[2] Before the growth of the African markets due to slave trading, the British gunpowder industry had been entirely located in London, with mills established since the Tudor and Stuart periods. It was sold domestically in small amounts for hunting and mining, but, ultimately, these privately owned mills were, in Radburn's phrase, 'a key weapon of the state, for the state is a voracious consumer of ammunition for its armies'.[3]

The Royal African Company obtained its gunpowder from these London mills in 1700, some of which were financed by the East India Company.[4] The mills supplied both the slave trade and a variety of other buyers, but the growth of the slave trade, firstly in Bristol and then in Liverpool, created fresh opportunities, and new mills were built in the surrounding countryside from the 1720s onwards to supply these ports more efficiently.[5] British merchant capitalists then established gunpowder plants to meet African demand. These mills, as Radburn elaborates, 'were established specifically to supply the slave trade, by slave traders themselves'. Radburn's research, conducted close to the major slaving ports, was on two mills near Bristol, one near Liverpool on the Mersey River, and two near Lancaster. He points out that, because of a need for running water, and their tendency to blow up, the mills tended to be in 'very obscure rural places' that were not, 'by any stretch of the imagination, the sort of locations that you would think would be politically plugged into a place like Liverpool, and then, by extension, to Africa'.[6] So this is also a story about the British countryside, and emerging rural–urban flows of people, goods and money.[7]

Gunpowder plants were expensive and required huge numbers of people from different industries to build, thus creating jobs. The capital to fund these mills came from investments from two sources: local merchant-capitalists, and slave traders.[8] Almost all mill owners were somehow involved in the slave trade, either as owners of slave ships or connected through business or family to the slave economy. Radburn's research showed that, of 'the two main branches of slavery, outfitting slave ships or selling people in the Americas, gunpowder [accounts for] about 10 per cent' of the profits. It doesn't sound like much, but it was enough to make those who invested very rich men – in fact, manufacturing gunpowder could be more profitable than investing in the slave ships themselves. This points to an interesting insight: that a lot of the money made from the slave trade did not come directly from the ships or from owning slaves, but from manufacturing goods for the slave trade. None of this, Radburn says, was accidental. 'Their whole reason for being was supplying the slave trade. That's why they were there, that's how they survived.'[9] We can see legacies of this wealth all round us – in the banks set up by mill owners that later helped to finance northern industry, and in the landscape in villages like Sedgwick that grew close to the works that supplied workers. These villages attribute their histories to gunpowder, but never to the slave trade. Vast country homes and estates, such as Sedgwick House in Cumbria (which later became a school and has now been converted into apartments), were also built from these profits, and still punctuate our countryside vistas, making their mark.[10]

Britain was locked into constant warfare between 1688 and 1815, both in Europe (particularly in France) and in the colonies. War was the backdrop to the Industrial Revolution, and the state was heavily reliant on a weapons industry and arsenal to ensure the survival of the kingdom.[11] Africa was without a doubt the largest export market for gunpowder before abolition in 1808, dwarfing demand in Flanders, Holland, Italy, Portugal, the thirteen American colonies, Canada and India. Between 1772 and 1808, 62 per cent of gunpowder exports went to Atlantic Africa, three times the quantity shipped to the Americas.[12] By the time of the abolition of the slave trade, Britain would have supplied approximately 200,000 weapons to Africa, every single year. The provincial British gunpowder mills developed specialist products, variously named 'Africa', 'Guinea' or 'Trade' powder, specifically for the African market, and which suited the climate and conditions there better than other compounds: durable, reliable and cheap.[13]

Guns were adopted willingly at first on the African continent for use in hunting, and were carried by bandits, warlords, kidnappers, merchants and caravans.[14] They were status symbols, representing prestige and masculinity from the very beginning, and were valuable and lucrative commodities for trading.[15] But the result of injecting mechanised weaponry into African society was devastating. Communities began using them as self-defence against both European slave traders and other African tribes and villages, who may have attempted to wage war or steal their villagers to sell as slaves. A vicious cycle emerged, in which West Africans needed guns to prevent their village members from being captured and sold, but to buy guns they needed to sell slaves. Villages were constantly violently preying on and attacking one another to steal human beings. Much blood was shed, and some kingdoms and city-states were decimated as a result. Others, like the Asante and Dahomey, grew rich and powerful. Dahomey (now Benin), which emerged around 1600, had, like many African kingdoms, a long history of slave-raiding and slavery, but it was the far larger and more professional system of transatlantic slavery that actually propelled Dahomey to vast wealth, creating an influential, centralised militaristic society from 1720 onwards. Raiding for slaves became a way of life that was key to the functioning of the kingdom. Ensuing rivalries, tensions and constant war prevented political stability. Historians and social scientists believe ethnic division that continues to this day almost certainly has its roots in this period.[16]

Holding people at gunpoint naturally made capturing and rounding up slaves more efficient and productive. At the same time, as the numbers of enslaved people sold from Africa grew, the more Europeans went there, thinking it to be a lucrative market, and the more guns were sold in exchange. Higher numbers of guns seemed to correlate with an acceleration in slave trading. This created a self-perpetuating *gun–slave cycle*, which all parties became entangled in.[17] If you track the financial records, the prices of gunpowder and cargo slaves go up and down in tandem.[18]

Historians have found significant evidence that the gun–slave cycle, and the slave trade at large, has had long-term negative consequences for West Africa.[19] There are numerous studies that evidence a clear negative relationship between areas that experienced high rates of population depletion and violence as their people were kidnapped and sold into slavery, with their social and economic outcomes in contrast to other parts of Africa, even today, centuries later.[20] On the whole, it seems that the exchange of guns for slaves was not a planned strategy to impoverish the continent. It was the result of centuries of participation in the trade and the hunger for profit on all sides. African societies were both complicit and fierce resisters of the system, in equal measure. As the trade eclipsed every other crop, commodity and industry in value, however, it became all-consuming. Those who did not join in would surely become impoverished: take or be taken. With an entire economic system built on the sale of human flesh, it is less a question of complicity than of need and survival, of ordinary people and everyday lives turning as small cogs in an epic system.[21]

But what happened when the 1833 abolition of slavery

ended the gun–slave cycle? There were few other places where gunpowder was so in demand as West Africa.[22] Initially, the mills pivoted towards miners – who needed it to blast out mines – or integrated themselves within a more global powder-making industry, finding new markets that would ensure their continuance through Britain's Industrial Revolution.[23] However, Radburn says that the biggest development was the continued viability of gunpowder as a currency for trade in Africa, but now, rather than people, it was exchanged for palm oil, which was used for soaps, candles and industrial lubricants. By the late 1830s, palm oil products were flooding Liverpool, and Radburn estimates that northern powder mills were actually providing more gunpowder to Liverpool than they did before abolition.[24]

Empire, slavery, violence and war all helped to catalyse the Industrial Revolution, and have therefore been fundamental to Britain's economic development and increased power. Yet we do not acknowledge them often and strongly enough as part of our country's legacy.[25] Radburn's important research is a demonstration of this: an ordinary-looking grey powder played a hand in shaping history, in state formation, conquests, slavery, mining, industrialisation and more.[26] He is certain that there is still much more to understand about the relationship between the British arms industry and the transatlantic slave trade, as well as important questions about how British businesses, merchants and manufacturers supplied and expanded the slave trade, and made fortunes that were poured back into this country's infrastructure in return. 'Such work', he tells me, 'is essential, if Britain is to fully reckon with the modern legacies of its slave-trading past.'[27]

Gunpowder is nowadays used primarily for celebrations on happy occasions, when we set off fireworks and write in the sky with sparklers on Bonfire Night, New Year's Eve and Diwali, at weddings and birthdays. Hearing this deeper, darker, vaster story from Radburn is uncomfortable and unsettling. I began to wonder why the story about gunpowder we know best is that of the Gunpowder Plot, where the gunpowder was never even put to use. Why have we barely heard the full story about how, and for what purposes, this country used gunpowder, and the impacts that reverberated around the world as a result? It seems to me that rather than Guy Fawkes, it's the gun–slave cycle that might be Britain's true Gunpowder Plot.

AL

3

The British Monarchy

It was during a visit to Jamaica in 2022 that Prince William said: 'Slavery was abhorrent and it never should have happened … I strongly agree with my father, the Prince of Wales, who said in Barbados last year that the appalling atrocity of slavery forever stains our history.'[1]

Before William visited Jamaica, which is part of the British Commonwealth, activists had demanded an apology from the royal family for their involvement in the slave trade. Tellingly, William's statement did not contain an apology – and it doesn't seem like one is likely to come soon. All prominent members of the British royal family managed to sail through the 2020 racial reckonings without addressing or even acknowledging their family's role, not only in transatlantic slavery, but as the figureheads of an empire that left a bitter legacy of inequality in its former colonies across the Commonwealth.

The royal family have a mixed effect on people. Some of us love them, even in former colony countries like Jamaica. My grandmother, for example, had Charles and Diana's wedding photos on her wall as though they were members of our family, and my aunt seems to have only good things to say about them. And then there are the countless people who lined Pall Mall and the route of the royal procession to watch King Charles's coronation, billed as a 'once in a lifetime' event. On the other hand, many believe the royal family to be an unnecessary drain on the British economy and that we would be better off as a republic. I have my own opinions of course, but one of my main concerns is their lack of accountability regarding the central role played by the Crown in promoting slavery. As discussed in this book, in recent years many large, well-known organisations and institutions have concluded that they must acknowledge their shameful histories in this regard, so why does the British monarchy – the literal heads of our state – get a pass?

The Royal African Company was a trading enterprise founded in 1672 by King Charles II, who granted a charter to the company giving it a monopoly over trade in West Africa (Edward Colston, whose statue was famously toppled into Bristol harbour in 2020, was a governor at a later stage).[2] The company's purpose was to expand in trade across the Atlantic, with a particular focus on mining gold from the Gambia, but it quickly turned to slavery as its biggest and most lucrative trade. The company was to establish a monopoly over this trade and split the profits with the Crown. Although Charles II was the founder of the company, the largest shareholder was his younger brother James, the Duke of York, who became King James II following the death of Charles in 1685.

During its time as the dominant mercantile force on the West African coast, the Royal African Company established trading forts and factories that helped facilitate the capture of slaves and goods pillaged from West Africa. A trading fort was a solid, fortified structure that gave merchants a stronghold in hazardous places, where they could safely conduct business, store goods and be protected from potential attacks. Slave forts were a critical part of the machinery of slavery: they were where recently captured people were taken and held before being forced into slavery and transported to a dangerous new life in the Americas. Looming over a port or an outpost, the Royal African Company's fortresses were potent symbols of European power, yet they also underscored European vulnerability, having then little to no sovereignty over the land as well as a terror of tropical diseases. Behind the safety of fortress walls, company agents primarily dealt with African vendors and worked hard to suppress independent traders who operated in the region illegally and without the company's permission. To maintain its precarious monopoly the company relied heavily on its royal and political backers in England, who could write laws and grant charters that stifled any competition.

Before he became king, the Duke of York was the governor of the Royal African Company, taking a direct role in its management and overseeing the transport of enslaved people. The company shipped more enslaved people to the New World than any other single entity involved in the Atlantic slave trade. Between 1673 and the 1720s, when the company maintained its monopoly on African trade, it transported almost 150,000 enslaved people, many of whom were branded with the letters 'DY', which is understood to stand for Duke of York; others captured by the Royal African Company would be branded with 'RAC' on their chests.[3] As the head of the company and its chief stockholder, the Duke of York insisted that buyers in the New World should know that enslaved people were his, and that the trade of these people was sanctioned and protected by the royal family, the highest of powers.

Under its monopoly, the Royal African Company was able to make substantial profits for its shareholders in England, which included several royals as well as prominent aristocrats and political figures. The average price the company paid for a slave in West Africa was three pounds, and after shipping an enslaved person to the British West Indies or the Americas it would sell them at a mark-up of around twenty pounds.[4] Using today's values, the RAC would have purchased an enslaved person for £614 and then sold them for £3,560. If we take these final sale figures and apply them to the average total number of enslaved people the company is estimated to have traded, over its sixty-plus-year monopoly, it would have earned just under an astonishing £534 million from enslaved people and associated goods in today's value. The Royal African Company's average profit on revenue was 34 per cent, and so £181,560,000 was paid directly into the pockets of the shareholders.

The modern royal family separates their income into two streams: personal and public. Personal income comes from private investments and the revenue brought in by land such as the Duchy of Cornwall, while their public income comes from taxpayers and the Crown estate. Any money that King Charles II, James II and later royals made via the Royal African Company would have been viewed as private income. This private wealth has stayed in the royal family, being passed down to future generations. It's not possible, however, to know exactly what was passed on or how much it was worth, as the law prevents sovereign wills from being made public. The royal family has been exempt from inheritance tax since 1993 'to prevent the dilution of the Crown's wealth and ensure the continuity of the monarchy's functioning'.[5]

Once James became king in 1685, Edward Colston became the governor of the Royal African Company, having been an employee since 1680 at the height of its profitability.[6] As the head of the company's slave trade, Colston earned a substantial fortune, and, for his complicity, his statue in Bristol was thrown in the river and his name taken off public buildings across the city. Yet unlike James, whose statue still stands in Trafalgar Square outside the Natural Portrait Gallery, Colston did not order enslaved people to be branded with his initials (as far as we know). Why has Colston's reputation borne the brunt of the public's disdain while the monarchy has so far avoided the same criticism?

The British royal family was able to build and retain a substantial amount of private wealth through James II, Charles II and others who played an active role in the transatlantic slave trade. Queen Anne, who succeeded James II to the throne, went on to receive 22.5 per cent stock in the South Sea Company, which she supplied with four ships to get them started in trading enslaved people for Spain (see chapter 4, 'The Church of England'). This mammoth British institution must address its family history as enslavers and profiteers from the slave trade – not least because so many people globally, including people like my grandmother, don't know this story. The royals are the heads of state for many Commonwealth countries, including several countries that are still rebuilding their economies in the aftermath of slavery and decolonisation. It's not enough for William or other royals to simply say slavery was abhorrent. Distancing themselves from the subject, and not owning their history, is unacceptable.

RR

4

The Church of England

Every town and village in England has an Anglican church, and, whether you're a believer or not, the Church of England is all around us. Most British schools contain an element of the Church, perhaps in hymns sung during the morning assembly, or in special activities like nativity plays, Easter egg hunts and so on. This isn't surprising, given that Christianity is the largest religion in the UK; worldwide, the Anglican communion represents over 85 million people in over 160 countries.[1] The Church of England, like so many of Britain's major institutions, has links to slavery, and in 2019 it began to conduct research into its own history, using forensic accountants and academics to get to the bottom of the story.

Established in 1948, the Church Commissioners are an authoritative body that administers the property assets of the Church of England, dealing with investment and income from the Church's various estates and holdings across the UK. Among other assets, the Commissioners are responsible for a much older fund, known as Queen Anne's Bounty, which was established in 1704 by Queen Anne to give additional income support to the Church's poorer clergy.[2] The Bounty was predominantly funded by taxes (in addition to voluntary donations by individuals, parishes and other organisations) to pay for clergy and upkeep on churches in smaller and poorer areas, and the funds were invested in order to create a reliable source of income to support the clergy long-term. The investments typically included mortgages, land purchases, government securities – and businesses like the South Sea Company and the Royal African Company.[3]

Dr Helen Paul was part of the research team tasked by the Church Commissioners to research Queen Anne's Bounty. Why, I asked her, did the Church want to find out more now? She identified the catalyst as the famous incident in June 2020 when a statue of Edward Colston was toppled during a Black Lives Matter protest in Bristol that took place following the murder of George Floyd in the US by Minneapolis police officers. The statue was pulled down from its plinth by demonstrators, then rolled down a hill on Anchor Road and pushed into Bristol Harbour. Often described as a philanthropist, Colston was a merchant and slave trader whose statue had become a source of contention among Bristol residents, although his name and crimes were much less well-known outside the city. The furore that erupted around the toppling of the statue drew attention to the details of Colston's life, especially his time as governor of the Royal African Company – one of Britain's biggest slave-trading ventures, which had been founded by the Stuarts (see chapter 3, 'The British Monarchy'). Colston was also one of the biggest donors to Queen Anne's Bounty.

Queen Anne, born 6 February 1665, was the last reigning monarch of the House of Stuart, and the daughter of King James II. Anne's reign, from 1702 until her death in 1714, was notable for the unification of England and Scotland into the United Kingdom of Great Britain in 1707.[4] After she had established the Bounty to support the Church of England's work in poorer parishes, Anne and the Bounty's governors invested in the South Sea Company.[5] Britain had been at war with Spain during the War of the Spanish Succession, and when it ended in 1713 with the signing of the Treaty of Utrecht, Anne, under the terms of the Asiento contract, was granted exclusive rights to supply enslaved Africans to the Spanish Americas.[6] Since the Spanish Empire had lacked the resources to run slave ships from Africa to their dominions in America, making the agreement profitable to both countries.[7] Anne passed the contract onto the South Sea Company, and was therefore directly responsible for facilitating Britain's involvement in the slave trade.

In addition to royal patronage, the South Sea Company had significant government backing as it was designed to convert the British government's foreign debt into equity shares that could be issued to naval contractors in lieu of back payment from the War of Succession.[8] The South Sea Company gained knowledge and advice on the slave trade from the Royal African Company, which had been founded a few decades earlier by Anne's predecessors, as the RAC held its own monopoly over West African trade and had established trading strongholds across the African coast. Queen Anne offered four warships to the South Sea Company to be used as slave ships, delivering captured Africans from West Africa to the Spanish Americas. In all, the South Sea Company is thought to have transported around 34,000 enslaved Africans to South America.[9] The money raised for the clergy by Queen Anne's Bounty came from the profits of slavery.

As well as Queen Anne's direct assistance to the South Sea Company, many of the private donors to Queen Anne's Bounty were themselves investors and directors of the company too. Alongside Edward Colston, many of the investors who contributed to Queen Anne's Bounty were others who had generated significant wealth through the transatlantic slave trade, and altogether the report estimated that 33 per cent of investments to the Bounty between 1713 to 1798 came from individuals who are very likely to have benefited from the slave trade themselves.

A question that was always on our minds while researching the history of slavery in Britain is: did the people who invested in slavery know what they were doing? Did they care? 'They don't seem to care', is Dr Helen Paul's diagnosis, and there must be some truth to this.[10] Either that, or the piles of money to be made nullified any moral concerns. The actual process of enslaving people occurred thousands of miles away and, unless you were actually on the ships, there's a chance that you could deny the grim realities. But the truth is that slavery was never invisible in Britain. There were slave ships in most of Britain's port cities that brought back the spoils of the trade and plainly advertised where their goods had come from. The wealth that slavery created was hard to ignore, and clearly difficult to resist for capitalists eager to make a fast buck. For ordinary people, too, slave-produced goods such as sugar, tobacco and chocolate were piled high in British shops. It was unavoidable, to some degree. In that sense, it is similar to how many of us don't have any real understanding about the modern slavery behind the production of chocolate and fast fashion today. And even if we do know, it's all too easy, in favour of convenience, to plead ignorance.

Many of the donors to the Bounty didn't consider themselves enslavers or slave owners. But it wasn't uncommon for them to own just one person, whom they might've inherited as the beneficiary of wills or when the ownership of people was transferred during a business deal. Dr Paul gave an example of a woman in a British colony who worked as a servant, and who ended up being given ownership of a person as some sort of pension. As the woman got older, the person she owned could take over her servant's duties while she herself still received wages to see her through retirement. There were many types of unconventional enslavement, which only make sense in a world where some people were seen as solely property, devoid of basic human rights.

More work needs to be done to expose the complex ways in which ordinary people and institutions in the UK funded, and profited from, the slave trade. The report commissioned in 2019 by the Church Commissioners only investigated Queen Anne's Bounty, and as one of the UK's largest landowners it's inevitable that the Church of England would have further links to slavery. Maybe one day this will be investigated. In today's terms, Queen Anne's Bounty invested around £443 million in the South Sea Company, and the Bounty continued its investments in the company until the late eighteenth century. The Bounty's total investments generated an income that today would be worth £1.4 billion.[11] That is an incredible amount of money. After the report published its findings, the Church of England created a £100 million fund to address its involvement in the slave trade. It is not using the term 'reparations' because the funds will not be used to compensate individuals, but will instead go to projects 'focused on improving opportunities for communities adversely impacted by historic slavery'.[12]

The Archbishop of Canterbury, Justin Welby, issued this apology following the release of the findings:

> The public report lays bare the links of the Church Commissioners' predecessor fund with transatlantic chattel slavery. I am deeply sorry for these links. It is now time to take action to address our shameful past. Only by obeying the command in 1 John 1:6–7 and addressing our past transparently can we take the path that Jesus Christ calls us to walk and face our present and future with integrity. It is hard to do this at a time when resources in many parishes

are so stretched, but by acting rightly we open ourselves to the blessing of God.[13]

Seeing established organisations like the Church of England addressing their dark history and trying to do relevant work to address legacy disparities in modern Britain is a step forward, and their example should inspire more organisations to do the same.

RR

5

The Colour Indigo

The world is embellished with colour. It is not just something we see, but an impactful, sensory experience, as well as something we use to describe and explain our understanding of the world to others, in words and in art. Colour is subjective, and we all experience and respond to colours differently. And yet scientists have tried throughout history to understand colour and pin it down. But we cannot understand what colour *is*, without understanding aspects of its history, and in so doing tracing a long, thorny past that intersects with slavery. I spoke to art historian Helena Neimann Erikstrup, whose research explores colour, paints and pigments in relation to race and emancipation in the Caribbean. Together we explored the rich and tangled histories of colour, empire and slavery.[1]

Neimann Erikstrup introduced us to the expansive, intricate colour world, explaining that 'colour exists in multiple forms. It is above all a visual experience, guided by our senses'. Colour was experienced through dyes and pigments, which were made by the hands and bodies of indentured and enslaved labourers on colonial plantations, and then shipped to Europe, where the dyes became part of tangible objects subject to fluctuating tastes and trends in Europe's art and fashion world. Colour also exists in relation to ideas, developments and practices of racial hierarchies based on divisions of skin colour, which the plantation regime relied upon.[2] Both physical objects (like paints, fabric dyes, or pigments for make-up) and theories and ideas about colour travelled around the world along the British Empire's trade networks, connecting people, plants, animals, laboratories and factories.[3] Neimann Erikstrup explained that we can see these links spreading across the globe most clearly in the story of one intense, dark, blue-purple colour: indigo.

Fabric dyes, produced from highly valuable natural resources, were at this time bound up in processes of slavery and empire, and deep blues were all the rage.[4] The indigo plant, and the organic blue dye that came from it, was an essential cash crop of the late-seventeenth-century Caribbean plantation, alongside the better-known sugar, coffee and tobacco. Used as a colourant since prehistory across many cultures, indigo took on a new life in the West Indies and Central America. It was originally introduced to the New World by the Spanish, but the English and French were quick to catch on in an attempt to create their own avenues for sourcing the dye.[5] It was extremely valuable, and was used as currency to trade for slaves on the coasts of Africa. Indian indigo was the most sought after, but was getting increasingly expensive, while the cheaper European version, woad (a kind of cabbage), created a weaker, less desirable blue dye.[6] Having learned authentic production techniques from India, the British took that knowledge to their plantations. Until 1655, a mixed labour force made up of enslaved Africans and indentured Irish servants who worked on seven-year contracts produced indigo for Britain. Within the first decade of British occupation of Jamaica, indigo became one of its chief exports, with forty-nine indigo enterprises operating in Jamaica by 1670.[7]

The path from plant to pigment begins with extracting colour from the leaves of plants, most popularly the *Indigofera* genus. On the Caribbean plantation, the first step in creating the deep, dark dye was preparing the ground and planting the imported seeds. After weeding and harvesting, the mature plant could be taken to be processed. The Caribbean indigo plantation combined rural agriculture with large and complicated semi-industrial refinements.[8] The indigo would first be immersed and pressed down in large water reservoirs to ferment before it was stirred, drained, boiled and finally strained to make a blue paste, which was then moulded into cakes ready to be shipped to the European market.[9]

Though a long and laborious process, indigo production actually required a smaller workforce than did tobacco and sugar. Indigo workers, however, were at much greater risk, as excessive inhalation of refinery fumes could be fatal.[10] Yet working with indigo could also afford the enslaved a few moments of solitude. Because of the lethal fumes produced during production, plantation owners and overseers often steered clear of the refineries, allowing the enslaved workers brief respite from ever-watchful eyes and the constant threat of violent punishment. Despite horrendous conditions, then, working in the refineries was not the most hated job, given the opportunity, however limited, for a kind of peace and freedom.[11]

Before 1700, trials of growing the plant in Virginia and South Carolina had been unsuccessful, but this changed in 1738 when the young Antiguan-born Eliza Lucas made a significant contribution to the British history of indigo. Returned from schooling in England to her father's rice plantation in South Carolina, the seventeen-year-old began experimenting with growing different seeds, sent from the West Indies by her father, a slave owner and military man. After numerous failed attempts, she and the family found that *Indigofera tinctoria* grew well in the climate and made a suitable rotation crop. They saved and distributed seeds and information to neighbours, and indigo sales from Carolina to England soon skyrocketed. Between the 1740s and 1770s, colonial South Carolina emerged as Britain's principal supplier of indigo, prompting surrounding states to legalise slavery and take up indigo too. In 1750, 87,000 pounds of indigo were exported from South Carolina, and in the lead-up to the American Revolution their exports increased tenfold, the value eventually hitting one million pounds a year.[12] And so indigo became the most expensive dyestuff in history.[13] As a woman shaping history, Eliza Lucas's story is now local folklore and has been influential for scholars. Nonetheless, we must also recognise the significant contribution of African workers, and their ancestral knowledge, in developing the industry.[14]

By 1800, however, the indigo industry had almost completely disappeared from the region, replaced by the even more profitable cotton, while India had once more become the primary site of indigo production (see chapter 6, 'Denim / Blue Jeans'). The crop would become virtually redundant after 1826, when the German chemist and merchant Otto Unverdorben extracted a substance, later named aniline, from indigo, thus inventing a synthetic dye that could be made in factories using far less labour. Unverdorben's discovery in the laboratory changed the economics of colour from an artisanal craft in the colonies into a mechanised industry.[15]

Thirty years later, in 1856, the British chemist and entrepreneur William Henry Perkin, aged just eighteen, accidentally invented another of the world's first synthetic dyes, the vibrant purple that came to be known as mauve, from coal tar. Purple had been a rare, expensive colour – few people had even seen such a bright colour before – until Queen Victoria wore a dress in 'Perkin's purple', triggering a fashion craze, a Mauve Mania.[16]

Before the Industrial Revolution and the advent of synthetic dyes, using insects and natural material such as indigo to create organic colours had been common. As its empire grew, Britain gained access to more flora and fauna that could be used to create new colours – many of which were already in use by the indigenous people of those places. Tyrian purple was found in the secretion of sea snails. Red was extracted from the cochineal insect from South America.[17] 'Indian yellow' was made from the urine of cows who had been fed mango leaves in India, and was perfect for British artists to paint the darker skin tones of people they encountered for the first time in the colonies.[18] Central American palo wood, or logwood, produced dyes of yellow, red, purple and – particularly sought after in seventeenth-century Europe – black. Black had until then been only poorly imitated through European dyes and paints, though it had long been used by the Maya in the Yucatan Peninsula. The British soon descended on the region to get rich from this inky black dye, forcing captured and enslaved African and Maya people to work on logwood camps. Both the environmental and socio-cultural impacts on the region reverberate to this day.[19]

Aristotle is credited with the first known theory of colour, which stated that all colours came from black and white – a theory that stuck for 2,000 years.[20] But, as Neimann Erikstrup says, it was Britain that developed a world-leading colour industry that shaped the world's relationship to colour, and this was tied to imperial trade networks. The first great development came from Isaac Newton when he created the famous 'colour wheel', having discovered that white light contains all the colours of the rainbow. Newton's theory was used to try to understand why people had different skin colours – in harrowingly violent ways – and to justify experimenting on enslaved people's bodies.[21] The American physician and slave owner

John Mitchell published a treatise in 1744 at the Royal Society of London about 'the Cause of the Colour of the Negroes'. In it, Mitchell outlines his experiments, including how he cut open the skin of an enslaved – and living – African man. Drawing on Newtonianism (see chapter 14, 'Isaac Newton /Gravity'), he proposed that African skin was thicker than European skin, meaning that light was unable to pass through it, thus making it dark. Mitchell was one of several colonial scientists and thinkers who investigated skin colour and racial difference, which stemmed from a deep fear that a white person's skin could turn black and vice versa. They hoped that if this was true they could find ways to prevent it.[22]

Today we may know that variations in skin colour are due to differences in the sizes and distributions of melanin, but attitudes towards skin colour persist and have varied over time.[23] From pale skin as an indicator of higher class (agricultural labourers would have had tanned skin), to emergent racial science and eugenics in the nineteenth century, colour has always been a marker of difference.[24] Access to the best, most accurate colour tones was important in pursuing the Enlightenment – and imperial – ideal of capturing and representing the world accurately.[25] But, as ideas about race, and the laws governing slavery, became more restrictive, scientists and artists started to dictate which pigments should be used to paint certain skin tones – for example, 'raw sienna should only be used for painting Negro skins'.[26] Some colours were even described using the language of race, such as 'Negro-Black', demonstrating the interconnections of colour, art, race and science.[27] By the eighteenth century, colour, race and slavery were firmly linked, and the word 'Black' became a synonym for 'slave', implying that all Black people were (or should be) slaves. Before this, people of all races could be enslaved or indentured, including Europeans, and particularly the Irish.

Now, only Black people were relegated to this particular form of dehumanisation. Thus racism was entrenched for years to come, with many people coming to regard its underlying assumptions as reflecting the natural order.[28] Neimann Erik-strup believes that at a time in which social, legal, health and economic (to name but a few) inequalities are still so strongly divided along colour lines, it is important to understand the many ways in which colour has made our world.[29]

AL

6

Denim Blue Jeans

'Denim jeans link the world.'[1]

Half a billion pairs of jeans are sold every year. But the thoroughly modern status of these garments conceals their violent roots in the Atlantic world and the wider British Empire, as well as their role in financing the Industrial Revolution.[2] Embodied in a humble pair of jeans are centuries of experimentation and contest, the all-consuming desire for profit at the expense of all else, and the exploitation of millions, without whom this fashion staple could never have become so widespread or so popular. Cloth, if we look closely, both reveals and conceals stories of people and places, labour and power.[3]

Driven by England's nineteenth-century Industrial Revolution and by empire, in particular the shifting, undulating global industries of cotton and indigo – white and blue gold – that link India with Caribbean and American slavery, the jeans you might be wearing right now tell us something about the development of modern industrial capitalism.[4]

Cotton was first grown in the Indus Valley 7,000 years ago, but a rich, complex artisanal industry, and later a mammoth enterprise, was to grow around it, fundamentally changing the world.[5] Europeans' first encounters with soft, delicate cotton fabrics made from a strange fluffy plant would have been thrilling, and utterly addictive, given that they were more accustomed to thick, itchy animal skins, wool and linen. The desire for constant access to this superior cloth was soon established and its value as a tradable commodity recognised.[6] The English began selling Indian cotton textiles to West Africa in exchange for slaves bound for the Caribbean, and this became the main trading currency for human beings in African ports.[7] These textiles sold best on the Gold Coast, the Bight of Benin and Angola, where, as in Europe, they became prestige symbols.[8]

The high prices the East India Company garnered in London for traditional Indian calicoes, also rich in their own history – and at least double in price – angered Indian artisans and manufacturers, who felt ripped off. In 1701, domestic pressure, in support of protecting woollen and silk manufacturers at home, succeeded in prohibiting the importation and wearing of most foreign cotton textiles into England or Wales (repealed in 1774).[9] This drastic measure, however, led to a dearth of cotton in the British Isles and inadvertently spurred the rise of a domestic cotton industry. Many resorted to imitating Indian plain and printed calicoes for sale in England, using knowledge gathered from observing the Indian process. Using slave-grown cotton kept costs low, and the British-run cotton industry was soon centred in Barbados.[10] The shift in cotton production from India to Europe also created a shift from the artisanal to the industrial.[11] The availability of raw cotton fluctuated with the political instability of the Americas, most notably following the Haitian Revolution, which promoted greater expansion into native lands on the North American mainland.[12]

The work of processing cotton was rapidly sped up and made cheaper by the invention of Eli Whitney's cotton gin in 1793, which could separate seed from fibre much faster than human hands.[13] By 1750, almost every single trading or manufacturing town in England was somehow involved with cotton and slavery.[14] Cotton became the first mechanised sector in England's economy and the first to use efficient machines cheaply in large quantities, through spindles, looms and steam power that developed over the next hundred years.[15]

A century later, in 1850, although slavery had been abolished in British colonies almost twenty years prior, 2.5 million slaves were producing almost 2.5 million raw cotton bales annually in the US.[16] The only reliable and affordable cotton was now produced by American slave labour, and Britain continued to source up to 88 per cent of its cotton from US plantations, laboured by enslaved people, until the late 1860s.[17] As new land was constantly needed to feed the demand for the crop, American planters pushed further west, forcibly displacing Native Americans as they went, the legacy of which can be seen today in the deep inequalities and poverty of many indigenous reservation lands. As with indigo fields, these monocrop plantations left indelible marks on the landscapes and ecosystems they subsumed. In their wake came agro-industrial plantations that sanctioned brutal workplace discipline and the earliest iterations of the global systems of modern industrialised manufacture that we can recognise today.[18]

Cotton was shipped to Liverpool and transported out to Lancashire mills, and weavers contracted from local villages. Men, women and children worked in mills in Manchester, while technological advancements in machinery, shipbuilding and countless other industries were all set in motion, touching the whole country.[19] Cotton has now come to be seen as the engine of the Industrial Revolution, with Manchester nicknamed 'Cottonopolis'. Indeed, in the 1860s, as much as 25 per cent of the English population was employed somewhere within the cotton industry.[20] The profits of this trade, and of slavery, built individual fortunes, were reinvested towards the modernising and mechanising of the industry, and were channelled into the nation's financial and political institutions, fuelling the infrastructural growth of cities like Manchester and Liverpool.[21] The outbreak of the American Civil War and the prospect of American slavery coming to an end in 1865 was hugely disruptive globally, and in England caused riots and protest, particularly in Lancashire. With the end of slave labour, Britain was forced back to India for its cotton, which, alongside Egypt, continues to be our main source for it.[22]

The first mention of the word 'denim' is in late seventeenth-century France, in the expression *serge de Nîmes*, which described a cotton fabric made in the French city of Nîmes. This was made into trousers in Genoa to clothe Italian mariners (which in turn gave rise to the word 'jeans') and the fabric was coloured blue using dye made from the Indian indigo plant, which was itself caught up in the transatlantic slave trade (see chapter 5, 'The Colour Indigo'). Also growing in popularity were boiler suits, called 'dungarees', which were more secure and made from coarse calico, also from India. They were made in Dongri in today's Mumbai, while the fabric came from Calicut in India. Denim became increasingly popular on the American mainland from the late eighteenth century for its solidity and resilience even after many washes, and was produced in American factories as early as the 1780s.[23]

The market for such sturdy and reliable workwear took off alongside the Gold Rush of the 1800s, when gold excavators from across the world flocked to the mines of the American West.[24] Taking advantage of this, a Bavarian called Levi Strauss arrived in California in 1853. Partnering with tailor Jacob Davis, they began supplying gold miners and cowboys with denim jeans, launching the still renowned brand of jeans recognisable to most of us today.[25] They began a now unstoppable revolution: worn by everyone from workers to military personnel to celebrities, by the 1920s, jeans were simple, classic, glamorous and rebellious all at once.[26]

When Levi Strauss's jeans were first made in California in 1873, they were done so using natural indigo dye. Things changed again when synthetic dyes were invented in the 1870s in Germany, posing a huge threat to the natural dye industry.[27] Now, indigo is almost exclusively a chemical, the colour no longer bearing the DNA of this illustrious plant, completing the full mechanisation of denim's production and its separation from its botanical origins.[28] All the same, denim would not be denim if it wasn't for its iconic yet neutral blue colour, and its soft, comfortable, easy wearability. Cotton, indigo and slavery are inextricably linked in the world's favourite garment.[29]

AL

7

Wool and Linen

Woollen clothing is seen as a quintessential part of surviving the cold, wet, British climate. Sheep are a staple of any stereotypical image of our 'green and pleasant' countryside. Our woolly jumpers, socks, scarves and gloves allow us to brave dark frosty mornings with fortitude. In the summer, we swap our woollens for lighter, more breathable linens that immediately put us into holiday mode. When they're good quality, both fabrics can be pretty pricey. Perhaps it's surprising then to learn that in the eighteenth and nineteenth centuries British woollens and linens were the hottest fast fashion items of their day – cheap, of poor quality, made in probably unethical conditions, and sold as rudimentary clothing for people living in even more unethical conditions – the enslaved populations of the British Americas.

It may be even more surprising to know that poor families living in small, rural, often isolated villages throughout the United Kingdom made their livings, however meagre, producing commodities that were sold into one of the first and largest truly global economic systems. This story takes us on a journey from mid-Wales to Northern England, to Scotland, to Africa and to the Caribbean, through cloth and clothing. This is not a shameful story, but a very human one, integral to better understanding the history of our nation.[1]

Wool, which we tend to associate with cold weather, was in fact supplied to hot tropical climates: until the cotton boom (see chapter 6, 'Denim/Blue Jeans'), there was no lighter or softer material for clothing. Between 1300 and 1850, Europe and North America experienced what was known as 'the Little Ice Age', which gave rise to exceptionally cold temperatures and freezing North American winters.[2] Yet until the late seventeenth century, slave owners often left their workers scantily dressed or even naked and barefoot while working the fields, leaving them vulnerable to cold, disease and death. Mortality rates were so high that slave owners were eventually forced to attend to the health of their workers, with medical care, better and more varied food, and an obligation to give them clothes.[3]

Laws governing slave clothing, such as the Jamaica Slave Code of 1696, ensured that the enslaved were clothed decently according to a minimum allowance, at the risk of penalty for violations.[4] Chris Evans, historian at the University of South Wales and expert on Welsh slavery links, describes this slave clothing as a prison uniform, introduced only out of necessity to keep workers productive.[5] The enslaved required new clothes every few years, as their garments quickly wore out under hard labour in sugar-cane fields. Approximately five yards of cloth was allotted to each adult slave, meaning that in 1812, around 7.7 million yards would have been consumed.[6]

Before cotton textiles became more prevalent, wool was a global textile, traded to purchase kidnapped Africans to sell in the Americas.[7] Though cloth was produced globally, Wales and Northern England became notorious for producing coarse woollen fabrics known as Welsh plains, Kendall cottons and Penistone cloth that became favourites in the New World to clothe the enslaved.[8] In Scotland, linen-making has always been an important industry, ebbing and flowing with the Scottish economy.[9] Linen was made from flax, both grown in Scotland

and imported from the North Sea and Baltic ports.[10] Scottish weavers began to produce Osnaburg, a knock-off of a German linen fabric, in the mid-eighteenth century. Osnaburg was made in many European countries at the time, including Ireland, but Scottish manufacturers did particularly well with it, to the extent that the village of Dairsie in Fife was renamed Osnaburgh in honour of the vast amounts of cloth it was producing.[11] It was cheap but versatile and could be used for bedding, sacking and clothing.[12]

The linen industry was scattered at first, but from around 1727 it became more formalised through spinning schools and local education, eventually requiring transport networks to ports and cities as it spread across Scotland. The main centres were on the east coast, including Montrose, Arbroath, Dundee and Edinburgh. The West Indies and North America both promised lucrative markets and fuelled the industry's increasing professionalisation.[13] By the 1820s, Dundee overtook Hull to become Britain's leading flax port, boasting thirty mills for spinning Baltic flax into linen. These mills employed 3,000 people in a city of 45,000, 600 of whom were aged under fourteen, with some as young as six or seven.[14]

Even after the American War of Independence, there was still strong demand for Osnaburg among the former colonies and the industry continued to profit from US plantations.[15] It sold its product in the port cities of New York, Charleston, Savannah and New Orleans, and in the Caribbean, as well as in Haiti and Brazil. Millions of yards of linen were exported every year right up until Britain ended the practice of slavery.[16]

According to the recently established V&A Museum in Dundee, 90 per cent of Scotland's coarse linen was exported to clothe slaves on plantations in the Americas.[17] So the production of Osnaburg boosted the Scottish economy to the extent that many of those involved were strongly against the abolition of slavery, particularly in Dundee, where loss of the trade would have been a huge threat to people's livelihood,[18] even while many in Scotland were fierce campaigners in support of abolition and Scots played an important role in Britain's abolition movement.[19]

As Nigerian historian Sati Fwatshak writes, cloth played two important roles in the slave trade: as currency for trading and as slave clothing.[20] Britain's Royal African Company also bought cloth in bulk for export to Africa's Gold Coast.[21] In Africa, cloth entered a sophisticated, competitive barter market, and so to attract sellers, merchants dyed their cloth in bright patterns and colours, particularly blue and green, with different colours preferred at different ports.[22] Competition was intense, for African traders knew their commodities well. Sometimes, the merchants would purchase European cloth and simply unravel it in order to improve the weaving, or they would dye it in brighter colours than could be achieved in Britain at the time.[23]

In the Caribbean, plantation owners ordered needles, scissors and thread for their enslaved workers to stitch their own cloth into clothing – jackets, waistcoats, smocks, petticoats and breeches.[24] The clothes were designed to be practical and hardwearing, so as to promote health and survival, but little more.[25] They were supposed to be loose and formless, and certainly not comfortable.[26] Osnaburg and woollen clothes were sometimes supplied together, to be worn as inner and outer layers, and were likely to be rough and itchy.[27]

Women's work, a crucial part of the plantation structure, was important here, particularly on larger estates where the plantation mistress would select some enslaved women to work as seamstresses.[28] Though strictly supervised, these women had some level of authority in clothing their fellow bondsmen, women and children according to their own traditions and tastes, and in this sense they had an important role in plantation society.[29] In making the clothes, they shared conversation and laughter, as well as their knowledge and expertise of different traditions of African clothing. Community and joy were also found at Sunday morning markets, which allowed the enslaved to buy their own cloth (particularly colourful cloth, including that dyed in Africa), buttons and other materials, using small amounts of money made by selling produce grown in front of their living quarters. Purchasing colourful, flamboyant clothing with their own money was a way for the enslaved to foster some sense of independence, style and individuality. It helped to resist the dehumanisation of being forced to wear drab, uncomfortable and impersonal workwear that was soaked in sweat and falling apart, day in, day out.[30]

Resistance, self-expression and cultural connection are part and parcel of this story. Headwraps and handkerchiefs were embroidered, folded or styled in ways that were known by other enslaved people to convey a call to revolt, or the secret, sorrowful goodbyes of a runaway.[31] In 1746, the English government banned the wearing of tartan in the Scottish Highlands. It was punishable by deportation, with many Scots sent to the Caribbean, India and other foreign shores. In response to an influx of Scotsmen in India, cloth-makers began printing tartan patterns onto their calicoes, both to please their customers and because they were inspired by the design. Tartan 'Madras' cloths became a favourite British Indian export to Europe and the Caribbean, where laws requiring women of French-Caribbean descent to cover their natural hair meant that patterned handkerchiefs were in high demand. The trend quickly spread across the region into the British islands. Today, checked tartan remains a familiar sight wrapped around the heads of Afro-Caribbean women, or sold as dresses and blouses at markets across the islands. Colonial officials seem to have grasped how important clothing could be for cultural connection and belonging, so they manipulated rules about what people could wear to help them exert greater control over people and their ability to express their cultural identity.[32] All over the world, dress and style have always served as a form of self-expression, creativity – even rebellion.[33] Fashion is intertwined with survival and resistance: our clothes tell stories.

Welsh, Scottish and English villagers did not grow rich from the cloth trade. Poor people on both sides of the Atlantic were engaged in an industry that primarily benefited a wealthy elite: child labour was common, incomes remained too low for rising rents and tithes, and weaving raw wool could cause illness and injury.[34] Cloth-makers were aware of their entanglement with slavery, but it was so normalised as a part of the British economy that it never presented a major moral issue. Even today, we find it easier not to consider the ecological and ethical implications of fast-fashion brands – many of whom have modern slavery and forced labour in their supply chains – because their products are cheap and easy to obtain. Nowadays, we constantly desire new clothing, but we don't consider the impact of its rapid consumption. Few of us can extricate ourselves from the pervasive capitalist system we exist within, or live a 'normal' and affordable life without consuming these things, at least sometimes.[35] In this story, culpability does not rest with any one party, and it is difficult to confront the fact that those from poor, rural communities were implicated within a wider, global system of ruthless slavery.[36] Yet doing so helps us to deepen our understanding of how we are all connected by capitalism. There is, of course, a fundamental difference between village weavers and enslaved people, which we must not ignore, but, as this story shows, disadvantaged people everywhere, in just trying to make ends meet, can become entangled in unjust systems that create poverty, suffering and violence.[37]

AL

8

Sugar

In his 2016 March budget, the then Chancellor of the Exchequer George Osborne announced the Soft Drinks Industry Levy (SDIL), colloquially known as the 'sugar tax'.[1] Paid by the packager to HMRC, the levy was to be applied to drinks produced in the UK or to the importer of drinks produced overseas. The levy raised the amount of tax that soft drinks companies pay on drinks containing more than 5g of sugar per 100ml, and after it came into force in April 2018 anyone who remembers how their favourite drinks used to taste will forever remember how the sugar tax ruined everything. The Soft Drinks Industry Levy was initially designed to help fight childhood obesity, with the revenue generated by the new levy to be invested into programmes tackling that issue. By 2020, just one year after the levy was introduced, it had raised £336 million.[2] However, after only a year, the money raised was no longer put towards childhood obesity programmes but absorbed into the general tax pot.

Although the SDIL ruined Ribena, the negative effects of high-sugar diets far outweigh the benefits of a sweet taste. Campaigns to reduce the sugar in our diets have been running for decades. Because sugar has been widely available and reasonably priced for over a century it has been a staple of any household or food producer, which is why, when we're looking to live a healthier lifestyle, sugar is one of the first things we try to cut out of our diets completely. Despite their abundance, sugary items have not historically been a byword for cheap, unhealthy foods; in fact, they've been markers of class and wealth. The story of how sugar became a fundamental part of our diets worldwide is one that is linked, notoriously, to the transatlantic slave trade.

It's believed that sugar was first used as a food in New Guinea around 8000 BC; references to sugar appear in Indian literature from the fourth century BC, about the same time that Alexander the Great was alive.[3] The knowledge of how to produce sugar spread across the Islamic world, and by the Middle Ages sugar was known as a valuable commodity in Europe. During the Crusades, Christian soldiers returning to Europe spoke of sugar as an exotic luxury, something extremely rare and expensive that could only be consumed by the very wealthy. Sugar was used as a sweetener for food and drinks, including alcoholic beverages like wine, and was also used in medicinal tinctures, as it was widely believed to have healing qualities.

As sugar consumption began to rise, so did demand. Sugar had been imported to Europe from the Middle East, often through intermediaries like the Venetians, who inevitably inflated the prices – and so by the sixteenth century sugar plantations became some of the most valuable enterprises for European colonists in the Americas. By cultivating sugar cane in territories that they could control, Western Europeans had the chance to break the monopoly from Asia and reap incredible profits for themselves. Soon, with the rise of American and Caribbean sugar plantations under European control, the availability of sugar in Europe transformed it from a luxury item for the wealthy to a dietary staple for most of the population.

As early as 1590, the first recorded sugar refineries had opened in Britain.[4]

Sugar refineries in Britain worked in tandem with sugar plantations in the Caribbean. The plantations were responsible for the cultivation and initial processing of the sugar cane – intensive agricultural labour mostly done by enslaved people or indentured servants. Harvested cane was then processed to extract its juice, which was then boiled and crystallised to produce raw sugar. This unrefined sugar was then shipped to Britain, arriving at ports around the country – though the majority went to Bristol, London and Liverpool. From here, the sugar would be received by the refineries to execute the final stages of processing. Sugar is refined in much the same way as crude oil, being subjected to intense heat to separate darker and heavier fractions from the lighter and finer sugars. Temperatures often reach above 100 degrees Fahrenheit and, especially before the advent of modern working conditions, working in a refinery would have been an intense, back-breaking job. Refineries were conveniently located close to harbours and waterways so that raw sugar could be delivered straight off the boats from plantations.

At their peak, in 1750, there were around 120 sugar refineries in Britain.[5] London was the centre of the industry, with more refineries than any other city, closely followed by Bristol.[6] In the Caribbean, sugar plantations had high profit margins because enslaved people were used at every stage of production, keeping operational costs low, and plantation owners would often measure their wealth in their sugar profits. So long as there was sufficient fertile land beside a plantation, and money to keep expanding, enslaved labour was obviously cheaper than employing paid workers. Slavery was thus adopted on sugar plantations throughout the British West Indies and in larger territories like Brazil and Cuba, and it's fair to say that the success of sugar plantations helped drive the expansion of slavery. Sugar plantations were initially established in the Caribbean, where its indigenous populations were all but wiped out, and its cultivation required a huge labour force, which led to the importation of more enslaved Africans. By the seventeenth century, the sugar industry accounted for a large part of the British economy, which was also true for other European countries with Caribbean colonies.

Until the nineteenth century, Caribbean colonies had a monopoly on sugar cultivation. However, things began to change when competition emerged from plantations in other regions such as Brazil, Mauritius, Cuba and India, as well as from domestic beet sugar production. This led to overproduction and a decline in prices, which left Caribbean plantation owners with diminishing returns. In France, meanwhile, the British naval blockade during the Napoleonic Wars led French sugar refineries to experiment with extracting sugar from sugar beet plants, as a cheaper alternative grown in Europe that could fulfil the now enormous demand for sugar without relying on colonial imports. Once the wars were concluded, and trade with France resumed, the effect of the blockade backfired for Britain's sugar industry as the influx of cheaper sugar from France and its colonies flooded the market. Despite this decline, the refining industry seemed robust and continued to expand. Sugar refineries were tied into the wider economic landscape, and were closely connected to the coal and copper industries, given the energy-intensive refining process. Sugar refiners also advocated for unrestricted imports on all sugar, regardless of its origin or method of production, so that they could receive the best deals on raw sugar from plantations even if they were outside the British West Indies. Imports from outside the British Empire were heavily taxed, and refiners argued that increasing costs diminished their profits and the overall health of one of the country's key commercial industries. Amid this climate, it's unsurprising that sugar refiners prioritised cheaper sugar and better margins over the moral arguments to abolish slavery on plantations.

Britain's economic policy was also changing during this period. At the height of the plantation system, the prevailing economic theory in Britain was mercantilism,[7] which emphasised a positive trade balance with the rest of the world and wealth accumulation through gold and silver reserves. Governments promoted exports and limited imports through regulation, by imposing tariffs and establishing British monopolies over certain commodities. This often led to colonial expansion as nations aimed to acquire resources and markets for their goods. However, in the late eighteenth and nineteenth centuries, more merchants and politicians began to favour a laissez-faire economic policy, which promoted free trade between individuals regardless of which nation they belonged to.[8] This philosophy advocated for a much lighter touch from the government when it came to economic interventions, and favoured free markets that were driven by supply and demand above all else. This approach aimed to enable businesses to act in their self-interest, which in turn would lead to economic prosperity – or at least prosperity among the businessmen who stood to gain from lower tariffs and lighter government regulation, to the chagrin of Caribbean plantation owners, who sought a greater degree of protectionism from the imperial centre.

Around the same time, plantations that had been running for decades in the Caribbean also began to exhaust their soil, leaving them unable to compete with newer and more fertile plantations in other territories. Although we're taught that moral arguments played a substantial role in the abolition of slavery, in the sugar industry it was economic decline that prompted the end of slavery on plantations. Simply put, enterprises that used enslaved labour were just not as profitable or efficient as they had been during their peak. In 1814, nineteen years before the Slavery Abolition Act, the British West Indies' share of British exports was one-sixth; by 1833 this had dropped to one-fourteenth.[9] Following abolition, the core of the sugar industry shifted to countries where slavery was still legal and the margins were better, further diminishing the British West Indian market. Exports from India and Brazil increased after slavery ended, and British trade and investments were shifted away from the Caribbean along with the market.

Sugar has a complicated past full of exploitation and capitalist greed. As with so many other products – from chocolate to tobacco, mahogany to cotton – Britain's need for sugar fostered the growth of the transatlantic slave trade, but it was the ill fortunes of the sugar industry that was ultimately one of the reasons it fell apart. While in Britain's telling, abolition was a triumph of humane reasoning, it was the economic strains that plantation systems were under and the move towards a laissez-faire economic policy that led to changes in attitude among the government and the wealthy. The story of sugar provides one of the most important answers to why the crime of slavery was committed for so long, and why it eventually stopped: money.

RR

9

Lloyds of London

The more you look at the history of slavery in modern Britain, the more you realise that insurance companies and banks have always been the staple that held everything together. Without the banks to lend the capital to buy enslaved people or a plantation, and the insurance companies to cover potential losses on human cargo travelling the merciless Middle Passage, there's a chance that the slave trade wouldn't have gained traction so quickly or have lasted as long as it did. Slavery might have been a niche activity for wealthy playboys rather than the profitable global industry that it became.

> We are deeply sorry for the Lloyd's market's participation in the transatlantic slave trade. It is part of our shared history that caused enormous suffering and continues to have a negative impact on Black and ethnically diverse communities today … We also recognise that the legacy of slavery continues, evident in the racial inequality that persists to this day.[1]

The above is a section of the statement that Lloyd's made as part of its 'Journey of Reflection'[2] concerning its involvement in the transatlantic slave trade. Lloyd's was one of the many

British institutions that looked inward following the racial reckonings of 2020. This is one of the only statements we've seen from a company that directly acknowledges the continued impact that the legacy of slavery has on Black communities today. It even goes one step further, and directly point out 'the lack of ethnic representation that still exists in the Lloyd's market today'.[3] It's no surprise that institutions like Lloyd's, founded at a time when Black people were barely seen as people rather than inventory, have a blind spot when it comes to race and how Black people navigate daily life today. Most companies who have acknowledged their ties to slavery would prefer that those associations remain in the past, instead of facing up to the harm they might be causing today.

Lloyd's Coffee House was opened in 1688 by Edward Lloyd.[4] In the seventeenth century, coffee houses were social networking spaces where people could gather to discuss business, politics and news. For drinking coffee and making deals, it was a less formal place than an office and a more social setting than someone's home. In London, business was officially done in the Royal Exchange on Threadneedle Street, but informal deals and networking took place in coffee houses throughout the City of London. Different coffee houses were frequented by specific tradesmen, for specific kinds of business, and Lloyd's became known as a place where sailors and shipowners would meet. The coffee house soon acquired a reputation as a place to obtain marine insurance, and where you could place bets on which ships would make it back to port after long voyages. In 1771, a group of merchants, who wanted to distance themselves from what they called the 'shameful practices' of speculative insurance and government securities, broke away from the old coffee shop and founded New Lloyd's Coffee House.[5] There were seventy-seven merchants, each of whom invested £100, totalling £7,700, to bankroll the new organisation.[6] This venture was more structured and was managed by a committee, and soon Lloyd's transformed how the marine insurance business was brokered in London.

Marine insurance – as you might gather from the name – is a type of insurance that covers all aspects of business done on the high seas. This includes insurance coverage for cargo and ships as well as insurance against the dangers of sea travel: from sinkings to storm damage, and including piracy, war and fire. Even insurrections were covered by Lloyd's, as up to 10 per cent of voyages carrying enslaved people or captured Africans resulted in uprisings.[7]

> The Anne, Clarke, from Leverpool, is Cut off by the Negroes on the coaft of Guiney – The Captain kill'd on the Spot, and all the Crew wounded.[8]

This is a quotation from the *Lloyd's List* newspaper, issue number 1539, Tuesday, 28 August 1750. It details an uprising that took place on a ship that had left from Liverpool. Although people tend to know about the horrific conditions enslaved people endured during the Middle Passage, these lesser-known stories of uprisings remind us that their spirit to fight never dwindled.

Lloyd's was integral to the development of marine insurance, as it evolved from a slightly morbid form of gambling into a regulated and essential national industry, one that could attract ever greater numbers of merchants to grow the trade. Lloyd's assembled capital for overseas trading by creating networks of intermediaries, like insurance brokers, who would act on behalf of shipowners and merchants. Only individuals were allowed to underwrite risk at the time, and so as overseas trade expanded there was a growth in the number of community brokers who specialised in insurance, who could act as mediators between merchants seeking insurance and individual underwriters. If you had something to insure – whether it was cargo, a crew or a slave ship – the brokers at Lloyd's would connect you with someone willing to underwrite the risk. These restrictions helped create the insurance system we still use today, where those seeking insurance cannot directly access underwriters but have to go through a third-party broker first. And so, an industry was born.

Lloyd's role in helping to create modern marine insurance was an integral part of the growing slave trade. The Lloyd's race report also established that some of the seventy-seven men who invested in the New Lloyd's Coffee House had individual connections to slavery. Robert Bogle Senior was a Virginia and West India Merchant from Glasgow who owned the Montreuil Estate in Grenada, a sugar plantation, along with property in Virginia.[9] Bogle was one of the famed 'tobacco lords' of Glasgow, and was part-owner of a slave voyage from Glasgow in 1720.[10] (See chapter 18, 'Tobacco Merchant's House, Glasgow'.) Another investor, Henry Wildman, was a merchant from London and the owner of the Esher Estate plantation in Jamaica.[11] Under his ownership, the Esher Estate produced sugar and rum and traded enslaved people. The estate listed 365 enslaved people as its property.[12]

Samuel Gist, another of Lloyd's founders, was a wealthy British American slave and plantation owner in Virginia who also traded tobacco. Unusually, Gist left money in his will for his 200 enslaved people to be freed and receive education after his death.[13] Under Virginia law, formerly enslaved people were unable to remain in the state when they were freed, and so before he died Gist purchased hundreds of acres of land to bequeath them in Ohio. Sadly, Gist did not provide them with any legal rights to the land, leaving them with another battle to fight. Following Gist's death, his former enslaved workers were escorted by federal troops to the land in Ohio. An agreement was made that if the now free men and women paid land taxes, they would be allowed to settle on the land. But the land was difficult to work, and it was extremely hard to make a living in the area, which led many of the families to move away. Today, most of the land is derelict and used as a dumping ground. Paul Turner, who was born on the Gist Settlement, has spent years steadily purchasing the land plot by plot and is determined to preserve its history.[14]

Lloyd's of London played a key role in the development of the transatlantic slave trade, through the insurance it offered to slave traders and in the personal dealings of its founders. In response to these discoveries, at the end of 2023 Lloyd's launched 'Inclusive Futures', a programme of initiatives to respond to the legacy of slavery by helping Black and ethnically diverse pupils 'progress from the classroom to the board-room'.[15] Many initiatives have been launched by organisations that have discovered their links to slavery since 2020, but only time will tell whether these schemes make an actual difference to Black people today. But one thing that all organisations can do immediately is educate their staff on such company histories, and explore why the structures and systems that historic organisations helped to develop may continue to negatively impact Black people in the workplace today.

In Britain specifically, there are so many glass ceilings yet to be broken by Black people. We still have not had a Black prime minister, and in 2024 David Lammy became the first Black foreign secretary. In the lead-up to the 2017 general election, the then Shadow Home Secretary, Diane Abbott, was found to have received nearly half of all abusive tweets sent to female MPs.[16] The Bank of England is yet to have a Black chief executive and although the BBC was founded ninety-one years after slavery was abolished, the institution is yet to appoint a person of colour, let alone a Black person, as Director General – the role has been male and white exclusively since its inception.

The link must be drawn between the system that treated Black people as nothing more than inventory and the unconscious biases that exist today, which undervalue Black talent and leave Black people in the fewest leadership positions, failing to progress at the same pace as their non-Black colleagues and disproportionately incarcerated.

RR

10

Bank of England

In the middle of the City of London, I held a gold bar for the first time. It's true – those things are much heavier than you expect. Inside the Bank of England, there is a museum that, until February 2024, included both the gold bar and an exhibit displaying the names of enslaved people listed as property as part of an estate the Bank owned in Grenada in the late eighteenth century. That the Bank was directly involved in slavery is relatively new information – uncovered in 2022 after the Bank commissioned research to gain a deeper understanding of its links to slavery. Previously, it was only known that the governors of the Bank had private investments in slavery and that the Bank had underwritten loans and insurances for others to purchase plantations and enslaved people.

A spokesperson for the Bank said:

In 2021, the Bank of England commissioned a researcher to explore its historic links to transatlantic slavery, working with the Bank of England Museum and archive. This research found that in the 1770s the Bank made loans to a merchant company called Alexander & Sons. When the business defaulted on those loans, the Bank came into possession of two plantations in Grenada which had been pledged as security for the loans. Our research has found that 599 enslaved African people lived and worked on those plantations. The Bank subsequently sold on the plantations.[1]

The 599 enslaved people were the names at the centre of the Bank's 'Slavery and the Bank' exhibition. Among them, the exhibit listed four 'unnamed infants'.

Michael Bennett, a research associate at the University of Manchester, was the head of the Bank's research team. In his blog following the release of the team's research, he explained that the two plantations were named Bacolet and Chemin,[2] which came under the Bank's control in the mid-1770s after the owners of the plantation were unable to repay the original loan. The Bank eventually bought out the other creditors and came into sole possession of the two plantations and their enslaved workforces in the late 1780s. The Bank then sold the plantations to the West India merchant James Baillie for £100,000 in 1790.

I was intrigued by what the Bank did during the roughly fifteen years when it owned the plantations. How much money did they earn? Who ran them? Was there someone from the Bank directly involved in overseeing operations? The sum of £100,000 was significant in the 1790s, and in today's money, adjusting for inflation, the plantations would be worth over £18 million. For them to retain their value over fifteen years must mean they remained operational under the Bank of England's ownership, possibly with limited interruption between takeovers.

There's a lot that we still don't know, but we can learn more by looking at the previous owners of Bacolet and Chemin, Alexander & Sons, which was a Scottish merchant firm based in Edinburgh.[3] William Alexander has been tentatively identified as the plantations' owner, having been a landowner in Grenada in the eighteenth century and who, via his firm, took out a mortgage loan with the Bank of England to buy the Bacolet and Chemin plantations. In 1774 the firm went bankrupt and defaulted on its loan with the Bank, passing on ownership of the plantations and the 559 enslaved people living there.[4] While the Bank was in possession of the plantations it still kept the books, and from the 1780s its records show that it received regular income from enslaved labour.

As well as directly owning two plantations, the Bank of England helped make slavery a viable industry through its financial services – much like Lloyd's of London, which we explore elsewhere. As well as providing loans to slave traders and would-be plantation owners, the Bank provided services to major slave-trading companies including the Royal African Company and the South Sea Company, offering company accounts with overdraft facilities and thus easing their business transactions. It also offered discounted bills of exchange, which enabled merchants to cash out agreements early. This was a particularly useful service for plantation trades. Cash-out agreements were helpful as they meant planters and slave owners could gain immediate liquidity by leveraging their assets rather than selling, which could be a timely and arduous process, depending on how much cash was needed.[5] The bank was more than willing to accept plantations and enslaved people as collateral for the loans it offered.

The Bank of England played a leading role in calming the market and restoring trust in Britain's financial institutions following the collapse of the South Sea Company in 1720, during the 'South Sea Bubble' financial crisis that rocked the British economy. The crisis was driven by rampant speculation that vastly inflated the share price of the South Sea Company, and when the bubble burst in late 1720 thousands of investors lost their livelihoods, causing widespread panic and anger.[6] Originally founded to service foreign debt after a series of costly wars with the Spanish, the South Sea Company had gained a monopoly known as the 'Asiento de Negros' to supply African slaves to Spanish colonies in South America. Although the Bank of England was nominally a rival of the South Sea Company, it still held interests in the company and stepped in to provide financial support for the slave trading business after the company's share price collapsed.

Under the terms of the Slavery Abolition Act, the Bank also helped facilitate the compensation scheme for former slave and plantation owners. Abolition in the British Empire was only secured with the promise to pay slave owners who would lose out financially. As part of the Slavery Compensation Act, the British government decided that a total of £20 million should be paid in compensation for the slave owners' 'loss of property', some of which was still being repaid by the government as late as 2015.[7] Those who were considered the property of slave owners, the enslaved people, were given nothing. Some £5 million pounds of the compensation was paid to claimants as annuities. This meant that these specific payments to slave owners in different colonies, including Barbados and Mauritius, were made in stocks that accrued an agreed interest rate of 3.5 per cent. The rest of the money was loaned by the Bank of England, and slave owners or their representatives could collect compensation certificates at the Office of National Debt, with which they could collect their money.

Following these findings from the Bank's research, the institution began reviewing its portraits of former governors and directors in order to identify which figures had a connection to slavery. Ten items (eight portraits and two busts) were found to have links and were swiftly removed.

Many of the Bank of England's governors profited from

slavery. Humphrey Morice – later found to have defrauded the Bank for £29,000 while serving as Deputy Governor from 1727–29[8] – invested in around 103 voyages and funded the transportation of 30,000 African people into slavery.[9] Sir Robert Clayton, a director at the Bank from 1702 to 1707, invested £500 in the Royal African Company, which is around £180,000 today.[10] Sir Gilbert Heathcote was a member of the Bank's Court of Directors from its inception in 1694.[11] He also served twice as a governor of the Bank from 1709 to 1711 and from 1723 to 1725.[12] Heathcote traded enslaved Africans to the Spanish colonies, and lobbied Parliament both against the Royal African Company's monopoly on slave trading and for the expansion of Britain's colonial ambitions.[13] William Manning served as governor between 1810 to 1812, and was the owner of several plantations across the Caribbean.[14] George Harnage, governor from 1810 to 1821, inherited the Boarded Hall sugar plantation in Barbados from his father John Lucie Blackman, a West India merchant. At the time of abolition there were 177 enslaved people at Boarded Hall plantation.[15]

Not all of the Bank's ties to slavery were negative, though, and not all of its governors were plantation owners or investors in the slave trade. Samuel Thornton was a governor of the Bank for two years from 1799 and was a prominent abolitionist. He was a member of the Clapham Sect, a prominent group of evangelical Anglican reformers, and the cousin of William Wilberforce. Thornton's brother Henry served as Chair of the Sierra Leone Company, which had been established by the Clapham Sect to establish a colony in West Africa that would be populated largely by formerly enslaved people.[16] The Sierra Leone Company was just one among many failed initiatives to establish settlements for freedmen in Sierra Leone, often led by evangelicals. Each of these schemes faced significant challenges, from the threat of re-enslavement to hostility from the

Royal African Company, which retained control of the land and refused to grant the settlers freehold, leading to conflicts and armed rebellions.[17] The Sierra Leone Company seemed to have good intentions – and Samuel Thornton was an exception among his pro-slavery colleagues at the Bank of England – but the need to create income in any new colony and the Sierra Leone Company's reluctance to let freed slaves own their own land made its demise inevitable.[18] Although the Royal Navy did transport hundreds of formerly enslaved people to Sierra Leone to start a new life as freedmen, the settlers found themselves bound by the apprenticeship system, which many saw as slavery in a different guise (for more on which see chapter 28, 'Treadmills').

Thornton's efforts aside, the research commissioned by the Bank of England revealed a stark truth about its role in facilitating the slave trade. Gestures like the removal of statues and public apologies show that the Bank's directors are aware at least of public feeling about their dark history. But how should such a major player in the slave trade atone for its actions? In 2024, the Government of Grenada demanded that the Bank of England pay reparations for its ownership of the Bacolet and Chemin plantations, writing: 'The Government of Grenada calls upon the Bank of England to make reparations to Grenada on account of the direct involvement of the Bank of England in the 1780s in the enslavement of Africans and their descendants in Grenada.'

The letter went on: 'the enslavement of Africans in Caribbean colonies including Grenada was atrocious. The work regime, punishments inflicted both physically and psychologically, and the immeasurable suffering endured have multiplier effects on our current populations of African descent.'[19]

In response, the Bank of England said:

We have received the letter and confirmed that, while there can be no doubt that the slave trade was an appalling aspect of British history, our position remains in line with that of the UK government, which has no plans to pay reparations.

The most effective way to respond to the wrongs of the past is to ensure current and future generations learn lessons from history and work together to tackle today's challenges.[20]

The Bank of England's response is extremely disappointing. Despite acknowledging that we must learn from history, it has done little, short of removing a few statues, to facilitate any such learning. It didn't even make its 'Slavery and the Bank' exhibition permanent. Given the Bank's legacy as an entity run by some of the biggest slave owners, one that propped up the financial system that made slavery possible – and having owned two plantations themselves – more should be demanded from it in order to put right historic wrongs. For the Bank not only to dismiss reparations but to also fail to have programmes in place that benefit communities and countries affected by the legacies of slavery is insulting, and shows that it has learned little from its own research.

RR

11

Chocolate

A tall, dark, handsome man stands on the edge of a cliff looking towards a small yacht. He has a small briefcase attached to his back, but it doesn't throw off his perfect dive. In the water, a shark is circling, but it doesn't stop our man, who ignores the shark and keeps swimming. Next, he's on the boat, his hair wet but still looking good; he's unfazed. He opens his briefcase and reveals the contents: a box of Cadbury's Milk Tray. He positions it on a bed, places his card on the box, and then leaves as though he was never there. He places a knife in his mouth and dives off the boat, moving on to his next chocolate delivery. Then we hear the famous words: 'All because the lady loves Milk Tray'.

This was an advert from the 1970s for Cadbury's Milk Tray, which for a long time in Britain was the height of sophistication in chocolate terms. Up until only a few years ago, chocolate was marketed to women as a source of adventure, sensuality and romance. It was a naughty, guilty but ultimately harmless pleasure. Women's magazines would ask their readers: was chocolate better than sex? According to advertisers, the answer was ... yes.

These days, chocolate isn't seen in quite such positive terms, even if the advertising is less sexist. Consumers often opt for fair trade brands instead of the mainstays like Cadbury, aware of accusations of modern slavery and exploitation in the industry's supply chains. Chocolate has also come under scrutiny for its sugar content, and where it could once be found in prime locations near the tills at supermarkets and petrol stations it's now been moved out of direct eyeline. No more spur-of-the-moment, cheeky purchases. But this isn't the first time that this simple pleasure has been revealed to have had a dark history.

The first evidence of people making chocolate is from over 4,000 years ago in Mesoamerica.[1] The Mesoamerican region was home to a diverse range of societies across the land that is now modern-day Guatemala, Honduras, Mexico, Belize, El Salvador, Costa Rica and Nicaragua. Cacao trees are indigenous to Mesoamerica, and the Olmec and Mayan people were the first to cultivate cacao, a practice that was later adopted by the Aztecs. Cocoa, which is made from the seeds of cacao trees, was a sacred food to Mesoamerican people, with the Mayans and Aztecs referring to it as 'food of the gods' and using it in many of their religious and ceremonial practices.[2] The cacao seeds were ground up, melted and mixed with spices and water to be consumed as a drink. It was an extremely special commodity.

During the sixteenth century, Spanish conquistadors encountered chocolate during their explorations of Mesoamerica. The Spanish took note of its religious significance and its luxury appeal among the indigenous population, particularly among the Aztecs, who also used the cacao bean as currency, and saw an opportunity to bring chocolate back to Europe as an expensive treat – one they would control a monopoly over. The Spanish, particularly the royal court, embraced chocolate and it became fashionable to consume it during elaborate royal ceremonies. Its popularity led to chocolate houses opening across Spain and later Europe, in imitation of coffee houses, and a greater demand for chocolate to be imported from the Americas.

Cacao production in the Americas soared to feed Europe's new appetite for chocolate, but the existing workforce was unable to meet the demands of merchants. The indigenous population began to decline due to the harsh working conditions and diseases brought over by the European colonists, to which Mesoamerican people had no natural immunity. Colonists thus began to lean on enslaved labour to ramp up chocolate production. In the Caribbean and Latin America, cacao became an increasingly lucrative cash crop, which led to the development of huge, commercial plantations across Middle and South America. The Portuguese were particularly notable for introducing plantation systems to their colonies in Brazil and later in West Africa, leading to the system of forced labour that is perpetuated in the chocolate industry to the present day. Chocolate plantations had a profound impact on the economic development of the regions where they were built, fundamentally reshaping the landscape and the commerce and labour of the modern countries they gave rise to. Enslaved Africans were forced to work on these plantations, where they cultivated the cacao trees and harvested the beans for export to the chic chocolate houses of Europe.

Cultivating cacao trees required huge swathes of jungle to be cut back with machetes to clear arable land before the trees could be planted and nurtured by enslaved workers. Harvesting cacao pods involved extremely delicate machete work, and care had to be taken not to damage the trees when cutting down the pods. It was a year-round activity rather than a seasonal one, with three annual harvests following seasonal rain. Enslaved people would also have to process the cacao, which involved fermenting and drying the cacao beans until they were ready to be crushed into a paste and cooked into chocolate. As well as tending the crops, maintaining the land and clearing forestry for new plantations, there were often animals on the plantations that enslaved people were also responsible for feeding, grooming and herding. Any failure to keep tools and machinery in working order, or any damage or neglect to the cacao trees, would lead to punishment from the plantation owners.

Life on cacao plantations was demanding and hard. Enslaved people were forced to work in the fields for long hours, particularly during harvest seasons, with little or no breaks. Enslaved workers lived under constant supervision, with overseers keeping an eye out for runaways and malingerers. As well as the physically demanding toll, workers also had to endure the mental strain of being compelled to work in these conditions, with no autonomy over their bodies, and at the mercy of indifferent overseers who might sell them or their loved ones to another plantation.

The profitability of a cacao plantation varied, not least because the size and quality of cacao trees varied significantly across regions and continents. In 1680, a cacao plantation could see a return of £480 per year from an area of 8.5 hectares of cacao trees.[3] That's the present-day equivalent of just under £108,000. By the end of the nineteenth century, cacao exports from Trinidad had expanded massively, and in 1894 were valued at £509,808 annually (just over £83 million today).[4]

By the seventeenth century, chocolate houses had begun to open in England. The first reference to one in London was in 1657, at Bishopsgate Street in London. As already mentioned, chocolate was initially consumed as a drink mixed with spices, as the natural flavour of cacao is quite bitter. As chocolate became more popular, chocolate houses began adding sugar (an increasingly available commodity) to the mix, turning a once bitter beverage into a softer, more palatable drink, one far more desirable to the public.

The Industrial Revolution played a significant role in the

expansion of the chocolate market, transforming it from an exclusive luxury treat for the elite into a cheaper, more accessible commodity for the general population. New machinery in the nineteenth century made it more efficient for cacao to be ground and for ingredients to be mixed. In 1847, Joseph Fry, part of England's pioneering chocolate family, produced the first chocolate bar by blending cocoa powder, sugar and cocoa butter.[5] In 1875, in collaboration with Henri Nestlé, a Swiss pharmacist best known for founding the Nestlé company, Daniel Peter produced the first milk chocolate, paving the way for the smooth and creamy product we prefer today.[6] But as the market grew, so did the need for bigger and faster production. This led to even more cacao plantations being founded across the Spanish and Portuguese colonies and an even greater use of enslaved forced labour, even after abolition in 1833.

The global chocolate industry is one of the most notorious factors in the prevalence of modern slavery as well as child labour. Well-known companies from Cadbury to Nestlé have been found to have sourced their chocolate from plantations that used enslaved labour to harvest their crops. Globally, the modern chocolate industry is worth over £95 billion annually,[7] with over 60 per cent of the world's chocolate originating in Ghana and the Ivory Coast, where 30 per cent of children labouring on cocoa farms do not attend school,[8] and the countries themselves do not benefit proportionally from the lucrative global trade.[9] Where we spend our money is important. We can all do our part to end modern slavery, just as we hope we would have done had we been alive during the transatlantic slave trade.

RR

12

Gardening

Gardening is a centuries-old beloved British pastime. Garden centres and nurseries, allotments, gardening magazines, books and guides and cosy television programmes are all inescapable aspects of modern society, despite our increasing disconnect from the natural world in our fast-paced urban, capital-driven, technological age.[1] But spending time with plants is not just a pleasant pastime: it is part of our history as human beings.

Plants are living archives. They hold histories, messages and stories from those who have interacted with them before. You need only look around your gardens and at your indoor plant pots to find them. You probably own, or have at some point owned, a brightly coloured orchid. You can grab one at the supermarket now, but that wasn't always the case. A British barrister named John Henry Lance collected and drew several new orchid species in the Caribbean colony of Suriname, as he travelled about, hopping from one sugar or coffee planta-tion to another, his primary role being to police and enforce the (very much unadhered to) abolition of slavery there by the Dutch after 1818. He sent his orchid findings home to nurseries in England, along with the message that slavery was alive and well in Suriname, and that Britain should allow it to go on, for it worked well and made everyone happy. It later turned out that most of the orchids were actually drawn by a mixed-race Surinamese man named Gerrit Schouten, who Lance declined to openly credit. In 1834, another collector, Thomas Colley, was sent to Suriname to gather orchids for English nurseries and botanic gardens. On finding a tree covered in orchids, Colley stripped off every single one, to ensure that no other British collector could take credit for his discovery. Orchids were snatched so unsustainably and irresponsibly that they were never found growing in that location again. Yet it is as a result of these activities and this environmental damage that we can keep these colourful tropical beauties in little pots in our distinctly un-tropical homes today.[2]

Another plant you might have at home or see in a botanical garden greenhouse is the *Dieffenbachia picta*, or the dumb cane – a plant with an exceedingly dark history. If it touches your mouth, immediate swelling and burns can make you permanently mute. Today, many people still end up at A&E having had an unfortunate accident with their dumb canes. The plant was a common vehicle of punishment for rebellious slaves who were seen to need silencing. It was also adopted, like many plants and herbs in plantation societies, as a method of suicide for the most desperate.[3] But plants have also been a form of strength and resistance in slavery: the mimosa plant, indigenous to the Caribbean and wider Americas, was used as a messaging system for enslaved people on the run. When touched, the fern-like mimosa leaves contract, folding up and drooping, remaining that way for a few minutes before unfurling. Escapees running through or hiding in thick forests could track the presence both of fellow runaways, perhaps creating or following routes for one another, and of slave hunters, by observing the position of mimosa leaves. The plants were ingenious alarm systems that kept people safe.[4]

The British were awestruck by the richness of the natural

world in the colonies, and colonial botany, along with techno-logical advancements, led to a rise in domestic gardening.[5] The influx of new plants inspired and sparked the imaginations and creativity of those who had never been abroad but were opened up to new worlds by the colour and life of imported flora. On both sides of the Atlantic, people gardened and found joy in plants. Some, on plantations, did so to guard against starvation and to experience freedom in the ownership of a few small, beautiful, living things. Others, in overcrowded, industrialising towns in Europe, took pleasure in the fruits of that back-break-ing slave labour, bringing close, containing and displaying foreign worlds.

Gardening and the keeping of houseplants were not, however, widespread pursuits in the British Isles until the sev-enteenth and eighteenth centuries.[6] Around this time, homes became brighter and greener as more people in towns and cities could afford glass windows, as well as balconies and gardens, facilitating outdoor and indoor plant cultivation. Many shared the same worries about losing touch with nature as we do today, living in polluted, sooty city air.[7] Plant and seed nurseries found business flourishing in response, with thirty nurserymen oper-ating in London by 1760. These began to feature specimens from the Americas and, later, Asia and Africa.[8] Returning colo-nialists and the owners of slave plantations had been bringing back other-worldly botanical findings and establishing country homes with gardens that sparked a trend and appreciation for 'natural scenery', landscapes and gardening.[9] Ordinary people bought cabinets and cases to display their indoor plants, mini home museums representing their worldliness.[10]

In the 1830s, while Caribbean slavery drew its final breaths, new inventions catapulted gardening forward. The 'Wardian Case' was invented by Nathaniel Bagshaw Ward, a London doctor with a passion for botany. This was the first ever greenhouse, and it could keep tropical plants warm and humid so they could grow in colder conditions. Protected from the elements and kept in a stable climate, plants could now be transported on ships without dying, and go on to thrive in grey, chilly England. Ward built a spectacular domed 'palm store' at Kew in 1848, giving Londoners the chance to experience all the tropical plants that had made the journey and to stand in simulated tropical air that they would never experience directly.[11] The Victorian thirst for tropical colonial plants was insatiable, from the zinnias first collected by slave-ship surgeon William Houston, who sent numerous plants to the Chelsea Physic Garden, to the later ferns and orchids, which experienced an ecological disaster in their native territories as a result.[12] Worlds collided, and through plants, the English were brought closer than ever to the rest of the globe.[13]

Botanical gardens themselves became key imperial assets that supplied, distributed and experimented with valuable plants.[14] They could create a sense of order out of the seemingly wild and uncontrollable colonies, and help to explain why these colonies were valuable commercial prospects by collating and displaying new findings.[15] Soon established at home and across the British Empire from Jamaica and Trinidad, to Calcutta, Sydney and Singapore, many were government-funded institutions, tying the infrastructure of botany to imperial governance.[16] By the end of the eighteenth century there were 1,600 botanical gardens set up by the European nations around the world.[17] They were often run using coerced labour: convict, indentured, enslaved and other. The first colonial botanic garden was established in St Vincent in 1765, and relied on enslaved Africans hired from local planters to do its work.[18] It followed the rules of plantation labour, reflecting the intimate relationship between botany and plantation slavery.[19] The work of enslaved Africans facilitated the garden's growth from

350 plant species in 1785 to over 3,000 in 1800.[20] There is little information about the lives, training or work carried out by the enslaved people who laboured there. Many of the botanical illustrations for superintendent Alexander Anderson (a Scottish surgeon and botanist) are, unusually, signed by a Black man, John Tyley.[21] Only two other of the workers are named in any of the records: men called Mazaran and Washington.[22]

The enslaved people of St Vincent were made to experiment with mass-growing breadfruit, a calorie-rich fruit brought over from Tahiti in the Pacific and believed to have potential as a cheap 'slave food'. As was the case with many of them, this garden's aims were scientific, but with a focus on developing plants for use as cheap, reliable foodstuffs to feed the enslaved, who often experienced chronic malnutrition.[23] This was known as generating 'useful knowledge' for 'economic botany', a term used at Kew Gardens from 1848 onwards, and it is indicative of a system that originally sought to sustain slavery and continue to profit from the colonies through exploitation.[24]

But the Victorian study of plants was more concerned with finding ways to uphold the industries of Britain's empire than the development of a radical new science to make Britain a progressive, modern society.[25] This was no secret at the time. The Royal Botanical Gardens at Kew was essentially a laboratory for imperial maintenance and expansion and for the education of those at home, 'a public symbol of the empire's control over nature'.[26] Thus, the botanic garden was also tied to the apparently benevolent colonial mission, the 'white man's burden' of 'improvement'; justifying empire through the rescue of people and nature from 'barbarity' and 'savagery', and bringing them to 'civilisation'.[27]

These pursuits relied heavily upon the slave trade's infrastructures for collecting and transporting specimens.[28] And while this was an era of death and disease – for white

Europeans, Amerindians, plants – there was also a growth in scientific knowledge.[29] Alongside the towering legacies of botanist Hans Sloane (1660–1753) or slave owner George Hibbert (1757–1837), was a slew of less well-known 'bio-prospectors', who had been contributing to this system for centuries.[30] James Petiver (1665–1718), an apothecary well connected with surgeons on slave ships, used his network to acquire an enormous botanical collection, still important in the study of natural history today.[31] Ship captains, surgeons and sailors collected shells, insects and plants along the West African coastline, while captives were onboarded at gunpoint.[32] Thomas Thistlewood (1721–86), an English slave owner in Jamaica, was a keen, esteemed map-maker and collector of plants. On the same pages of his notebooks, intertwined with his scribbled scientific observations, he records his sexual interactions and clear admissions of numerous rapes of his enslaved women.[33] Control (and harm) of nature and people went hand in hand.

Historically, however, Africa and African people have not been given a central role in these stories, as producers of science, knowledge and historical developments.[34] Thankfully, this is beginning to change.[35] Historians have now found that Africans facilitated the migration of many vegetables, seeds and roots by bringing them aboard slave ships, sometimes sewn into their headwraps, or carried as surplus food for the journey, and giving them new life on the other side of the world. These included watermelons, okra, greens, plantains and bananas, black-eyed peas and sesame, to name just a few. They brought agricultural, botanical and medical knowledge and skills from their homelands to apply to the crops of the New World, knowing better than many Europeans how to produce the best yields or cure tropical ailments, thus saving lives.[36] Slave ships were spaces of both unimaginable human suffering and of science, and transported botanical reminders and memories of

Africa to new horizons, reminding us of the continent's many important contributions to the modern world.[37]

Incidental details in the archives provide glimpses of enslaved humanity, and even of moments of resistance.[38] John Edmonstone, a formerly enslaved Guianese man, emigrated to Edinburgh, where he met a young Charles Darwin. They studied together, and Edmonstone taught the skill of taxidermy to Darwin, knowledge central to the latter's groundbreaking work later on.[39] Englishman Henry Smeathman collected for four years in West Africa, using the slave trade's travel routes. In a painting, he depicts unnamed enslaved Africans pulling down termite mounds to collect insects, and records that they shared local knowledge with him for his studies.[40] African-born Surinamese slave Graman Kwasi earned money healing people. Amerindians showed him the benefits of quinine for treating malaria, knowledge we still use, and the soon-famous Kwasi was paid copiously by the most eminent taxonomist of the day, Carl Linnaeus, who shaped modern classification systems of the natural world. Linnaeus named the plant *Quassia Amara* in his honour.[41] Kwasi was freed, allowing him to travel to Europe, and returned to his own plantation replete with slaves; he is a now controversial figure for his own subsequent role as a slave owner. Kwasi's story, just one of probably countless similar but unrecorded ones, shows the fusion of scientific and economic gain: was he a scientist, an entrepreneur, an opportunist? These stories lead us to ask further questions about what science is, and what makes it authoritative and rigorous; can we call these enslaved and indigenous people scientists too?[42]

As well as inspiring green fingers across the British Isles, botanists were also agents of empire, bringing wealth to Britain and Europe at the expense of others, and taking credit for knowledge that was not their own.[43] The tropics are the world's most diverse regions in terms of plant life, though covering only 6 per cent of the earth's surface. Despite centuries of exploration, extraction and exploitation, less than 0.5 per cent of all flowering plant species have been studied today. This puts into perspective the delusions of Europe, which, in its bid to understand and control nature, and the world, had, it believed, 'unearthed' the Caribbean.[44] In studying, collecting, climbing, measuring, mapping, deforesting, clearing and domesticating the land and its flora, Britain attempted to tame nature, to order it, and to exert man's mastery over the natural world. A much larger force, however, nature continues to grow and fight back, and remain elusive, mysterious and wild.

AL

13

Hans Sloane

On the east coast of Northern Ireland, there's a little village called Killyleagh, best known for its twelfth-century castle. It's a small, lusciously green village on the shore of Strangford Lough, with a population of just under 3,000 people. Killyleagh is also the birthplace of Sir Hans Sloane, best known as a doctor, collector and naturalist, and a name more commonly associated with London and England than his birthplace of Ireland. But his obsessive, acquisitive interest in the natural world began in Killyleagh, where he would collect plants and birds' eggs from the shore as a child.

Sir Hans Sloane's collections ultimately formed the nucleus of the British Museum and Natural History Museum, and he also funded the Chelsea Physic Garden. An eminent man in his own time, he was also the president of the Royal College of Physicians and the Royal Society (succeeding Isaac Newton) and was commemorated in several places and monuments in London, most notably Sloane Square. He's also credited with being the first person to mass-market chocolate in England, with bringing drinking chocolate to Europe, and even, some say, with having invented the practice of drinking chocolate hot with milk – which is entirely wrong as there is evidence that the indigenous people of Jamaica had made a similar drink, blending cocoa, cinnamon and milk, at least as early as 1494.[1]

Born in 1660, Sloane was a wealthy doctor who had a passion for natural history. He studied chemistry in London and anatomy, medicine and botany in France. Sloane is known for collecting a vast number of plants, animals and cultural artefacts during his time as a physician to the Duke of Albemarle in Jamaica.[2] The duke had been appointed governor of Jamaica by James II, and so Sloane's posting to the Caribbean colony would have come with privileges and connections to those in authority. They set sail from Portsmouth in September 1687 and towards the end of the voyage made a ten-day stop in Barbados before arriving in Port Royal, Jamaica, in December.[3] On this initial trip, Sloane spent a total of fifteen months in Jamaica, where he served as a plantation doctor and surgeon to the West Indies fleet, alongside his duties to the duke. During his time in the Caribbean he gathered over 800 plant specimens, as well as live animals, shells and rocks, and he also wrote in detail about the lives of enslaved Africans.[4] Sloane's Herbarium, which is a collection of dried plants typically mounted on paper, was one of the first extensive collections of Jamaican plants, a collection that served as a foundational resource for botanical studies and classifications in history.

Sloane made use of enslaved labour to collect samples and relied heavily on local knowledge and skills for his collecting. In many cases, his progress would have been hampered without this help, and it's unlikely that Sloane's assistants, as enslaved people, would have had a say in the matter. Sloane also collected enslaved people's possessions as cultural artefacts, which included several musical instruments. 'Collecting' in this context is of course a polite way of saying that things were taken without consent. And while there is a possibility that these items were bought or given freely it is also true that if Sloane had wanted to 'collect' one of the few belongings of an enslaved person they would not have had a choice about it.

While in Jamaica, Sloane became deeply involved in the local environment and economy. He invested almost all of his physician salary in Peruvian bark, which was thought to have healing qualities as a treatment for fevers and was highly valuable back in London.[5] He sold the bark for a substantial profit when he returned to England. From his time on plantations, it's clear that Sloane used his time as a sort of fact-finding mission, both for his scientific research and for investment opportunities such as the Peruvian bark trade. He would learn from enslaved people what plants and botanicals had value and uses, knowledge that he then went on to exploit. As well as Peruvian bark, Sloane brought drinking chocolate back to the UK and claimed it as his invention. Although he clearly relied on the knowledge of indigenous and enslaved people in order to build his collections and wealth, what's not clear is how Sloane felt about the slave trade itself, as he only wrote and expressed feelings publicly about his collections and the vast resources he was able to uncover on his travels. Yet it was the network of slave ships and the captive labour that the slave trade created that allowed Sloane to make his name and conduct his research.

Following the Duke of Albemarle's death in 1688, Sloane returned to London where he opened a medical practice and was appointed 'Physician Extraordinary' to Queen Anne and King George I.[6] Back in England, he also met and married Elizabeth Langley Rose, who was a wealthy heiress and widow of Fulke Rose, a resident plantation and slave owner in Jamaica, and it was his wife's inherited fortune that enabled him to continue his work as a collector.[7] Sloane built his vast collections in the decades following his time in Jamaica by absorbing collections created by others, often his friends, such as James Petiver, who was a London apothecary, and by purchasing natural and artificial 'curiosities' from travellers and colonial settlers.[8]

Sloane originally housed his collection in No. 3 Bloomsbury Place but as it expanded he outgrew the original building and had to purchase the property next door. The collections included 32,000 coins and medals, and a herbarium that included 334 volumes of dried plants from around the world, both of which are now in the Natural History Museum in London.[9] The collection also included 1,525 'things related to the customs of ancient times'.[10]

During his time in Bloomsbury, many notable people visited, mostly scholars and dignitaries. The composer Handel is said to have outraged Sloane during a visit by 'placing a buttered muffin on one of his manuscripts'.[11] In 1742, Sloane and his collections moved from Bloomsbury to Manor House in Chelsea, which was a former residence of King Henry VIII, on what is now named Cheyne Walk. Sloane also became a significant landowner in the area, and following his death his residence was commemorated by landmarks such as Sloane Square and Hans Crescent, which is located on land still owned by his descendants, the Cadogan family.[12]

Today, Sloane is credited with helping us understand tropical flora and with bringing the stories of enslaved people to life through his collections. But what's not often spoken about is how he was able to gain such access to build the collections in the first place. Miranda Lowe, principal curator and museum scientist at the Natural History Museum London, and a founding member of Museum Detox, said that Sloane 'most definitely would have used enslaved labour to collect plants for him'.[13] How this should be recognised is still something that needs to be figured out, however, and I'm not sure if words are enough to reflect the value of the work enslaved people contributed.

Hans Sloane

Sloane remains a towering figure in British history, and attempts to contextualise his legacy have met with pushback. But Sloane's contribution to British life – and the research made possible by the museums and collections he left to the country – would have been impossible without slavery and the labour and knowledge of enslaved people at the time. By ignoring this fact, we are saying that the benefits to botany and science, and the profits made, outweigh the damage done by the participation in the brutal regime of slavery. Is the answer to tear down the monuments erected to Sloane, or to add plaques and historical context to explain the background to his career? Currently, we as a society seem unsure about how to proceed – but not acknowledging the actual human resources he relied on to build his collections does a disservice to us all.

RR

14

Isaac Newton

Just think, milord: without the voyage and experiments
of those sent by Louis XIV to Cayenne in 1672 ...
never would Newton have made his discoveries.
Voltaire, letter to Lord Hervey (1740),
prefacing the Siècle de Louis XIV.[1]

At the V&A Museum in London is a portrait of Francis
Williams. Born in 1690, Williams was a Black Jamaican astronomer and free man – rather unusual for his time.[2] Williams's
father had been freed from slavery just before his son was
born, giving Francis unimaginable privilege for a Black person in eighteenth-century Jamaica. Williams took advantage
of this in controversial ways, himself becoming a plantation slave owner. He also travelled to study at the University
of Cambridge in 1720, where he read Latin, astronomy and
mathematics, including the transformative new theories of the
English mathematician and physicist Isaac Newton. When he
returned home, he set up a revolutionary school, imparting his
knowledge to other free Black children.[3]

In 1745, he posed for a portrait in his study, standing with
an open copy of Newton's *Philosophiae Naturalis Principia
Mathematica* (1687), or *Principia*, a compass and a globe.

Surrounded by books, the room is dark and dim, like the library of any eighteenth-century scholar. Williams stands confidently, gazing straight at the viewer, paying homage to a scientific genius, while also asserting his own knowledge and authority, the whole world within his reach: an ideal cosmopolitan gentleman, despite his dark skin.[4] But through the window behind him stretches an unmistakably 'tropical' landscape, that of Jamaica's Spanish Town – green mountains, blue winding river, swaying palm trees.[5] Gazing up at him, we are reminded of how entirely atypical Williams was for his time, a free Black man with command of cutting-edge science. We are also reminded of how vast and extensive the interactions between slavery and science were at the time, and in the making of the modern world. The man credited with discovering gravity, Isaac Newton, lies at the very heart of these connections.[6]

The Enlightenment was a seventeenth- and eighteenth-century movement begun by European intellectuals and philosophers that sought to break with traditional religious and superstitious ways of understanding the world and to stress the importance of science, logic, evidence and rationality instead. Kick-started by the publication of Newton's *Principia* itself, it is often seen as a purely philosophical and scientific age. But the Enlightenment was also an age of flux, of fledgling empires, exploration, slavery and war between European powers, Eastern dynasties and peoples of the New World.[7] Empire and science went hand in hand, growing together and expanding in tandem.

History has tended to portray Isaac Newton as a solitary, immobile figure, a genius who sat at his desk solving the world's great mysteries. He never saw the sea, and the only places he ever visited were Lincolnshire, where he grew up, Cambridge and London. Newton, however, did not work in isolation. Though he never travelled, he was connected to the outside world by the growing colonial system at the time, which was founded on the backs of slaves. It was the system of slavery that allowed Newton to collect the masses of data that proved his theories and made his legacy.[8]

Science came into being as a professional pursuit in 1660 when King Charles II granted two royal charters: to the Royal Society (a 'learned society' that brought together and sponsored scientists to conduct and publish research and experiments), and to the Royal African Company (the commercial vehicle for trade in Africa for slaves). This was the first time a formal, organised, state-sponsored system had been created for either science, or for slavery. They shared members and fellows, and invested money into one another. Not unusually, Isaac Newton was heavily involved with both.[9] Furthermore, along with shares in the East India Company, Newton purchased over £20,000 worth of shares in the South Sea Company, an amount worth over £2 million today. Established in 1711, the South Sea Company traded around the world to pay off British national debt after years of war. In addition, 60,000 enslaved Africans were transported across the Atlantic by the South Sea Company between 1713 and 1737.[10] In 1703, Newton became President of the Royal Society, later succeeded by Hans Sloane, the botanist and collector whose vast wealth came from Jamaican plantations (see chapter 13, 'Hans Sloane'). Newton was significantly less involved in the slave system than many of his counterparts; however, as the historian of science Simon Schaffer argues, both Royal Society presidents were connected by a similar obsession with collecting and science, and both were aided immeasurably in this pursuit by colonialism and slavery.[11]

One of Newton's great pursuits was to ascertain the earth's shape. His famous pendulum experiments, by which he was able to establish that the earth was indeed a sphere, required measurements taken in the tropics to see whether its gravitational pull was weaker near the equator. There were very few specially commissioned vessels for cross-ocean scientific investigations at this time, and so the majority of scientific agents travelled free of charge on commercial or slaving ships.[12] Newton simply could not have advanced his theories without the masses of international data that became possible to obtain through slavery.[13]

Still in their infancy, the British and French empires were very much entangled at this point and the work of French astronomer Jean Richer was central to Newton's arguments. In 1672 and 1682, Richer undertook three French and British state-sponsored expeditions to the French colonies of Cayenne in French Guiana, the island of Gorée in West Africa, and Guadeloupe in the Caribbean, which he travelled to aboard a slave ship holding 250 Africans.[14] All of these were slave colonies, places that functioned through the buying, selling and labour of enslaved people. In Gorée, Richer's office was just above the holding cells of hundreds of imprisoned people awaiting their uncertain fates on the Middle Passage and faraway plantations. In these colonies, Richer collected astronomical information and pendulum data at different distances from the equator.[15] Newton also cites data collected in Martinique by the Catholic priest and traveller Louis Feuillée, who was on the island from 1703, in his 1713 updates to the Principia, a work he continually revised as he gathered further data.[16] His results also contain the astronomical observations of close childhood friend, Arthur Storer, who emigrated with his family to the fledgling North American colonies before 1673, becoming a slave owner in Maryland in the same county that George Washington's family also owned slave plantations.[17] These facts have always been hidden in plain sight. The Principia states clearly the origins of its data (though usually not the names of people who produced it), yet this legacy has not been questioned or acknowledged for hundreds of years.[18]

Newton struggled to trust non-European information. He feared that tropical heat might skew the pendulum results, reflecting consensus at the time that the only genuinely trustworthy and objective knowledge came from Europe, where more pleasant temperatures and fresh winds gave rise to calmer and more rational thinking. In addition, he thought that tropical heat was conducive to laziness and slowness in its (coincidentally, Black and brown) people. Newton also worked at the Royal Mint, where he developed the means to rigorously test coins made of gold from Guinea, in Africa, because he was convinced that Africans were likely to have provided fake gold dupes.[19] These prejudices reflected the racism of the time as well as commonly held apprehensions about 'darkest Africa' and the unknown colonies, and the notion that Africans were cunning, evil and untrustworthy. It is also characteristic of the Enlightenment belief that proper examination, experimentation and evidence could reveal the objective 'truth' about anything.[20]

Throughout the eighteenth century Newton's theories were the subject of numerous controversies and debates. Global expeditions and explorations were organised to collect data to test, confirm and cement his theories, which depended even further on non-European skills and knowledge. Indigenous Inca in the Andes were relied upon by French scientists to find the true shape of the world, confirming that Newton was correct. Tahitian knowledge about star constellations and their use for sea navigation, particularly the work of a Tahitian astronomer, navigator, priest and historian named Tupaia, was essential to measuring the size of the solar system, and to providing the British with stellar geographical knowledge of the Pacific.[21] Explorers and scientists could not have made Great Britain a powerhouse of knowledge and progress without indigenous knowledge, or the infrastructures of empire. In turn, this knowledge helped them to travel further and to conquer, colonise and control more and more foreign territories, creating a cycle of knowledge and power. [22]

It is rare to see the names, stories and experiences of Black bodies and scientists in the historical record, but much exciting work is now connecting science with slavery, centring on African knowledge.[23] Just one example of this is how the role of seventy-six Afro-Jamaican slaves who worked as pioneering metallurgists (the art and science of creating pure metals, which was important to many of Britain's technological developments in this era), has recently been revealed. Their intricate generational knowledge of iron brought over from West Africa accidentally fell into the hands of English ironmaster Henry Cort, who is still credited for these patented 'discoveries' today.[24] In our chapter on colour, we detail the cruel, racist and unethical eighteenth-century experiments, which hinge upon Newtonian theories of light and colour, into why the skin of African people is 'black' in colour, experiments during which Black enslaved bodies, dead and alive, were cut open and dissected for 'research'. Newton's entanglements with slavery continued long after his death.[25]

Newton catalysed the Enlightenment, and his legacy has survived today not solely because of his individual genius but thanks to the global connections that made his breakthroughs possible.[26] This has been a story of a world in which slave ships are sites of science; a story of trust, authority and who has the right to be remembered. It speaks not only to the ubiquitousness of slavery in building the world we know today but also of what is taken for granted, what is ignored and erased in the making of modern society.[27] There is much more work to do, but expanding and enriching the story of Isaac Newton marks just one of many excellent beginnings.

AL

15

Gynaecology

Birth is a dangerous business: as I write this, maternal death rates in the UK are the highest they have been for over twenty years. This is shocking enough before you realise that the risk of maternal death is almost four times higher for women from Black and minority ethnic backgrounds compared with their white peers.[1] The reasons are complex, but most healthcare providers believe that structural racism plays a part, and it is certainly true that gynaecology and obstetrics, two branches of medicine that should be about protecting and healing women, have some very grim secrets of their own.

In April 2018 the New York Public Design Committee voted unanimously for a statue of J. Marion Sims to be removed.[2] J. Marion Sims is often credited as being the 'father of modern gynaecology', and he was able to develop his gynaecological techniques by operating on enslaved African American women throughout the 1840s. His most prominent victim was Anarcha Westcott, who lived in Alabama and suffered terrible damage to her vagina and rectum after a three-day labour to deliver a stillborn child. She then underwent around thirty experimental and non-consensual procedures over four years to correct the fistulas without anaesthesia – readily available at the time – which allowed Sims to develop the first surgical techniques to repair rectal and vaginal fistulas. Many consider Sims's procedures a medical atrocity.[3]

We spoke to Professor Kathleen S. Murphy at California Polytechnic State University, author of *Collecting Slave Traders: Natural History and the Eighteenth-Century British Slave Trade*. Kathleen pointed out that many scientific discoveries that have shaped our modern world have insidious roots in slavery and oppression. While the white, Western, mostly male scientists are recognised for their contribution to human knowledge, the Black enslaved people they operated on – and without whom these discoveries would have been impossible – are very rarely remembered. An example of this is Henrietta Lacks, who, following treatment for cervical cancer at Johns Hopkins University Hospital in 1951, had her cervical cells taken without her knowledge or consent by Dr George Gey.[4] These cells, nicknamed 'HeLa' cells, are used widely throughout the medical world for research. Johns Hopkins Medicine appears to be proud of the discovery and boasts on its website about the cells' multiple uses:

> Today, these incredible cells – nicknamed 'HeLa' cells, from the first two letters of her first and last names – are used to study the effects of toxins, drugs, hormones and viruses on the growth of cancer cells without experimenting on humans. They have been used to test the effects of radiation and poisons, to study the human genome, to learn more about how viruses work, and played a crucial role in the development of polio and COVID-19 vaccines.[5]

Henrietta Lacks died later that year at the age of thirty-one. In an online statement, Johns Hopkins acknowledges that they could have and should have been in better communication with Lacks and her family out of respect for her and her privacy.[6]

You will certainly have used medicines or products that have been tested on the HeLa cell line. So what do we do about this kind of complicated ethical situation? Murphy doesn't think the answer is to simply 'throw it out'. 'It's not even really possible. We can't stop using Newtonian theories of physics', for example, although Newton had investments in the slave trade and used slave ships to conduct many of his famous experiments (see chapter 14, 'Issac Newton /Gravity').[7] The answer, Murphy thinks, lies in acknowledging the contribution made by the subjects of those experiments, even when the contribution was coerced or unwilling.

It's especially hard to separate women's health and gynaecology from plantation slavery because there was a particular interest in enslaved women's reproductive health, which created a supercharged environment for medical discoveries. We spoke to Dr Annabel Sowemimo, author of *Divided: Racism, Medicine and Why We Need to Decolonise Healthcare*, who explained that the links between gynaecology and slavery came down to money: 'Slavery obviously was very profitable, and is where a lot of people made their fortunes. A lot of middle-class individuals became very, very wealthy. And maintaining an able-bodied slave workforce was quite imperative to the whole enterprise and also for the production of more slaves.'[8] Plantation physicians came into being partly because there was a need for them to ensure that enslaved women could continue to bear children, who would themselves be enslaved and produce more profit for the plantation owners.

Although obstetrics and gynaecology have always been a branch of medicine, the advent of plantation slavery created a sudden availability of a huge group of women, 'thousands upon thousands of people that were not seen as people, and did not have autonomy.'[9] This led to a huge number of advances in medical research, over a relatively short period of time. It wasn't just enslaved women, as Sowemimo makes clear: incarcerated individuals, people with mental health conditions and poor women, particularly those of Irish descent, were also experimented on.[10] Nonetheless, the combination of financial incentives and the sheer number of enslaved women is 'really how the speciality developed and came into being'.[11] Effectively, plantations provided physicians with a medical playground in which they could experiment, trying to prove theories such as 'Black people don't feel pain',[12] and 'Black people aren't as intelligent as white people', along with general surgery practices and methods. Sara Baartman was a South African woman who became enslaved in the nineteenth century, and was taken to Europe under false pretences to appear in 'freak shows' that specifically focused on her large buttocks.[13] Baartman was exhibited in these shows across London and objectified as an exotic species. Following her death at age twenty-seven, her body was dissected and preserved for scientific study by French physician George Cuvier. J. Marion Sims also experimented on an enslaved woman, known simply as Lucy, to treat her vesicovaginal fistula. During an excruciatingly painful operation, in which she was offered no pain relief, Sims commented that Lucy bore the operation with 'great heroism and bravery'.[14] Another brutality visited upon non-consenting women by medical practitioners was forced sexual acts, and rape was common in so-called medical experimentation as a way to test a women's reproductive health.[15] These rapes led to higher birth rates among enslaved women and increased the number of complications during birth.[16]

Josiah Nott was a physician in the nineteenth century known for his espousal of race science. In addition to other pro-slavery physicians of the day, for example Samuel Cartwright, Nott produced studies aiming to prove that Black people were not only inferior to white people but in fact belonged to an entirely different race.[17] Physicians like Nott used their experiments on enslaved people to develop race-based science, which they used to justify the enslavement of non-white people and to support discrimination against other races. The polygenesis theory, which was at its most popular in the late eighteenth and the nineteenth century, held that different races evolved from different origin species – and that some races were genetically superior to others.[18] Proponents of polygenesis and supporters of slavery used such arguments to suppress those who believed slavery to be cruel and exploitative, declaring that a certain skin pigment or the width of someone's nose not only signified low intelligence, but also denoted a physicality that would benefit from manual labour.[19]

We can see remnants of this type of thinking in contemporary discussions about athletes. During the 2024 Paris Olympics, the words used to describe certain gymnasts had a very similar tone. Whereas white gymnasts would be described as graceful, elegant or beautiful, for instance, Black gymnasts were called powerful, dominant or robust. This was particularly evident during the performance of Team USA, led by Simone Biles, the most decorated gymnast in history, who also happens to be a Black woman. Even though the arguments behind race science have long been disproved, its legacy within our language remains.

The evidence and techniques developed on plantations are still in use today, but the voices of those who were experimented on and used to progress medical research have been lost: we will never know what they thought and felt about what was happening to them. And the racist myths that underpinned race science are still in play – in modern medicine a discrepancy persists between the treatment of Black people and that of other patients. Black women in pain are still not listened to. In a report released by Pew Research Center in the US in April 2022, 70 per cent of Black women aged eighteen to forty-nine said that they had 'experienced at least one negative interaction with care providers', which included the dismissal of their pain.[20] Following the death of Kira Johnson in 2016, a Black mother who lost her life following a routine caesarean section, the 4Kira4Moms campaign was founded in order to draw attention to the fact that doctors were not taking Black women's pain and medical care seriously. Her story has been portrayed in medical dramas *The Resident* and *Grey's Anatomy* in an effort to highlight the issue of Black women not being heard.

The ideas underlying race science also influenced colonial attitudes to birth. The perception that Black people were physically stronger than white people gave rise to the belief that Black women were 'better' at giving birth. Dr Annabel Sowemimo points out that this 'is not true, [but] again shows us how medicine is so socially constructed. It fit their narrative that childbirth should be easy for Black women because they were exploiting Black women to make more slaves, and they needed Black women to birth.'[21]

There is an interesting parallel today, where, by contrast, some commentators have speculated that the higher mortality rate for pregnant Black women is actually on account of some sort of anatomical 'deficiency'. It seems particularly cruel that not only is the contribution of Black women to the progress of gynaecology obscured and dismissed – when their lives and bodies were put on the line for medicine – but that Black women today are still being put in danger and being subjected to unnecessary pain and interventions because of the same racist perceptions that harmed their predecessors. Medicine is another example of a modern system built on racist views, experimentation, practices and preconceptions, all of which continue to shape how doctors are trained and how procedures are carried out. Unconscious biases are real, and they affect the outcomes of modern-day patients. To fix the systems, we must understand how they were created.

RR

16

Blood Pressure Monitoring

If you're over eighteen and have had any medical appointments, there's a good chance that your blood pressure will have been checked at some point. It's a pretty standard medical practice and something that we will all experience in our lifetimes. Blood pressure is the force of blood circulating against the blood vessel walls. It's measured in millimetres of mercury (mmHg) and is usually expressed using two numbers: systolic pressure over diastolic pressure. When the heart beats and pumps blood, the pressure in the arteries is systolic. Diastolic pressure is the pressure in the arteries between heartbeats when the heart is at rest. A typical blood pressure reading would be something like 120/80 mmHg, while a high or elevated blood pressure reading would be anything over 140/90 mmHg,[1] although the parameters for what is deemed 'high' changes depending on age and where the test is taken.

One of the earliest modern researchers into how blood pressure could be measured was English scientist and clergyman Stephen Hales. Hales was born in 1677, and throughout his life he made significant contributions to medicine, plant physiology and chemistry.[2] Despite having no formal scientific or medical training, Hales was able to conduct extensive studies on blood flow and blood pressure, ultimately helping to develop one of the most basic principles in general medicine.

In 1698, Hales co-founded the Society for the Promotion of Christian Knowledge.[3] The society aimed to spread Christian teachings and education across the British Empire, and in Britain's North American colonies there was a particular focus on the moral and spiritual instruction of individuals, which included efforts to convert the children of enslaved people. Hales was also one of the founders of the Georgia colony in North America, which was established by the British in 1732 and was intended to be a refuge for those fleeing persecution in Europe and a place for impoverished people to start a new life. Its founders, led by James Oglethorpe, believed that starting a new life in America was the best way to 'reform' the urban poor in Britain. Interestingly, the Georgia colony banned slavery (and rum) from 1735, three years after its founding – though economic pressure from a group of pro-slavery colonists known as the 'Malcontents' led Parliament to lift this ban in 1751.

Although he would later pioneer the measurement of blood pressure, Hales was first interested in ventilation and, being acutely aware of the poor, unhealthy conditions that enslaved people were forced to endure on slave ships, he began developing a ventilator for use on the ships around 1741, with the aim of reducing mortality rates. When enslaved people and prisoners were transported across the Atlantic, they were stacked together in the ships' holds, in horribly tight and dark spaces. Hales understood that in these cramped conditions the air became 'vitiated' or spoiled after being breathed for just a short period. Deaths were common on the Middle Passage, and Hales recorded significant improvements on ships that used his ventilators. On two Atlantic crossings, ships with his ventilators carried 575 men without any loss of life – and the fact that this was a rarity speaks volumes.[4]

Although Hales was an eyewitness to the plight of enslaved people on ships sailing the Middle Passage, there is no evidence that he was overtly against slavery. His primary concern was improving public health, and we have no record that the specific impact of the misery of slavery registered with him. But, given that so many people who worked on plantations or in refineries back in Britain could ignore the reality of the slave trade, it is perhaps not surprising that a scientist like Hales was able to do so too.

Hales's ventilators were also used in prisons, where he recorded similar results. In London's notorious Newgate prison, Hales's ventilators reduced the annual death rate by more than one hundred people.[5] At the Savoy Prison, a military jail, the ventilators reduced the annual death rate from between fifty and one hundred to just one.[6] That was a remarkable difference. Prisons had the same problems as slave ships, where prisoners were treated with a basic level of humanity and held in extremely cramped and poorly ventilated conditions.

While he was working on ventilation and educating enslaved children, Hales began to experiment on live animals and, through a series of observations that were innovative at the time, he was able to manipulate their blood flow. He called this approach a 'statistical way of investigation' and he aimed to measure the force of blood in veins and arteries.[7] In one of his first experiments, Hales tied a live female horse on her back and cut her left crural artery after first binding the horse's leg, before inserting a brass pipe that was connected to a glass tube. When he loosened the bind, Hales noted that the horse's blood rose significantly in the tube, which demonstrated the blood pressure exerted from the heart. Similar experiments were conducted on sheep and dogs. To refine his measurements Hales used a lateral manometer, a device used to measure the pressure of fluid. This enabled him to record blood pressure more accurately by measuring the height to which blood could be forced from the brass insert up to the glass tube. Thanks to Hales's work, later scientists and doctors were able to build on these discoveries and refine the study of blood pressure.

As mentioned earlier, Hales never explicitly expressed any thoughts in his writing on the morality of slavery. Although he was a member of the Board of Trustees for the Georgia colony during the period when it had banned slavery, it should be noted that the Trustees were motivated principally by the desire to promote an austere, hard-working lifestyle among their own colonists, many of whom had been debtors in prison back in the UK. And rather than prohibiting slavery on humanitarian grounds, the Trustees in fact repealed their ban in 1751 following pressure from colonists eager to catch up with the planter aristocracy in neighbouring Carolina. Accounts about Hales and his work focus solely on the advancements he made in the various sciences. He is considered a philanthropist for improving the conditions under which people lived, whether they were free, enslaved or imprisoned, and his advancements in medicine are used every day by medical professionals. It's rare that people recognise his connection to the slave trade as part of his legacy, or that research conducted on enslaved people played a crucial part in the history of medicine. Hales worked and lived aboard slave ships, and though his work did some good for enslaved people, it also benefited those who captured and enslaved them.

Olaudah Equiano wrote about the despair he felt when first captured and boarded onto a slave ship:

When I looked round the ship too and saw a large furnace or copper boiling, and a multitude of black people of every description chained together, every one of their countenances expressing dejection and sorrow, I no longer doubted of my fate; and, quite overpowered with horror and anguish, I fell motionless on the deck and fainted. When I recovered a little I found some black people about me, who I believed were some of those who brought me on board, and had been receiving their pay; they talked to me in order to cheer me, but all in vain. I asked them if we were not to be eaten by those white men with horrible looks, red faces, and loose hair.[8]

When he realised that his fate was sealed, he said

I now saw myself deprived of all chance of returning to my native country, or even the least glimpse of hope of gaining the shore, which I now considered as friendly; and I even wished for my former slavery in preference to my present situation, which was filled with horrors of every kind, still heightened by my ignorance of what I was to undergo. I was not long suffered to indulge my grief; I was soon put down under the decks, and there I received such a salutation in my nostrils as I had never experienced in my life.[9]

For many, death was a preferable fate to making it across the Atlantic, the only salvation they could hope for. Hales found a way to prolong life aboard slave ships, but this also made it easier for enslavers to carry millions of captured Africans to a life of enslavement.

The close history of scientific advancement and slavery should be acknowledged more widely. In modern medicine, the kinds of biases this research can produce are still in evidence. It's commonly believed that Black and South Asian people are at a higher risk of developing high blood pressure than the rest of the population, a 'fact' repeated by charities like Blood Pressure UK and elsewhere. As people from Black and South

Asian backgrounds tend to have a diet that contains more salt and fat (a leading cause of hypertension) there's a presumption that they are more susceptible to high blood pressure than others. But all this tells us is that high blood pressure has more to do with diet than it does with ethnicity. On a global scale, no ethnic group is more affected by high blood pressure than any other. There is clearly more work to be done to recognise the legacy of slavery in modern medicine. In the words of Dr Kathleen Murphy, an author and a historian of the slave trade, 'What we haven't fully done is to understand just how deep these connections are, and how insidious and wide-reaching they are.'[10]

RR

17

Mahogany

It is rare to find a brand-new piece of mahogany furniture for sale today, but if you've ever visited or stayed at an old hotel or country house, you are likely to have encountered the sturdy, dark, shiny wood fashioned into tables, chairs, cabinets and countless other furniture pieces. Mahogany is immediately reminiscent of an old world, a bygone time of stately homes and unimaginable wealth. Long-lasting yet rare, and thus expensive, it is suited for flooring, stairs, furniture and ships. Lord Nelson's iconic flagship at the Battle of Trafalgar, HMS *Victory*, was one of many to flaunt mahogany upper decks, entrance ports and interior fittings.[1] Plantation owners, merchants, mariners and colonists were constantly worried about the decay and rot of wood on the slave ships that made the beginnings of industrialisation and globalisation possible.[2] Mahogany provided the perfect solution. It is a rugged, resilient hardwood found in the tropics: dense, heavy, and resistant to rot and insect infestation.

Strong and striking, yet allowing for delicate, intricate carvings and details, mahogany was (and still is) also a popular wood for railway cars and musical instruments, such as guitars, keyboards and drums.[3] While the earliest recorded use of mahogany in European furniture was in Philip II's El Escorial

Palace in Madrid in 1584, and at Nottingham Castle in England in 1680, it was not until 1725 that mahogany really burst into the public consciousness.[4] From there ensued a golden age lasting one hundred years, followed by endangerment and decline – a period correlating directly with the major rise and fall of slavery in the Caribbean.[5]

Mahogany comes in two main forms: the short-leaved West Indian variety, and the larger-leaved Honduran mahogany found in an area of South America that stretches from Colombia to Brazil. For 300 years mahogany was harvested primarily using enforced African labour.[6] Long before this, indigenous Taino Amerindians used the tree for carving sacred objects and for medicine, while the Miskito of Central America crafted it into canoes.[7] 'Mahogany' derives from the Yoruba word *m'oganwo*: newly arrived slaves recognised the tree as similar to a West African variety, the khaya tree, and the worms living in it as edible.[8] Guided by indigenous people, the earliest European settlers felled mahogany for building houses, and for flooring, shingles and simple furniture.[9] The knowledge of indigenous and African people was fundamental to mahogany's ascension as a precious resource in Europe.[10]

Enslaved men, women and children were placed in gangs contracted out from different plantations, in groups ranging from ten to fifty people and working on rotation for three months at a time.[11] Men cut and hauled logs, women dragged and cleaned heavy branches and the children bundled them together.[12] Gangs were isolated far out in the forests with nothing but food, livestock, a white overseer, their work and each other.[13] Camps were set up among the trees with small, rudimentary dwellings for sleeping. The enslaved workers selected promising trees, then constructed raised wooden platforms around each one. Men were made to stand around the trunk, painstakingly hacking it with axes. After felling enough trees, pathways were cleared back through the forest along which trunks were dragged out, in itself some of the hardest and slowest work. Paths and later roads penetrated thick forest, opening them up for the first time and thus changing them forever.[14] Burning, clearing and hacking the forest away with machetes, the workers then dragged the logs for many miles to a water source and floated them downstream in the cool dark night alongside canoe-paddling slaves. Such brutal, dangerous work naturally caused deaths and injuries. Larger gangs were organised around regimented timetables, and strict discipline and punishments kept order: fifty strong slaves to one white overseer – deep in the forest – would require it.[15]

England's consumer revolution provided many people, for the first time, with rising disposable incomes, leisure time, and a thirst for shopping and luxury.[16] Mahogany became a status symbol for wealth and power; it was so expensive and opulent that many, including American Founding Father and slave owner George Washington, painted pinewood furniture dark and shiny in imitation.[17] The wood arrived in England aboard slave ships, and was awaited by craftsmen in Bristol, Liverpool, Lancaster, Sheffield, Leeds and Hull. Also popular in Scottish mercantile communities, in Leith, Dundee, Montrose and Aberdeen, it was all the rage in great country houses and castles.[18] From a small local craft, the mahogany industry grew into a major international business popular in England, its North American colonies, and even with Caribbean great houses, to which 'Windsor Chairs' were shipped – back to the very islands where the wood had originated. Popular craftsmen, reliant on the slave trade for their raw material, thrived: over 17,000 pieces have been attributed to the renowned Chippendale workshop, now found in prominent country homes and museum collections on both sides of the Atlantic.[19]

At the peak of the transatlantic slave trade, Parliament

passed the 1721 Naval Stores Act, which removed duties on specific imports stored on naval ships. Planters wishing to dispose of wood felled to clear plantation land and to make money from its sale pushed for mahogany's inclusion. Tree-less land left more open vistas from which to survey the countryside, limiting hiding spots, shelters and the distance a runaway could go before capture.[20] Coinciding with a shortage of walnut trees (another desirable timber) in England, this removal of duties fast-tracked mahogany's attractiveness, accessibility and affordability for British and American craftsmen.[21]

With the fashion for mahogany growing, sugar planters rapidly worked through the colonies' naturally occurring stocks. As early as 1735, Jamaican and other nearby mahoganies had been exported at such alarming rates that they were already becoming scarce along the coastlines, while inland mahogany in the mountains was too dangerous and difficult to access.[22] New, plentiful supplies of mahogany were soon found and heavily exploited by British-owned enslaved Africans in Belize by 1765, an area known as the 'Mosquito Coast' after its indigenous Miskito people.[23] The Miskito cleverly manipulated warring Spanish and British forces in the region, and chose to provide the British with highly valuable and useful knowledge on effective mahogany extraction in exchange for military and political protection. In doing so, they were also complicit in the suffering of enslaved Africans. The knowledge, labour and oppression of Africans and indigenous peoples were closely entangled, but they did not always act in support of one another.[24]

Attempting to curb mahogany's decline, the Company of Apothecaries' Physic Garden tried and failed to cultivate mahogany trees in England, while the British attempted in vain to introduce or tame wild mahogany in other colonies, such as Tobago. The only solutions came with pasting mahogany veneers over cheaper woods in an effort to preserve supplies, and using technological developments such as steam-powered sawmills to cut labour costs. From a once-precious resource, mahogany became mass-produced, and mass-marketed.[25]

Requiring decades to mature, mahogany would never be an efficiently renewable resource.[26] Continued attempts to grow and log this 'green gold' in places like West Africa, the Philippines, Peru, Venezuela and the Brazilian Amazon remains controversial and problematic today. Mahogany has even become an invasive species, attracting strong protest in many of these places.[27] Meanwhile, deforestation continually threatens the delicate balance of vulnerable biodiversity on the Caribbean islands, which have experienced repeated extinctions and the endangerment of forest rodents, insects and birdlife.[28] Concerns about Caribbean deforestation for plantation use, and what would happen to the native people and the forests' abundant flora and fauna, have, however, been expressed in text from as early as the 1650s. Yet these warnings went consistently unheeded.[29] Barbados's deforestation and habitat collapse had been caused by English Royalists in just twenty years, 'as planters submitted nearly 80 per cent of the landmass to sugar cultivation – a fate that the small colony would quickly share with neighbouring islands'.[30] Deforestation was no new issue, and had been a concern in England since the sixteenth century, which saw early attempts at conservation and protection of its own forests, through programmes, books, pamphlets and parliamentary acts.[31]

In Jamaica, forests remain under threat today. Bauxite mining across the island thwarts conservation aims and penetrates contested lands owned by the Accompong Maroons – descendants of slaves who escaped into forests and island interiors, fostering independent communities, cultures and languages. The Accompong Maroons believe that their land constitutes an independent indigenous territory, making this mining illegal, a fact that the Jamaican government contests. To defend such land claims, and protect their right to clean water and safety, the Maroons are willing to enact violent resistance. Once again, the West enriches itself from extraction in the Caribbean at the expense of local communities and the environment, whose right to thrive on their own terms is repeatedly denied.[32]

Natural resource extraction depends upon the disruption of the landscape, rendering it inhospitable to the animals, plants and people that once dwelled within it. Nature is put to work, made into a factory.[33] And yet Europeans never achieved their goal of cultivating mahogany on a mass scale on plantations, and instead irreversibly depleted the supply. Mahogany laughed in the face of the Enlightenment belief that man could one day exert total mastery over nature. The story of mahogany binds together the pleasure of Europeans with the trauma of the enslaved: past and present, ecology, exploitation, capitalism and luxury walk hand in hand.[34]

AL

18

Tobacco Merchant's House, Glasgow

There are lots of hints around Glasgow that point to the city's historic links to the transatlantic slave trade, but they're subtle. There's Jamaica Street, of course, named after Britain's largest plantation island. Completed in 1763, the street was home to many warehouses full of imported goods from the Caribbean ready to be shipped all over the world.[1] Merchant City is an area of central Glasgow that was rebranded in the 1980s by developers, its name a reference to the area's historic concentration of prosperous tobacco merchants and their associated businesses. Then there's Tobacco Merchant's House, built in 1775, on the east side of Merchant City at 42 Miller Street.[2]

The house at 42 Miller Street was built by John Craig, although the land itself was feued to Craig by John Miller, a land investor who first laid the street in plots in the 1750s.[3] The Scottish feudal system, long abolished, was similar to the lease-hold system of England and Wales. Under the terms of a feu, John Craig would have paid a fee to John Miller annually and if the terms of the agreement were broken by Craig, Miller would have had the right to evict. The house, which was relatively modest compared to the extravagant mansions of tobacco merchants at the time, was bought by Robert Findlay of Easter-hill in 1782.[4] Findlay and his son, also named Robert, gained their wealth from tobacco in Virginia, where other Findlays ran plantations. It was as the Findlay residence that 42 Miller Street earned its name 'Tobacco Merchant's House', and its place not only in Glasgow's history but in Scottish history too.[5] The building still stands and is the only house from the peak of slavery that has survived in Merchant City.

Scotland has a contentious relationship with the history of its involvement in the slave trade. The country's history is often framed as one of struggle against oppression and invasion from its English neighbours, while its place as part of the British Empire is often viewed at a distance. In reality, the Scottish were heavily involved in the empire, as administrators, financiers, doctors, lawyers and merchants, to name just a few of the roles occupied by prominent Scots.

Before Scotland's union with England in 1707, the Navigation Acts restricted the trade that Scotland could do with England and its colonies.[6] Dating back to 1660, the Acts were designed to tip the scales of global trade in England's favour by requiring imports from its colonies to come to England first before they could be shipped to other countries.[7] As an independent nation, Scotland was seriously disadvantaged by this. Unlike England and many other European countries, Scotland's small colonies in Nova Scotia and America did not produce enough wealth to compete with its neighbours, which led the Scottish economy to fall behind its European counterparts. Scottish merchants were unable to fully exploit the triangular trade without direct access to England's colonies. Following the Acts of Union, these restrictions were dropped and Scotland was able to trade freely, giving its merchants access to new markets and a chance to take part in the slave trade.[8]

Once the Scots were able to trade directly with British colonies in the Caribbean, tobacco and sugar became the dominant imports to Glasgow. For consumers on both sides of the Atlantic, tobacco was a popular social and recreational drug, usually smoked in pipes or rolled in cigarettes, and occasionally used within medicinal remedies. For merchants, tobacco was a 'cash crop' grown mostly in the southern states of America, and tobacco was often bartered to buy enslaved people, retain indentured servants, pay local taxes and on occasion to buy manufactured goods from England. Even after slavery was abolished in the British colonies and America, the scale of tobacco production did not decline, indicating that the work continued at the same rate, carried out by the same people. It was simply 'slavery by another name'.[9] The Scottish Oswald family are a good example of how lucrative the tobacco trade could be, and how becoming a so-called 'tobacco lord' – merchants who'd made fortunes trading tobacco across the Atlantic – could solidify your place among society's elite.[10] Richard Oswald was a notorious slave trader and plantation owner who built Auchincruive House in South Ayrshire and became known as Oswald of Auchincruive, and his nephew, George Oswald, was a prominent tobacco lord. Exact figures detailing George Oswald's wealth are not readily available, but as a politically influential family the Oswalds were able to shape government policy, invest in infrastructure around Glasgow and significantly shape Glasgow's development.[11] The tobacco trade also meant that the Oswald family remained wealthy for generations. Oswald's brother, Alexander, was also a merchant and was one of the founders of the Royal Infirmary, while George Oswald's son, Richard Alexander, was an MP for Ayrshire between 1832 and 1835. George Oswald went on to inherit Auchincruive House, and eventually two tobacco plantations, for which he claimed compensation upon slavery's abolition in 1833.[12] Richard Alexander Oswald was awarded £4,080 for the Pemberton Valley estate and £865 for the Boscabelle Pen Estate, both in Jamaica.[13] His second wife, Lilias

Oswald, was also awarded the same amounts for both estates,[14] alongside Lilias's sister, Lady Jane Montgomerie,[15] and Lady Jane's brother-in-law, John Hamilton of Sundrum Jr.[16] In total, the family were awarded £21,780 in 1835, just under £3.5 million today.

Glasgow was not the only British city whose buildings and streets have been shaped by tobacco and slavery. As one of Britain's most vital port cities, Bristol, like Glasgow, has the legacy of slavery etched into the bricks of its streets and grand houses. Tobacco plantations typically had between seven to twelve labourers, some of them free men and some enslaved. Bristol's docks frequently received hogshead barrels of tobacco harvested and packed by enslaved labourers, and you can track the rise of the commercial tobacco industry by following the records of houses built and family fortunes made. In Bristol, the Wills family were a typical example of this growth. Henry Overton Wills arrived in Bristol from Salisbury in 1786 to open a small tobacco shop with his business partner, Samuel Watkins.[17] The shop was called Wills, Watkins & Co, and would eventually grow to become one of the biggest companies in the world.

In 1791, after Watkins had retired, Wills partnered with Peter Lilly, a prominent figure in the tobacco industry. This partnership led Wills to scale up his commercial tobacco store and open a first tobacco plant in Bristol where they manufactured their products, a significant investment that indicated their ambitions to meet a rising demand for tobacco. Compared with the capital needed to open a sugar refinery at the time, a tobacco plant was relatively affordable, needing a much smaller upfront cash injection of between £200 to £1,000 depending on business size.[18]

Typical start-up costs for a tobacco plant in the late eighteenth century are given in Table 2:[19]

TABLE 2

	£	S	D
Cutting engine and wheels	60	0	0
3 Large presses	42	6	0
3 Jack presses	34	18	6
2 Spinning tables and wheels	7	0	0
1 Chop engine	7	0	0
2 Saddle horses	30	0	0
1 Black cart horse	8	0	0
1 Snuff cart	8	8	0
	197	12	6

The new business with Peter Lilly was called Lilly, Wills & Co., but like its earlier counterparts, the company went through various name changes as additional partners came and went. By the time Henry Overton Wills had retired, his sons had renamed the company as W. D & H. O Wills and had expanded the business, with greater investment, a larger market to sell to, and new machinery that ramped up production capacity. By the end of the nineteenth century, W. D. & H. O. Wills was one of the largest producers of tobacco goods in the UK.[20] When it merged with other British tobacco companies in 1901 to form Imperial Tobacco Company, it managed to resist competition in the market from the American Tobacco Company to become the seventeenth-largest company in the world.[21]

This legacy – of enormous capital growth and family dynasties built on the backs of enslaved workers and their exploited descendants – links Glasgow and Bristol, but this is something barely acknowledged on either side of the border. The only clues lie in buildings like Tobacco Merchant's House in Glasgow, which has only survived in Merchant City due to restoration work by the Scottish Civic Trust, and in the names of streets and the buildings where the tobacco lords once toasted their success. In 2017, three years before the toppling of the

Edward Colston statue in Bristol, students at the University of Bristol petitioned to remove the Wills name from the 'Wills Memorial Building', which is the university's most prominent building. The Wills family gave land and property to the university worth about £1.37 million in the first half of the twentieth century, and the institution refers to them as 'the founding family of the university'.[22] The university's statement on the Wills family goes on to explain that 'They were not enslavers, but their business and financial success benefitted from slavery as they traded in tobacco grown by enslaved Africans and their descendants.'[23] At the time when the petition was started – as is still the case today – there was growing frustration among residents and students over Bristol's failure to acknowledge the city's many links to the slave trade and how its economy and infrastructure had benefited. In the words of historian Madge Dresser, 'There really was a denial of the history of slavery in Bristol. In the mid-1990s there was the Festival of the Sea, a celebration of the city's maritime past, and not a dickie-bird was mentioned about the slave trade.'[24]

Fortunately, this is no longer the case. Although the Wills family name remains on the building, the University of Bristol pledged £10 million in 2023 to 'address racial disparity'.[25] Vice-Chancellor and president of the university, Professor Evelyn Welch, added: 'I am deeply sorry for these damaging and hurtful experiences which continue to the present day, and I apologise to everyone impacted by those injustices.'[26] The money will be used for a 'Reparative Futures' programme, which will invest in schemes including Bristol's current Black Scholarship programme.[27]

RR

19

Salt Fish

Fish is a staple of the British diet, battered and crispy on a Friday night, in a steaming winter pie, and as a quick source of protein for lunch. One of the most popular ways to buy fish is where it has been preserved (and processed) in some way: tinned tuna, sardines, anchovies and mackerel are national pantry favourites. More 'elevated' forms include smoked salmon and haddock. Salted cod and other dried, salty fish are increasingly sold at mainstream British supermarkets, particularly in the 'World Food' aisles that allow Britain's Caribbean diaspora (and foodies of all origins) to access a staple tenet of West Indian cuisine. Salted fish is also sold as a luxury deli item across the Scottish Highlands and Islands. In fact, many Scottish Highland towns gained their wealth from an unexpected source: selling salted herring into the transatlantic slave system.

According to David Alston, historian of Scotland's slavery links, yearly exports of herring from Scotland to the West Indies were between 50,000 and 80,000 barrels until emancipation.[1] In 1798 around 61 per cent (around 51,892 barrels in that year alone, and typical of the decades preceding abolition) of salted herring sent to the West Indies from Britain was exported from Scotland, offering huge opportunities to Scottish merchants.[2]

The herring trade turned sleepy northern fishing villages into small hubs of activity, industry and trade. Known as the 'Silver Darling' at the time, herring were sold to many places, but by the late eighteenth century, almost two-thirds of exports went to the Caribbean, where they were bought in order to feed the enslaved populations living on plantations.[3] Curing cheap, low-quality fish with salt enabled them to be stored for months in barrels without spoiling on the journey across the Atlantic. Fish was brought in from most northern of points of Scotland, such as Lewis and Lochbroom, before being processed in towns like Campbeltown and Greenock (which is where most of the profits ended up).[4]

The trade was also the cause of conflict, with some people wishing to adopt new advanced technologies for fishing, to increase yields and make the process more efficient, and others fiercely opposed to this apparent drive towards innovation and profit, preferring to protect small fishing communities and their vulnerable herring populations, which could be quickly impacted by overfishing.[5] Fishing went from being a seasonal activity that supplemented income to an occupation that could keep the town going all year round. Multiple men could hold a share in a small boat and split its profits, meaning one or two fishing vessels could support a whole community: an attractive prospect.[6] Demand for these herrings was so high that Clyde merchants reported West Indian vessels patiently waiting in harbours for weeks longer than they wished in order to pick up their supplies. This created tempting opportunities for many local seamen employed in the fishing 'busses', who, with their useful knowledge and skills, would jump ship on to Caribbean-bound slaving vessels. Alston writes that 'legions of women' worked in fish curing, a mark of how the industry touched every part of society.[7]

Salted foods were ideal for feeding the enslaved in the

Americas. Another major export from the British Isles was salt beef from Ireland; essentially beef jerky, which had been exported for over one hundred years.[8] As well as feeding slaves, this cheap meat formed the basis of naval diets on slave and trading ships in the Atlantic. Surprisingly, this product did much better in the French Caribbean than in the British, and was mentioned copiously in French sources regarding plantation slavery. Salted beef was 'only one of the many foodstuffs of a thriving Irish provisions trade' to the Americas 'and operated on a scale unmatched by any other single country trading in the Atlantic world', according to one historian.[9] These foodstuffs included salted pork, butter, fish, hides, skins and tallows, cheese, beer, bread, candles and pickled tongues, often consumed on ships heading towards the Americas. By the 1680s, the salt beef industry had settled and become centralised in the port towns of Cork, Dublin and Belfast, where people worked seasonally for low wages, producing tens of thousands of barrels of beef that were sent overseas.[10] The provisions trade immediately and profoundly impacted Irish port towns such as Cork, which soon became Ireland's wealthiest and best connected port of the eighteenth century, with a booming population.[11] Salt beef was a staple for planters and their slaves in the French colonial diet, and despite attempts with salting local tortoise – and of course importing salt fish – nothing seemed to beat beef for the French islands.[12] The influence of the salt beef and salt fish trade shows how enslaved people were not only the *producers* of popular, valuable commodities sold to Europe, but also profitable *consumers* who shaped trade and markets around the world. Enslaved people were, then, important and influential figures in these complicated circles of trade.[13]

The best Scottish fish went to Europe or to other colonial ports, and so the dry, tough, heavily salted fish that arrived in the West Indies was the poorest quality available.[14] At first, though, salted herrings were not intended for food. Fish was originally used as a fertiliser, and the salt was meant to deter hungry, desperate, enslaved people from stealing them to eat – though many still did. If those caught were not punished by being whipped, shot or having their tongue cut out, they were likely to die of dehydration from consuming so much salt. It was thus eaten only by the most malnourished, and today it is still seen by some as a food for the poor. But over time, enslaved communities found that they could make stolen salt fish safe by processing it (washing, soaking and boiling it to remove the presence and taste of salt). It eventually became a common slave food, and as it was long-lasting, was stockpiled for inevitable periods of food shortage.[15] It was edible, just, but certainly not enjoyable.[16]

Salted herrings provided a protein- and vitamin D-rich, non-perishable source of food that was cheap, quick and convenient.[17] A 1737 account of plantation provisions in Barbados by a man called John Woolman claims that slaves were provided with 'six pints of Indian corn and three herrings' as their full week's menu.[18] Jamaica appears to have consumed the greatest amount of Scottish herring, perhaps because of the links provided by its substantial Scottish population, particularly from 1740 onwards. Other islands also ate salted cod from North American markets such as Chesapeake, New England, Nova Scotia and Newfoundland.[19]

In the earliest days of slavery, European colonists, indentured servants and enslaved Africans generally all ate the same things: salted fish, salted beef, salted turtle, tubers and root vegetables like cassava. Food insecurity was a defining aspect of enslavement, due in part to geographic isolation, weather fluctuations, hurricanes and war blockades, but also due to the poor provisioning of plantation owners who did not want to spend money or give up profitable land to grow food for the enslaved.[20] Enslaved people almost certainly did not have access to enough protein, and the majority were malnourished. As food historian and archaeologist Peggy Brunache explains, 'the desire for animal protein was strong and thus ... enslaved communities actively exploited their environment whenever possible for sources of meat'.[21] Forced to develop creative and innovative strategies of survival, subsistence practices included fishing and foraging in the sea and rivers for aquatic creatures and foraging wild plants – subversive activities that increased resilience, energy and community.[22] Stewed dishes known as gumbo, callaloo or pepperpot were popular and effective as dishes to which small amounts of fresh or salted meat could be added when available, but which were otherwise eaten vegetarian.[23]

Increasingly, in addition to their meagre diets, slaves on larger plantations were given small plots of land, or 'provision grounds' on which they could cultivate a few crops of their own, such as starchy roots and greens. This led to internal trade and exchange between slaves within and between plantations, providing opportunity for some self-sufficiency and autonomy over what was done with, and went into, their bodies outside of their harsh working hours. African food and growing practices could be mimicked, remembered and preserved on these plots, giving them a non-violent means by which to both resist the all-encompassing domination of the slave master and to assert their own culture and identity.[24]

These were a huge success, ensuring food stability in the face of the political, geographic and environmental instabilities of a region so reliant on imports. Foods like ackee, cocoa, mangoes, breadfruit and others were all experimented with to provide alternative forms of cheap nutrition.[25] Slaves grew yams, cassava, corn, eddoes, okra, potatoes, plantains and pigeon peas, and raise livestock (which they could raise, but not eat themselves) to sell at weekend markets.[26] With the money, they bought wood, eggs, fruits, salted fish, beef and pork for dietary variety.[27] Markets created slave-run economies that kept the whole colony fed, Black and white. Even when the land provided by plantation owners was tiny, provision gardens improved the health, mood and morale of the enslaved. It was believed that having something of their own to care for would discourage runaways.[28] Old cookbooks and receipts also show that traditional African dishes were cooked in the homes of planters and in the slave quarters, particularly by women, fusing foods, tastes and cultures and bridging European, African and Amerindian traditions.[29]

Demand for salted herrings did not die off completely after the end of the slave trade in 1807, as there were still slaves who needed to be fed in the colonies. Petitions against the ending of slavery, which would eventually kill off the demand for salt fish, were, however, sent from the towns of Wick, Cromarty and Tain in 1824 and in 1836. These communities knew that the end of the trade would result in a loss of income, and perhaps even livelihood. The industry provided employment in fisheries, curing stations, shipping vessels and ports. Indeed, after 1838 when slavery and the later apprenticeship system were fully abolished, there was a collapse in the market.[30] These facts complicate an accepted narrative of Scotland's past and its national identity today as a nation disadvantaged due to English colonisation and with long-held dreams of independence. Accepting that at least parts of Scottish society profited from, and perpetuated, both slavery and the expansion of the British Empire challenges this narrative. As the journalist Yvonne Singh writes, 'this view of Scotland as the victim is enmeshed in politics, in Scottish nationalism (of a Scotland bullied by its large English neighbour), which is perhaps why it has been so difficult for Scotland to address its past.'[31] It is not always easy, throughout history, to disentangle the oppressed from the oppressor. Often, as in the case of Scotland, it is possible to be both a brutalised victim and a brutal villain at the same time.[32]

Scotland's slaving legacies can be found in our food cultures at home and abroad. Salted fish, available at open-air markets and in supermarkets and often still imported from abroad, remains a part of the Caribbean diet today. Each island has its own traditions and ways of eating it. In the former British West Indies, salt fish is the national dish of Jamaica and Barbados, where it is enjoyed with cornmeal called cou cou. Trinidad and Tobago mornings are characterised by bake (a fried bread) served with shark meat or buljol, a salted cod salad. Salt-fish cakes and fritters called accras are well-loved staples in every household and restaurant across Grenada, St Vincent, St Lucia and beyond. Salt fish is a major culinary and cultural symbol, born of bondage and starvation, and of the resourcefulness of hungry and impoverished, but determined, enslaved people and their ancestors.[33]

AL

20

Cromarty

When we think of Britain's involvement with the slave trade, Scotland is often left out of the picture, and it's easy to understand why. It might have something to do with the way that 'British' and 'English' are often used interchangeably, but the public's awareness of slavery is much stronger in connection to the English cities of London, Bristol and Liverpool than it is to Glasgow, for example (see chapter 18, 'Tobacco Merchant's House, Glasgow'). Liverpool, in particular, has openly acknowledged its slave-trading history, and is also the home of the International Slavery Museum, which in 2023 was awarded £50 million by the National Lottery Heritage Fund.[1] These port cities were a key part of the triangular trade, the point at which ships loaded with goods produced by enslaved people would dock in the UK ready to be traded.

In Liverpool there is an obvious legacy, in the warehouses and slave ships, but Scotland's ties to the slave trade are much more deeply hidden. In this chapter, we're going to focus on a small town named Cromarty, about an hour's drive from Inverness. If you were to close your eyes and imagine a picture-perfect coastal town, there's a chance that the image you'd come up with would be just like Cromarty, one of the Highlands' quaintest towns. With just over 700 residents, Cromarty is around 117 square miles in area, a touch smaller than Milton Keynes or Canterbury, but despite this the town has multiple links to the slave trade, and especially to Guyana, where there's another town called Cromarty.[2] Although Guyana is located on the northern coast of South America, sandwiched between Venezuela and Suriname, it is still considered a Caribbean country as it was once a British colony, although it was first colonised by the Dutch who called it Berbice. Aside from the Falkland Islands, no other South American country was ever under formal long-term British rule.[3]

Many Scots had been drawn to settle in Berbice in the late 1700s to found plantations, eager to make a fortune in cash crops like cotton. Those who came worked as plantation owners and managers, and as merchants trading enslaved people or exporting the crops they produced to Europe and America. The Frasers of Reelig, a family from Cromarty, were slave owners who ran plantations in Berbice.[4] Edward Satchwell Fraser inherited a share of a plantation and owned another outright. At the height of his wealth, Fraser owned 171 enslaved people in Berbice.[5] He later became part of the plantation union, which he acquired in 1800. The Plantation Union was both the name of a sugar plantation in Berbice and a partnership between Fraser and other plantation owners, including James Fraser of Belladrum and Colin Mackenzie of Mountgerald.[6] Edward Satchwell Fraser's sons trained as overseers and ran the family plantations following their father's death. In a property register for Berbice dated 1818 the family estate is unnamed, but the most likely candidates are plots 23 and 28, which were registered under Fraser's name.[7] The Frasers were typical of hundreds of Scots who emigrated to take part in the slave trade or who held investments in plantations from afar, though you'll not find a statue acknowledging this in Cromarty.

In the centre of Cromarty, there are some beautiful

sandstone buildings dating back to the 1770s. Now social housing, in their Georgian heyday these buildings served as the town's hemp-weaving factory. Hemp was woven into sacks, which were vital to keep the global slave trade running, and the north of Scotland was a popular place for textile manufacturing as factory owners could take advantage of cheap – mostly female – labour in this economically deprived region. Hemp sacks were needed on plantations to package goods such as cocoa and cotton for export, as well as for clothes and other materials that were used by enslaved people. The Scottish hemp industry is just one of many examples of people working in Britain to supply an integral service to plantation owners abroad. The production of Welsh cloth, which was also known as 'Negro cloth' in Powys, Wales, is another (see chapter 7, 'Wool and Linen').

The hemp industry was a hugely significant part of the Highlands economy, and stretched from the Caribbean to the Baltic. Merchant companies like the British Linen Company imported hemp from St Petersburg into Inverness, from where it was distributed to women to be spun at home, before the yarn was shipped to Cromarty to be woven into bags. Technology was also advancing at this time – the invention of the spinning jenny and spinning frame, which were larger, more mechanised versions of the original spinning wheel, cut production times substantially and led bosses to demand a greater quantity of finished product in a shorter time. This impacted the women's lives dramatically, increasing the toll of work and confining workers to a static place beside a spinning wheel, whereas before they could be mobile while spinning.[8] Being in a position to exploit female labour, merchants saw the opportunity to make a coarse cloth out of hemp.

Although the Cromarty factory was a 'slow-producing factory' and not a mechanised one, its workforce still made around 1,000 yards of hemp cloth a day, which is equivalent to the total output in the much larger Inverness.[9] The factory employed up to 250 workers within its premises and around 600 home workers in the town. In total, there would have been over 800 people employed in hemp production, more than the number of people living in Cromarty today.[10] These employees weren't necessarily the poorest in society, but they did include former agricultural workers who had been displaced during the brutal Highland Clearances, as well as people for whom the idea of emigrating to the Caribbean and setting up as land and slave owners was a distant prospect. But although these workers would never travel to the West Indies, they were still entirely dependent on trade there.

David Alston is a historian who writes about the legacies of slavery and the Scottish Highlands. He's also a Cromarty resident. When I spoke to him, he was keen to establish just how important hemp production was for the local population – so transformative that the poor relief otherwise provided by the church to struggling parishioners ceased as soon as the factory was up and running. The factory employed the whole community, from the age of four (small boys who delivered the spindles to the weavers) to the age of ninety. The factory was vital for the people who lived there. But what did they think about the system they were involved in? 'They would have known but I'm not sure they would have known what it meant in practice. It's quite a difficult question, but once you've watched the social scale, there were certainly lots of young men from poverty who went to the Caribbean. Lots of them died, but lots did well, and came back.'[11]

This is difficult to grasp: most of us would like to believe that, if we'd been alive during the time of slavery, we would have been vocal abolitionists, condemning it strongly and having no part in it. We certainly wouldn't want to think that we would profit from it, however indirectly. But the fact is that the global networks of trade that connected Cromarty and Guyana are still in place today, but are even more complex and opaque to the ordinary person. How much do we know about the people who grow and pick our food? Where are our pensions or savings invested? Who made the trainers you are wearing? Chocolate, for example, is a product that many of us consume every day but it has serious problems with modern-day slavery and exploitation in its supply chains. Ynzo van Zanten, a representative from Tony's Chocolonely, a Dutch company that bills itself as 'slavery free', had this to say: 'Anybody in front of a chocolate shelf, or any shelf for that matter, needs to realise that they have the opportunity to vote for the world they want to live in every day. You vote through your shopping basket.'[12]

As Alston explained, the coast of Guyana was particularly suitable for growing cotton, especially a variety called sea cotton, a type of long-staple fibred cotton that could be used in mechanised production. Cotton was key to the Industrial Revolution in Britain, but before it could be grown in Guyana, the rich coastal land needed to be reclaimed from the seas.

These reclamations were 'massive works of engineering, on a colossal scale, all carried out by enslaved African labour', Alston told me. The process would have involved the construction of dykes and elaborate drainage systems. Land was reclaimed from the sea so that plantations could be built, and, if the land was fertile and the plantation was a high producer, owners would want the option to expand. The connection between Guyana and faraway Scotland that originated with a few key early planters resulted in a sizeable Scottish population in Guyana, when those from Scottish rural areas went there to seek their fortunes.[13]

Cromarty was, and is, a small rural town whose workforce was once reliant on the slave trade, and therefore on the suffering of other human beings many thousands of miles away. Their community thrived and their families were fed – but at what cost?

RR

21

Swimming

When the sun is shining in the UK, there is always one guarantee – the queue to your local lido will be around the block. It is no different at Cleveland Pools, the UK's oldest lido, which dates back to 1815.[1] A grade-II listed building on the banks of the River Avon, it is something of an architectural marvel. Most lidos in the UK were built around the 1930s, but Cleveland Pools is not only grand in age but also significant in history: it is the only swimming pool in Britain that is known to have direct links to the transatlantic slave trade.

The pools were built on land owned by William Vane, the first Duke of Cleveland. In the aftermath of the Slavery Abolition Act of 1833, many slave and plantation owners were awarded a share of £20 million in compensation, paid out by the UK government to ease the hardships of elites who were no longer able to profit from the forced labour of enslaved people. Vane owned 233 slaves in Barbados and was awarded £4,854 in compensation.[2] This may not seem like much, but that figure would be worth just under £725,000 today. On 9 February 2018, the official HM Treasury Twitter account posted a 'surprising #FridayFact':

In 1833 Britain used £20 million, 40% of its national

budget, to buy all slaves in the Empire. The amount of money borrowed for the Slavery Abolition Act was so large that it wasn't paid off until 2015. Which means that living British Citizens helped pay to end the Slave trade.[3]

The post was swiftly deleted following a backlash. The tweet confirmed that the descendants of slaves, including myself, actually contributed to the compensation paid to slave and plantation owners. Why anyone thought that this would be a 'fun fact' to share on social media goes to show how confused our understanding is of Britain's role in the slave trade.

Aside from Cleveland Pools, what connections link slavery with the activity of swimming itself? The idea that 'Black people don't swim' is a long-standing stereotype, and data released by Sport England in 2024 backs it up, to some extent: they found that 95 per cent of Black adults and 80 per cent of Black children do not swim.[4] I'm in the 5 per cent of Black adults that can and do swim, but I learned when I was in my thirties after completing the Swim London programme, a twelve-week course that targeted non-swimmers in London. The course was led by Swim England's teacher of the year Harley Hicks and was championed by BBC presenter Ayo Akinwolere. The classes, because of where they were based in North and East London, were made up of a diverse group of working-class and Black and brown students.

Even now, every time I'm at the pool I'm usually the only Black person doing laps, even if things are slowly changing and, at my two-year-old daughter's swimming lessons, we are, thankfully, not the only Black family participating. But where does this apparent aversion to swimming come from?

I spoke to Kevin Dawson, a history professor of the African diaspora at the University of California, about his research on enslaved swimmers and underwater divers. He shared his own experiences, pointing out that the US also has 'this perception that Black people don't swim', even though, as Kevin told me, 'I'd grown up swimming, and I'd grown up surfing.'[5] But when he brought his academic expertise to bear and went to the sources, he found something fascinating: not just stories about enslaved people swimming to freedom, and using boats to escape to freedom, but 'very rich sources on Africans with really exceptional swimming and underwater diving abilities'.[6]

This suggests that the myth that Black people can't swim (rather than don't swim), is a relatively modern phenomenon, albeit one that has somehow stuck around for generations. As with many Black athletes, a subject we cover in more detail in chapter 36, the focus is on the body, and the supposedly inherent qualities that make Black bodies different: Black people have even been told by swim instructors that due to their muscle-dense bodies, they are unable to float. When Kevin mentioned enslaved people swimming to freedom, I thought of the Middle Passage, the route slave ships took from West Africa to the New Americas. The voyage would often take between six and eleven weeks and would result in many deaths. In chapter 16, on blood pressure monitoring, we learned of the stifling conditions aboard slave ships. People were piled on top of one another and were stuffed on to the ships as cargo. As you can imagine, sanitation was extremely poor, sickness was common, and the air was thick and putrid. The sick and weak – no longer valuable cargo to the enslavers – were often thrown overboard, because it would be too costly to care for them. Once land was in sight, some even made a bid for freedom by jumping overboard.

Kevin Dawson provides more detail, revealing both the possibilities open to those who could swim and the complexity of the attitudes to slavery at the time. Some of the islands in the West Indies are only a mile apart, close enough to swim between. Also, as Dawson says, 'If there was a ship that was offshore, you could swim out to that ship and stow away. Or that captain might have agreed with that person, "Alright, I'll take you to freedom if you can get to my ship".'[7]

Why would a captain offer to help an enslaved person? The answer lies in the uneven way that slavery was abolished, and the subsequent patchwork of regulations around slavery in the region. A ship's captain from Mexico – where independence had been obtained from Spain in the 1820s, and slavery abolished – might be 'appalled by slavery and would be perfectly willing' to help an escapee.[8] Similarly, when, after centuries of profiting from the slave trade the British abolished the practice, they became 'perfectly willing to take people from Cuba, from Puerto Rico, from French islands, or Dutch islands. And so people are swimming out to those places, to those ships to obtain their freedom.'[9]

Slave owners and traders might have been aware that this was happening and sought to prevent it. Dawson has found some examples of enslaved people being punished for swimming – including a woman who was enslaved in the American South whose owner would beat her if he 'caught her swimming, but she loved to swim so she swam anyway'.[10] And a horrifying case from St Vincent, the 'most sadistic form of punishment I think I've ever seen', in which the slave owner

> takes this guy, he puts them in a barrel, nails the lid onto the barrel and drives hundreds of nails into the sides of the barrel, then turns the barrel over on its side and rolls [it] down the hill into the ocean. So the guy would be impaling himself as he's trying to break out of the barrel. You would think that that would discourage people from swimming, but it doesn't.[11]

The fact that swimming was going on despite these brutal

punishments suggests that it was of huge importance for enslaved people. Swimming wasn't just a skill to improve the quality of their lives, as well as to potentially change their fates, they also swam recreationally – for fun.

To return to Kevin Dawson's research, he has found that plantations both big and small were mostly established on waterways, so that their produce, such as sugar, indigo, rice, tobacco or cotton, could be loaded directly onto ships. In both the Caribbean and the American South, colonies tended to sprout up around the perimeter of the islands, or around the lagoons, bays and deltas of larger countries. The people who loaded and unloaded ships were enslaved – not only did they spend a lot of their working life on the water, but they also had direct access to waterways. They could swim to relax, cool down, and could even fish and set traps to supplement their meagre diet. Dawson notes that 'these beaches and waterways became cultural spaces, social spaces for the enslaved'.[12]

The ability to swim and catch fish for your own dinner must have represented an important freedom. The water became a way for some enslaved people to earn cash and gain some agency by hiring out their skills, whether by becoming divers or by participating in dangerous work that the planters didn't want to do themselves.

This took lots of forms, as Dawson has found. For example, sometimes crews of enslaved people would be sent out to catch fish or sea turtles, perhaps with only a captain in charge (the obedience of the crew was ensured by the fact that their families were on the mainland, effectively being held hostage in return for docile behaviour on board). But opportunities to make a little money might have sometimes occurred on these trips, and there are examples of enslaved people offering to navigate for ships that had got into trouble, or helping salvage wrecks, and diving for conch and sponges.

Some enslavers even valued slaves with diving skills higher than those without, as they could reach wrecks and salvage otherwise lost goods, which could be extremely lucrative. Spanish treasure ships would leave Cuba in late summer and early autumn – hurricane season in the Caribbean – and, as Dawson says, 'sometimes an entire fleet would go down with tonnes of silver'.[13] Squads of enslaved divers would go out, fifty or sixty at a time, and strip the wrecks, producing millions of dollars' worth of income for their enslavers in just a few weeks. Dawson notes that, in the 1850s in the American South, an enslaved person who was considered a 'prime field hand'[14] would be worth around a tenth of that of an experienced diver.

Interestingly, although the divers would often be hired by another enslaver, they would also be paid something themselves, evidence of just how complicated slave economies could be. If Mr Smith owned a slave who he knew was a great diver and another enslaver, Mr Jones, needed someone who could dive, Mr Jones could approach Mr Smith and hire his enslaved diver for a specific task. The available profits encouraged both parties to do something that, as Dawson says, was 'technically illegal. It's illegal to hire people out because enslaved people can't enter into contracts. This gets disputed all the time. Slavery is supposed to treat people like property, not labourers.'[15]

The consequences of these arrangements could be huge for enslaved people, not just because of the inherent risks they ran but also because of the rewards. Diving was effectively 'incentivised labour', in which the diver might sometimes secure a wage, or might earn a share of the profits instead. At the end of a profitable salvage trip, the enslaved diver could earn 'spectacular amounts of wealth', 'enough money to buy his freedom, the freedom of family members', as well as ships and property.[16] This would be equivalent to hundreds of thousands of dollars in today's money.

Salvage was hard, and incredibly risky. For everyone who managed to earn their freedom, many more died or were horribly injured. However, it's easy to see why people took the risk: swimming could offer a literal route to freedom for enslaved people with very few other options. So how did an activity that Black people not only participated in but also enjoyed and were valued for, and which was considered an important, even transformative, ability, turn into the 'Black people can't swim' stereotype just over a century later?

Following the abolition of slavery in all countries, it still took well over a hundred years before Black people were seen as anywhere near equal to white people – a process that is, sadly, still ongoing. And where Black people did gain access to the same legal rights as white people, even then integration wasn't smooth.

In countries like America, Canada and Britain there were rules – both official and unspoken – that prevented Black people from mixing with white people in public and in private. This included public swimming pools, which were not places that were welcoming to Black people – something that is still true today. There are stories of white people throwing bleach in the water when they saw Black people swimming in 1950s and 1960s America. My grandfather saved for months to take his family on holiday to a famous British holiday camp, which included several water parks. When he called up to book, he was told, 'We don't take your kind'. This was in the early 1970s. Experiences like these leave lasting scars, and the generational memory persists. So it's possible that the reason fewer Black people than white people learn to swim is because they were denied the opportunity – not because they can't.

RR

22

Football: Liverpool and Everton

In 2017, Everton Football Club began a long-awaited project to move away from their long-time home ground to a new £500 million, 52,000-seater stadium, built on the Bramley-Moore Dock in Liverpool, a city that once served as the centre of Britain's slavery-derived wealth. In February 2021, the historian Joe Mulhern sparked controversy by publishing an article exposing the extensive and shocking profiteering from slavery in Brazil, which went on far beyond abolition in Britain's own colonies, of Liverpool's one-time mayor and the stadium's new namesake, John Bramley-Moore (1800–86).[1] It turns out that the stadium's name is not the only link between slavery and Merseyside's beloved Liverpool FC and Everton FC: the entanglements go much deeper, all the way back to the founding of the clubs as professional institutions in the mid-nineteenth century. Even though football, our national sport, wasn't professionalised until at least two decades after slavery's abolition, it's possible to find the insidious traces of wealth drawn from that terrible industry seeping into every aspect of our national life.[2]

In response to Mulhern's article, Everton FC decided in August 2021 to remove Bramley-Moore's name and association from the stadium, instead promising a 'lasting memorial to the historic crime of slavery' at the club's future visitor centre.[3] Publicly memorialising slavery in Liverpool and elsewhere in the UK has always been contentious and difficult, with some believing that statues, place names and memorials should remain as they are so as not to 'erase' history, whether that history is regarded as good or bad. Others believe that changing place names or removing statues from public spaces and placing them in museums puts those histories in context, thus avoiding the implication that the individuals they commemorate are worthy of unambiguous admiration. Making such changes allows us to acknowledge that our relationship and understanding of the past is always evolving. When preserved and labelled appropriately in a museum, these figures are thus not erased but are instead positioned as relics of how our society once saw things, and of why we have moved on. Football has faced repeated accusations of racism against its Black and ethnic minority players, and so many people saw this move of Everton's as a commitment to take seriously issues of historic slavery and racism, conversations which exploded after the 2020 murder of George Floyd in the US by the police and the resulting upsurge in the Black Lives Matter movement.[4]

John Bramley-Moore, or John Moore, was the owner of one of the largest British-Brazilian merchant houses, a giant that exported slave-produced coffee and also directly invested in the illegal slave trade, slave-worked gold mining and other manufactures and industries.[5] But, as Joe Mulhern makes clear when I speak to him, 'Moore is not just involved indirectly in the export of slave products. He's a slaveholder himself, owning enslaved people on his coffee estate and his urban commercial premises.'[6] Best estimates say that he owned between five and fifteen Africans, and is also rumoured to have profited from a large sale of newly arrived African slaves. Mulhern says the truth of this is unclear, but it could explain 'how an ordinary man of fairly modest means becomes such a wealthy and well-respected merchant later on in his career'.[7]

Mulhern explains that Brazil is a key site of what historians have called the 'second slavery'. After abolition, the world was rapidly industrialising, and Britain was at the centre of this. New opportunities and conditions arose for slavery to continue covertly in more peripheral places, away from areas the British government generally kept watch over. Many industrialists felt justified in continuing to use forced labour: it was needed, it seemed to them, to fulfil the working classes' new hunger for sugar and caffeine.[8] These peripheral zones included the US South for cotton (see chapter 6, 'Denim/Blue Jeans'), Cuba, Brazil, St Croix in the Caribbean, Suriname and others.[9] The British state tried in vain to shut down this activity, but foreign slave traders were quick to remind Parliament that removing 'rightfully owned' property was illegal and would require compensation, such as had been received by slaveholders in the West Indies in the 1830s. They cunningly played upon the nation's increasing commitment to free trade and property protection as the British government became more committed to capitalism, individualism and liberty. Though the government refused to give compensation, they did allow Brazilian merchants to retain currently enslaved people, as long as they did not purchase any new labourers. Always finding loopholes, British merchants simply hired slaves from one another on temporary contracts to work on coffee plantations, gold mines and railways. They also supplied Brazilian slave traders with goods to barter for illegal slaves in Africa on their behalf, bolstering Brazil's heavily entrenched slave society, and making their fortunes in return.[10] British involvement in Brazilian slavery lasted until 1888, when the trade was finally abolished there.[11]

Like many rich men of his day, Bramley-Moore also tried his hand at politics, becoming mayor of Liverpool in 1848 and later serving two terms in Westminster as an MP. Here, in the 1860s, he came under fire from Britain's abolitionist lobby for actively and passionately defending the Brazilian government's continued support for slavery, for which he was awarded the Imperial Order of the Rose, one of Brazil's highest honours of the state, in 1863.[12] Nonetheless, Mulhern says, Bramley-Moore lied about his associations with slavery, and 'quite cleverly obfuscates and sanitises his own legacy. He creates this legacy as a self-made man, like a lot of men at the time. Even his 1901 entry in the Dictionary of National Biography makes no reference to slavery, only calling him a "Brazilian merchant", which masks all sorts of direct and indirect connections to exploitation.'[13] He covered his tracks so completely that even Mulhern, who has dedicated years of his life to studying these links, missed the connection between the slaveholding company John Moore & Co., oft-mentioned in the archives, and the John Bramley-Moore for whom Liverpool's famous docks are named, until the announcement of the new stadium. Mulhern laughs at himself, but emphasises that 'this story definitely speaks to a much larger erasure of slavery from Britain's history in the way that we remember it today. So many of these former slaveholders were able to rewrite their own histories, write slavery out of their own personal stories. Eventually, these connections were written out of British history as a whole.'[14]

Ten years before the abolition of Brazilian slavery, Everton FC began life under the name St Domingo's FC in 1878 – strange, given that Everton is an English team, and St Domingo was the name of the former French slave colony, now Haiti. In fact, the club was named after a Methodist church with that name, built in 1758 by George Campbell, a prominent West Indies sugar boiler who spent much time on the island and later became mayor of Liverpool, in 1763. A slew of other places in Liverpool were also named St Domingo by Campbell. In

1877, the new Minister of the Church set up a cricket team for children during the summer, which morphed into a football club in the winter, birthing the club in 1878.[15] And so although the name came from slaving activities more than 100 years before the club's birth, it reveals much about the ubiquity of slavery's legacies in Liverpool. In the growing, industrialising city, as more and more urban youth fell into gambling and alcohol, football had been promoted as a moral mission that would involve young men in exercise and camaraderie.[16] The game had shifted over time from an upper-class recreation to one for workers who wanted an escape from harsh industrial mining and factory conditions.[17] Nonetheless, in order to professionalise it, with teams, leagues and tournaments, the sport depended for funding on society's elites – politicians, aristocrats, merchants and slavers, eager to attach their names to rising cultural institutions.[18] Football benefited immensely from Britain's economic growth, which was brought about by urbanisation, industrialisation, slavery and empire.[19]

Perhaps unsurprisingly, given how many Britons continued to deal in slavery after abolition, four out of the eight original patrons of the fledgling Liverpool and Everton football clubs, like Bramley-Moore, also maintained direct and indirect slavery interests abroad after 1833. Dudley Ryder, Viscount Sandon, 3rd Earl of Harrowby and an MP for Liverpool between 1868 and 1882, was grandson of a plantation owner, the son of a former Liverpool MP and 'one of the most formidable pro-slavery voices', who turned to Brazilian slavery when he failed to prevent British abolition, and fought for its legality in Parliament.[20] Dudley Ryder took over his father's work promoting Brazilian slavery, famously campaigning for the Brazilian government to pay compensation to British subjects for the loss of property and slaves following a major rebellion of enslaved people.[21]

Scottish merchant, shipowner and football patron Robert Galloway profited from the slavery in Peru even after its abolition in 1854.[22] Galloway's shipping line's principal cargo was guano, calcified bird manure, the trendiest natural fertiliser in Europe. David Kennedy, the researcher who uncovered these links, elaborates: 'Before abolition in 1854, Peruvian guano mining was carried out exclusively by African slaves. Subsequently it was mined by kidnapped ("blackbirded") Pacific Islanders, or else by Chinese "coolie" labour – 100,000 of whom were transported to Peru between 1849 and 1874.'[23] It was incredibly dangerous work: guano collectors experienced lung damage, accidental burials and commonplace violence. Having knowingly profited from unfree labour, in 1888 Galloway became a Tory city councillor for Everton.[24]

Another Everton patron was Liverpool city coroner Clarke Aspinall. His grandfather had been a founding member of the African Merchants Company in 1750, aiding Liverpool's slavery expansion and profiting from 113 slave voyages up until 1807. In total, he was involved in facilitating the transportation of 68,000 African slaves from the Bight of Biafra to the Americas. Clarke's great-uncle James Aspinall was also the co-owner of the slave ship *Zong*, on which one of the infamous and horrific events of the transatlantic slave trade took place; one that galvanised abolitionists and is still widely taught and discussed today. The 1781 *Zong* Massacre saw 131 humans callously thrown overboard and drowned by its British crew, to 'conserve' dwindling water supplies after the ship got lost at sea.[25] James Aspinall actively sought compensation for 'lost property', triggering one of the most significant criminal investigations in history. The investigation concluded that the company had lost property through no fault of its own, and had not committed the murder of any human beings. Clarke Aspinall himself (no doubt successful in part due to his family's wealth, which also derived from slave plantations owned by his mother's side of the family) was involved in post-abolition pivots towards African palm-oil trading, another industry dependent on 'slavery-like' coercive labour in West Africa.[26]

Finally, there was David MacIver, who ran a 'commercial colossus in Liverpool's maritime power', the D&C MacIver Shipping Co. and the Cunard Steamship Company.[27] He conducted shipping activities in support of the pro-slavery Confederacy during the American Civil War, which determined the future of slavery in the US. Probably with his business interests in mind, MacIver openly expressed his support for the Confederacy, and the company was also known for having denied first-class passage to the famous former African American slave Frederick Douglass when he travelled to speak in Liverpool in 1847.[28]

Connected from their inception, and sharing the same heritage, this story is about both Everton *and* Liverpool football clubs. They began as one institution and split into two in 1892, so the money from these four patrons kickstarted both clubs. Liverpool FC's founding father and first owner, John Houlding, founded the second club when he was dismissed from Everton in 1892, but before that he had been an important figure in bringing these patrons on board.[29] Moreover, he himself was indirectly connected to the slave trade through his in-laws, who were prominent St Kitts sugar plantation owners known to have hanged and burned many of the enslaved workers on their estates who had staged revolts against their treatment. Houlding supported the Tory Party's electoral machine in the north of the city and became chairman of Liverpool Working Men's Conservative Association, another indication of how many pots these elites had dipped their hands into.[30]

It is hard to overstate the far-reaching impacts of 'second slavery' upon our nation, past and present.[31] Beyond football,

Mulhern says, the political and commercial impact of the trade was substantial, with the monies derived from it reinvested everywhere in the British economy: in mining and industrial property, and in railways in Brazil (worked by slave labour), in north-east England along the River Tyne, and in Scotland. Slave-worked gold- and copper-mining in Cuba were incredibly fruitful for Wales in particular.[32] Lloyds Banking Group, for instance, began life as 'the London and Brazilian Bank', and many other merchant banks emerged from it.[33] Mulhern feels that this undoubtedly 'complicates that self-congratulatory narrative still strong in the UK about our important role in the abolition of the international slave trade and global slavery', something that is undeniable but also, clearly, only part of the story. Liverpool's slave links have been copiously explored, but the story is usually neatly parcelled up and concluded at one of three dates: 1807 (the abolition of the slave trade), 1833 (the abolition of slavery), or 1865 (the end of the American Civil War and American slavery). An examination of the origins of Liverpool and Everton football clubs reveals the deeper connections (subtle but harmful) between Britain and non-Anglophone slavery, something that is overlooked in this story, as is Britain's need to reckon with 'its indebtedness to enslaved Africans', as Mulhern emphasises.[34] Given the city's dark and complex history, it is unsurprising that these beloved Merseyside football clubs also bear its traces.[35]

The narrative of football's entanglement with race and empire usually begins with Black British players emerging on the pitch from the 1970s, along with skinhead hooligans and mobs, and includes abuse hurled at three Black players after England's defeat in the 2021 Euros final.[36] But the first Black British football player, Andrew Watson (1856–1921), who stepped onto the scene and revolutionised British football nearly one hundred years before this, has received little celebration. His mother had been born a slave, and his father was a slave owner. The mixed-race Watson was taken as a child to Scotland from Guyana by his white father, living and studying among the country's elite. He married the white daughter of an East India Company merchant, and worked aboard Liverpool ships for some time. An unsung hero, he is credited with transforming football in its early days, bringing Scottish football customs down to London that are still in effect today.[37] Watson's own first club, the Corinthian-Casuals, were themselves responsible for introducing Brazil to the sport. Its Scotch-Brazilian player Charles Miller, an engineer embroiled in Brazilian railway-building and probably slavery before its abolition, took two footballs back to Brazil after his 1894 stay in England, igniting an enduring craze.[38] Generations later, Andrew Watson's unwitting descendant, Malik Al Nasir, grew up an infatuated Liverpool supporter. But he was driven away from his beloved club after suffering racial violence at Anfield in 1977, and has felt unable to return ever since.[39] Al Nasir's life was shaken by unexpectedly discovering his blood ties to Watson. Through both his academic studies and his involvement in the arts, he began the long process of tracing his family's connection with slavery, a story in which his forebears both experienced terrible suffering and gained unimaginable wealth. For a man whose ancestor was Britain's first Black footballer, there is a certain irony in being a supporter of a club founded by slave owners, and whose enjoyment of the game has been clouded by racist abuse.[40]

Mulhern believes that this is a story with profoundly serious legacies, most crucially the legacy of racism. 'If we are talking about Britain's role in expanding and entrenching the second slavery, then Britain bears responsibility not just for racism in the UK, but also people who are descended from formerly enslaved populations in Brazil. Britain had a paradoxical role in the eventual ending of Brazilian slavery, but also its survival for a long time. I'm no sociologist', Mulhern admits, 'but it doesn't take much research to understand how pervasive the system of colourism is there, or to realise that Afro-Brazilians have the fewest opportunities, face huge education and health-care barriers, and are the largest victims of state violence in the country. Brazil was one of the first sites of slavery in the Americas, and was the last country to abolish it as well. It's an incredibly long and difficult history.'[41]

AL

23

Dictionaries

The *Oxford English Dictionary* was potentially one of history's earliest and largest experiments in crowdsourcing. It was collated through letters and notes from people who put forward words and their definitions as dictionary entries, sent in from all over the world. It took more than sixty years to put together and was finally published in 1928. The *OED* was immediately regarded as a national treasure, a collation of all that it means to be British, for it defines and sets our language, phrases and even attitudes towards life and the world apart, both from other languages and from other forms of English, such as American English. As the entries themselves show, however, the dictionary could not have been compiled without the empire, as so many of its contributors lived in the British colonies and had strong ideas about what it meant to be, and to not be, English.[1] By 1900, the British Empire ruled over 400 million people, 126 million of whom were English speakers (the figure was just 26 million in 1800). English by this point had naturally incorporated words from its colonies, claiming them as its own and forgetting their origins – from the indigenous Caribbean 'canoe' to the Hindustani 'bungalow', the indigenous Australian 'budgerigar' and countless others.[2] As we have seen throughout this book, in Great Britain what is national is also, inevitably, imperial and global.[3]

Slavery is an inescapable part of this. In 1828, one of the first ever Gaelic dictionaries was published by the Highland Society of Scotland and was felt to be an important national project. Writing down the Scottish language was a way to preserve it forever and show it off as a complete, sophisticated, official language that could be a source of pride for Scots all over the world. It was funded by donations and subscriptions from enthusiastic Scots who believed in the value of the dictionary, some whom resided in the Caribbean, among them prominent plantation and slave owners. James Fraser held 374 enslaved people on his plantation, called Golden Fleece, in Berbice, while Demerara's William Monro owned more than 160 people on the Novar Estate, and donated £100 (equivalent to £13,000 today) to the Gaelic dictionary.[4] The Scottish Highlands and the Caribbean were deeply connected by slavery, and by the profits from it that flowed back into Scotland produced by those who wished to make the nation strong, wealthy and united (see chapter 19, 'Salt Fish' and chapter 20, 'Cromarty').[5] The intensely national and patriotic mission of protecting and celebrating a language through the compilation of a dictionary was in fact a global, international one because the desire to connect languages with national identity occurred simultaneously with other transformative processes: slavery, empire, rising literacy rates, and the development of transport and the printing presses.[6] This meant that books could be produced in huge numbers for the first time in history. Books, holding new information drawn from all over the world, made knowledge both portable and able to be shared.[7]

When I spoke to the historian of slavery, Christine Whyte, from the University of Glasgow, I was plunged into the deep linguistic histories of slavery and empire and its lasting but under-appreciated impacts on the dictionary. Although dictionaries might be considered a bit dull, when you delve deeper they are neither boring nor static.[8] The historian Lynda Mugglestone writes that 'humans have long since been captivated by words, with even the early civilizations attempting to provide comprehensive lists of words and their meanings'. Dictionaries have a long history, and were first found on ancient clay tablets and in medieval Latin books.[9]

It was only really in the eighteenth century that English itself began to be written down, with the first English dictionary compiled in 1755 by the Englishman Samuel Johnson. Johnson's *A Dictionary of the English Language* was the standard English dictionary for over 150 years. Whyte explains how this was all part of the Enlightenment mindset, something we have referred to throughout this book. Before this, Whyte says, 'spelling is all over the place, people can just do what they want. There's no central authority dictating how words are spelt. But this all began to change.' By the end of the nineteenth century, printed dictionaries were widely sold to the public and taught to children in all schools, which standardised English as one unified language for the first time. So, over the course of a hundred years, English words became solidified, cemented and fixed into particular spellings, which, Whyte reminds us, 'is why the Americans spell differently than we do. They went through that process of standardisation on their own.'[10]

As we saw in the chapter on Isaac Newton, men like Newton and Johnson are often regarded as singular geniuses to whom we are indebted for major societal contributions. But, as we will see, dictionary-writing was far from a solitary pursuit, for it was contingent on knowledge and unpaid labour facilitated by empire and slavery.[11] All lexicographers relied on helpers and assistants in the compilation of any dictionary. Sometimes these people were credited, but often they were not, their contributions erased from history. Helpers were usually unpaid, friends or volunteers, people that the lexicographers had encountered and learned from.[12] They could also be indigenous and enslaved people.[13]

Lexicography, dictionaries, nations and empires all developed in concert in the eighteenth and nineteenth centuries.[14] Some of the first modern dictionaries were often bi- or multi-language lexicons – that is, a dictionary used to translate between two or more languages – and often began in slave colonies. Various short word lists were compiled of West African languages and emerging Creoles in the Caribbean, such as in the Danish West Indies, Haiti and Suriname, using the knowledge of enslaved people who remembered their mother tongues.[15] At the time, Africans forced together from different regions and cultures could not communicate with one another or the slave traders, owners and overseers they were forced to labour under. Plantation slavery also sought to eradicate African languages and identity in order to create docile, powerless workers, though people did manage to hang on to their connections to their homelands, and many African words have been passed down and survive in the Americas centuries later.[16] As Whyte pointed out, even though fifty or sixty different languages may have been spoken by the population of enslaved people on one plantation, English was the language of wider society and the legal system, so they would have been forced into speaking English for practical purposes.[17] On plantations and slave ships, enslaved African interpreters taught English, Christianity and the Bible to new arrivals, as well as preventing insurrection and maintaining order, so African languages would have been heard and used on plantations until after the abolition of the slave trade.[18]

Over the coming century, in the context of a larger European colonial agenda, missionaries and lexicographers extended into Africa, as the imminent abolition of the slave trade inspired the search for alternative revenue streams from the continent, and thus the need to converse with and learn from its people.[19] When I spoke to Whyte, she stressed the fact that 'an awful lot of conquest involves understanding the place you're in'. In India, there was an even longer tradition of British missionaries, researchers and scholars learning and studying ancient texts. By contrast, she explained, 'most oral African societies didn't have those written texts to study. The texts were instead the people; enslaved, and then later, emancipated people.'[20] In West Africa, unlike in the Americas, speaking only English would have put you in a dangerous and weak position as an authority figure, and so it was essential for the British to learn African languages. There were probably always individual Europeans who had learned African languages, but in the nineteenth century the rise of cheap publishing and higher levels of European settlement on the African continent led to a far more sustained and systematic linguistic effort.[21]

Throughout the nineteenth century, Whyte continued, missionaries became very involved in recording and translating African languages, partly because it was hard to convert people without speaking their language. At first, with no formal alternative, British missionaries would learn from village children, who were faster than their parents at picking up English. Some of the most effective communications between Europeans and Africans relied on child intermediaries and go-betweens and Scottish missionaries would capitalise on the linguistic abilities of the children, who were often multi-lingual.[22]

Some West African rulers sent their children to the missionaries' schools, which they saw as an opportunity for learning English and gaining international connections. But vulnerable children such as orphans were actually kidnapped from their families and were trafficked either to mission stations to live or taken to Britain, particularly Scotland.[23] From the age of seven, mission station children would be put to work, doing menial tasks, tending to the gardens and growing vegetables to eat and sell.[24] Other children, trafficked and enslaved, were set to writing grammars and vocabularies and to constructing dictionaries. Children learned English to translate the Bible, dictionaries, childhood stories and other texts into their native languages, and vice versa, to enable British officials to understand their cultural values. Larger mission stations would even have their own printing presses, which children would be placed at to run. So, as Whyte points out, children provided both the intellectual and physical labour in the production of these linguistic aids. This work improved the ability of imperialists to understand the places they colonised and to exert a system of control that was tailored to specific locales.[25]

The flow of dictionaries, and people, back to Britain built up resource repositories with which to train soon-to-be missionaries and colonial administrators, who were increasingly taught language courses *before* embarking. This equipped them, essentially, to convert and rule better. Whyte says that places such as the School of Oriental and African Studies in London and some departments at Oxford University were founded to specialise in training colonial officials for government service abroad. In the twentieth century, handbooks were increasingly made for colonial officials, with both practical and linguistic information, 'things like, "carry my hammock" or, "pick up the suitcase": commands and useful phrases in different languages'.[26] Thanks to the foundations laid by missionaries and the children they exploited, future generations of colonisers heading overseas had half their work done for them, creating a well-oiled imperial machine.

Colonial dictionaries would come to shape and change the languages, too, rather than just record them. This is particularly so for oral languages, where 'new' sounds and tones are written down for the first time, requiring the invention of new alphabets or adaptations to Roman characters to form writing rules.[27] Dictionaries were, and are, important in this sense: they authorise a 'real' language, of high or low status, versus a mere 'dialect', vernacular or regional variety, as well as 'acceptable' accents and pronunciations.[28] They reproduce social class, as well as prejudices around gender and race, and they reflect the values and priorities of nations. American dictionaries written after its independence from Britain were the first to define concepts such as 'monarchy' and 'democracy'. The *Oxford English Dictionary*'s original definition of 'a canoe' was 'a kind of boat in use among uncivilised nations', perhaps based on an entry sent in by a Brit in the Caribbean or another colony, and shows how interpretations and assumptions were always part of dictionary making, no matter how 'scientific' the process.[29]

Whyte encourages understanding of the history and evolution of the dictionary because, despite advancements, we still inherit languages based on the ideas, decisions, technologies and innovations of these nineteenth-century developments.[30] The rise of the digital world, in which everything is available at the touch of a button, obscures the centuries of conflict and contestation that preceded our free, easy access to knowledge. Knowledge is something we like to consider democratic, rights to which are held equally by all.[31] But the knowledge we take for granted today has a history. It had to be compiled and gathered, often through unimaginable violence and oppression, while that very knowledge often came to be used as the justification for further imperial expansion.

AL

24

Greene King Brewery

Going to the pub is possibly the activity we are most known for around the world. Brits love a pint. Pub culture is figured to be so important to British health and well-being that during the COVID-19 lockdowns, pubs reopening was a key part of government policy. But who knew the British pub started as an Italian wine bar? Thousands of years ago, in AD 43, invading Roman armies brought roads, towns and what were known as *tabernae* to the British shores.[1] *Tabernae* were essentially shops that sold wine and they were built along Roman towns and roads to help quench the thirst of the troops. Back then, water was rarely guaranteed safe to drink and so fermented, alcoholic beverages were often safer.[2] And as ale was the local brew of choice, *tabernae* adapted to supply the locals with their favourite beverage. These places, later known as taverns, adapted to their ever-changing customers as the Roman roads brought successive Saxons, Jutes and Vikings with their own thirsts to quench.[3] Fast-forward 600 years, to the reign of King Henry VIII, and alehouses, inns and taverns had come to be known collectively as public houses, a name that was shortened further simply to 'pubs'. But how is such an ancient British tradition linked to the transatlantic slave trade?

These days, most pubs in the UK are owned by large chains – and one of the biggest is Greene King Brewery, based in Bury St Edmunds in Suffolk. Greene King was founded in 1799 by Benjamin Greene, who owned sugar plantations in the Caribbean where he profited from the labour of enslaved people.[4] Greene King's own website, which has been updated many times in recent years with different versions of the story, acknowledges that 'even in the 1800s, his views on slavery were deeply unpopular – he wrote columns in his own newspaper in Bury St Edmunds, criticising abolitionists'.[5] But it still stops short of admitting the benefits of Benjamin's plantation investments in growing a thriving business, which was passed on to Greene's son Edward in 1836 three years after the abolition of slavery in the British empire.

Following the 1833 Slavery Abolition Act, Benjamin Greene received £4,033 in compensation (around £500,000 in today's money), for his 'losses' in emancipating the labourers on his properties, and the following year he gave his two plantations in Saint Kitts to his son Benjamin Buck Greene, at which time there were 220 enslaved people inventoried as plantation property.[6] Many of Greene's descendants went on to hold prominent positions in British society, and the Greene family counted among its ranks a governor of the Bank of England, a Conservative MP, and a Director General of the BBC – as well as the novelist and British Museum chair, Graham Greene.[7]

In 2020, when many companies began to publicly grapple with their histories in the wake of the Black Lives Matter protests, Greene King's CEO, Nick Mackenzie, said this:

It is inexcusable that one of our founders profited from slavery and argued against its abolition in the 1800s. We don't have all the answers, so that is why we are taking time to listen and learn from all the voices, including our team members and charity partners as we strengthen our diversity and inclusion work.[8]

Mackenzie also stated that the firm will 'make a substantial investment to benefit the BAME community and support our race diversity in the business'; that it now employs people 'across the UK from all backgrounds', and that 'racism and discrimination have no place at Greene King'.[9]

Along with a collaboration with Liverpool Slavery Museum, and the renaming of four pubs, three called the Black Boy and one named Black's Head, Greene King made a number of commitments as part of their 'Calling Time on Racism' manifesto.[10] A phased action plan was set out with clear goals by 2022, 2025 and 2030. No update has been made on how they are progressing with these commitments.

In January 2024, Carla Astaphan, chairman of the St Kitts and Nevis reparations committee, told the *Sunday Telegraph* that reparations should be made, and that 'discussions are planned to look at some form of reparatory justice for St Kitts and Nevis'.[11] Talks were planned with Greene King but, as of now, there is no further information publicly available.

But the Greene King chain aren't the only pubs with links to the slave trade. During the eighteenth century, the Royal Navy were notorious for using pubs for impressment, a scheme by which recruiters would get sailors drunk and then force them to join the navy.[12] Forced recruitment had been common since the Elizabethan era and was often justified by the Admiralty as a necessity in order to man the navy appropriately.[13] This was, of course, a particularly urgent issue during times of war. Men aged between eighteen and fifty-five, who had seafaring, or similar experience, were typically targeted by impressment and this enabled the navy to maintain its strength during colonial expansion and in conflicts like the American Revolutionary War.[14]

Impressment was obviously unpopular among sailors, who didn't much like being kidnapped and shipped off to war, but it was especially egregious as naval salaries were less than half what a merchant seaman could expect to earn. Merchants were typically paid around 55 shillings per month, compared to the paltry 24 shillings given to naval sailors.[15] Merchant sailors were in demand, especially during the slave trade, when crews were needed for the risky Middle Passage transporting enslaved people from Africa to America. Nevertheless, slave ships weren't always popular choices for sailors – the threat of disease was high (see chapter 16, 'Blood Pressure Monitoring') and there was often the threat of pirates.

The Hole in the Wall pub, once called the Coach and Horses, is a well-known Bristol landmark just on the water by Queen Square. During the eighteenth century, the pub, along with others, was frequently full of seamen drinking and gossiping between voyages. But during this period seamen were susceptible to kidnap by press gangs when there was a high demand for their labour, and the Hole in the Wall was a prime location for it.[16] There was a spy house on the dock, where lookouts would watch out for likely press-gangers. They would also look out for slave ships, which, although they did not use press gangs, would often employ underhand methods to get the sailors on board. It became fairly common for pub landlords around docks to receive money from ship owners in order to get seamen drunk, which made it easier to get them aboard the ships.

Although slave ships were notorious for sickness and death, seamen were more reluctant to join the navy, where, along with the low pay, there were strict rules and less autonomy. Royal Navy ships often escorted slave ships through dangerous waters where there could be threats of violence from pirates, and they were the first line of defence for merchants and colonies in guarding precious slave-produced crops such as sugar and tobacco. Pub landlords, and the press gangs they assisted, were responsible for manning those ships.

In recent years, some pubs have changed their names to avoid racist connotations or to disavow links to the trade. The Colston Arms in Bristol was renamed, as you might expect. Locals petitioned to have the William Gladstone in Liverpool change its name to distance itself from Prime Minister William Gladstone, who had familial links to slavery, but the pub has kept its name.

Our society was built upon the shoulders of the enslaved. Those who were able to build up their businesses by exploiting the enslaved saw their wealth grow and their social standing rise. Benjamin Greene used his abolition compensation to not only boost his business enterprises but also to enhance his family's social position. Pubs are not just places in which to relax and have a drink – they're a significant staple of our culture, one that we perhaps take for granted. They were places that were used to enact business and to build empires, just as happened in coffee and chocolate houses in the past. Maybe we are less critical of pubs because they are such a big part of everyday life, and they seem so quintessentially British and domestic that we find it hard to associate them with the crimes of slavery that happened thousands of miles away.

When slavery was outlawed those who had profited from it were nonetheless compensated. Yet when the subject of reparations is brought up it is almost immediately dismissed as nonsense, even though it is clear that countries like St Kitts and Nevis continue to deal with the economic consequences of slavery nearly 200 years on. And while acknowledging history is certainly important, changing the name of a pub or making an online apology is not enough.

RR

25

Pirates

Captain Jack Sparrow, Captain Hook, Blackbeard, Robinson Crusoe, Long John Silver – all names that immediately call up iconic imagery: maps with clues to buried treasure, swashbuckling drunk and bearded men swearing through missing teeth, hooks for hands, eye patches, parrots galore. They are your favourite Halloween costume and your kids' birthday party theme. We know they gallivanted around the Caribbean, but have we ever truly considered their connection to the trade of human beings?

Eighteenth-century naval and merchant ships were brutally disciplined environments, described as floating factories and prisons, their crews trapped and isolated at sea, dreaming of escape.[1] Today, what were effectively criminal gangs have been romantically recast as havens for rebels and revolutionaries, the oppressed and the downtrodden.[2] Popular tropes in novels, plays and films since the nineteenth century, pirates have always existed, even in ancient times, in North Africa and in southern Europe. But it was during the period of transatlantic slavery that they really came into their own, and took on the form we think of today – the Pirates of the Caribbean. Piracy's 'Golden Age' lasted from 1650 until 1720.[3]

A pirate can be defined essentially as a thief or opportunist primarily operating on water and in coastal areas, attacking and taking over ships and waterside towns. For ordinary people who had fallen into poverty, joining a pirate's crew and conducting criminal activity was a straightforward means to money, security, community and an occupation. The label was also sometimes applied to anyone living outside the norms of Caribbean society, from prostitutes to convicts and escaped slaves.[4] All kinds of people became pirates, for a variety of reasons: destitute people, poor fishermen, formerly enslaved runaways, religious outcasts, disgruntled sailors, planters, slave owners or even a lieutenant governor, in the case of Jamaica's Henry Morgan.[5] People of all ethnicities and origins could be pirates, from Europeans, Indians, North Africans and Chinese people, to indigenous Americans and Africans, free and enslaved.[6] Women were also important members of pirate ships and societies, either dressing up as male pirates, or helping to meet the crew's dietary, social and sexual needs.[7] They entered piracy to survive, to escape the bounds of class and religion, or just to get rich. Previously enslaved African pirates like 'Calico Jack' were critical to the trade and to daily ship functioning, but they were also able to take advantage of a more egalitarian society to gain their own freedom, sometimes with the support of their crew. Piracy was a fluid lifestyle in which an ex-slave could create a new life for themselves.[8] Pirate ships were cultural and linguistic melting pots, developing their own cultures and ways of life, and even their own languages. In the transatlantic world, 'pidgins' and Creoles were often formed from a mix of European and African languages and were more commonly used than English, producing the stereotypical crass turns of phrase that we think of as distinctively piratical today.[9] Piracy shaped on-land societies too, as pirates spent their plundered money at taverns and brothels, and replenished their supplies for their next journey. As they came to dry land more frequently than did naval ships, pirates were actually often healthier and better fed than most at sea.[10]

Piracy was sometimes legal and sometimes illegal, and popular acceptance for it was constantly changing. There were many types of pirates, too.[11] Privateers were authorised by the English Crown to attack ships flying under foreign flags, and were immune from the punishments usually doled out to pirates and entitled to keep half of the profits not sent home to the monarch. Corsairs harassed European ships and coastal cities out of the large African ports of Tripoli, Tunis and Algiers, and then later operated out of England, the Netherlands and elsewhere. For 300 years (from the sixteenth to eighteenth centuries), Barbary corsairs captured between 800,000 and 1.25 million people as slaves for Arab slave markets, including from the south-west coast of England.[12] By the seventeenth century, buccaneers (European adventurers, mostly hunters selling meat smoked on a Native American wooden frame called a 'boucane') settled throughout the Caribbean islands and routinely attacked Spanish vessels. By the eighteenth century they were ravaging trading vessels and coastal plantations. Piracy developed over time, from individual raiders like Francis Drake sailing from the Old World to the New, to Caribbean-based raiding companies that travelled around the globe.[13]

Piracy's rise directly correlates with a global transition from haphazard forms of trade and slavery into more tightly structured global networks. Before establishing its own official colonies, the English behaved like pirates themselves, and regularly plundered the Spanish and Portuguese. Places like Jamaica were heavily fought over for many years, creating unstable conditions and ungoverned islands whose indigenous populations were decimated by genocide.[14] Piracy was vital to colonial economic functioning, and was seen as necessary and acceptable.[15] Slavery was a highly profitable industry for pirates, and vessels containing humans were frequently attacked by them, being large enough to accommodate huge pirate crews, which were essentially sprawling professional criminal gangs. Malnourished and traumatised enslaved people – and ship crews with their own grievances over their living conditions – were not always opposed to pirates taking control of their ships.[16] The most famous of all pirates, Blackbeard himself, was known to have five formerly enslaved Africans serving in his crew when he died in 1718. During piracy's height, it is estimated that nearly one-third of pirate crews were Black, probably liberated slaves.[17]

The growth of Black populations in many English colonies before1720 is difficult to explain without the plundering and reselling of twice-kidnapped, twice-stolen enslaved people by pirates. Pirates came ashore, flaunting enslaved Africans for sale, providing many colonies with their first taste of the profitability of free labour. This led many to eventually adopt slavery as an official legal practice in places where it had not previously been supported. Fundamentally, piracy helped disseminate the logic and mentality of slavery across the Americas: slavery helped pirates thrive, and pirates helped slavery thrive.[18]

Piracy also depended upon the indigenous world of the Americas. Piracy historian Arne Bialuschewski explains that the 'most successful buccaneering expeditions were at least facilitated by, if not entirely dependent on, indigenous assistance', but were also hindered by their resistance.[19] Moreover, many indigenous hunter-gatherer groups worked as pirate bands themselves, in opposition to English and French invaders. From the sixteenth century until the end of the Seven Years War in 1763, north-eastern American tribes attacked and plundered early English settlements.[20] By contrast, in Central America, the Maya of the Yucatan, the Miskito of Nicaragua and Honduras,[21] the Cuna of Panama and others actually supported French, English and Dutch pirates, seeking protection against the Spanish, and vice versa.[22] Indigenous people were enslaved by pirates too; buccaneers raided settlements along the Mexican coast, looting from, abducting and enslaving indigenous Maya people, selling them into colonial slave markets or putting them to work on pirate ships.[23] These dynamics changed indigenous societies forever, bringing in new goods and wealth, and altering the balances of power within their social structures.[24]

Another trade network was also beginning to emerge, spanning the worlds of the Atlantic and Indian oceans.[25] As piracy became more heavily policed in the Caribbean Sea, the lure of 'exotic' Asian goods such as silver, gold, diamonds, porcelain, sandalwood, silks, cottons, spices and tea were hard to resist, and were fiercely demanded by New York merchants.[26] European and over a thousand Atlantic-born pirates travelled from the New World to the Indian Ocean, using Madagascar as a base for rest and refuelling. Ignored by Europe's mainstream shipping and trading routes until the 1640s, Madagascar was rich in provisions, fresh water and natural reserves; it made the perfect refuge for illegal traders who wanted to avoid government detection.[27] Piracy soon came to shape Malagasy society, just as it had Amerindian ones, bringing new languages, material wealth, skills, weaponry like muskets and pistols – and, subsequently, warfare – in exchange for protection from colonial governance and the rule of law.[28]

Madagascar was also a rich source of potential slaves.[29] English raiders soon became the largest importers of Malagasy slaves to plantations in the Americas, especially Jamaica and Barbados.[30] These journeys could take up to a year and a half and were incredibly dangerous, but still profitable given how cheap Madagascan slaves were (ten shillings, around £40 today) relative to West Africans (three or four pounds sterling, around £300 today).[31] Slaves were both commodities to be traded and labourers supporting the system by working on ships, even earning their freedom for it.[32]

In the 1710s, the Madagascar slave trade grew rapidly, soon becoming legal, and important for populating what is now French Mauritius. This meant that licensed British and French slave ships began trading around this time, putting pirates out of business. Over the following decades, pirates tried to move out of piracy, settling and marrying in Madagascar and other colonies, or participating more heavily in the slave trade, finding more 'acceptable' lifestyles.[33] Ultimately, these pirates were less like rebels than opportunists just trying to make money. Whether within or without the dominant system, piracy was a temporary sojourn for as long as it worked.[34]

By 1722, it appeared that almost all existing pirate crews had dissolved and established new lives for themselves.[35] Golden-age piracy was quashed through a combination of changing attitudes, pirate hunting and blockading, new approaches to corruption and justice, and the absorption of pirates into other professions.[36] Pirates in a larger sense, though, did not disappear, nor did piracy's connection to slavery. Barbary, Malay and other pirates remained a threat to European colonisers until the mid-nineteenth century.[37] When the transatlantic slave trade was abolished in 1808, illegal slave trading was itself labelled an act of piracy (a derogatory, shaming term) by governments and abolitionists well into the late nineteenth century. As noted by the scholar Lydia Fash, 'both were fundamentally about stealing'.[38] Somali and Yemeni pirates operating in the Gulf of Aden, between the Red Sea and the Indian Ocean, are today's modern archetype for the criminal at sea.[39] Many who struggle to get by now make their livelihoods by chasing and capturing vessels, kidnapping, and smuggling drugs and other contraband items. Modern piracy is well-organised, large-scale and – now, as in the past – engaged in by those with few other options, who become trapped in its cycles.[40] Pirates can still be found across the seas, in East Africa, the South China Sea, South America, the Caribbean and in the Serbian and Romanian stretches of the Danube River.[41] It seems unlikely that these modern forms of piracy will disappear, despite attempts to police the waterways by employing modern technology and weaponry. Pirates, too, have speedboats, missiles, night goggles, GPS devices and AK-47s.[42]

Today, the pirate fantasy is the rags-to-riches story, the idea that anyone can find their pot of buried treasure, thus connecting piracy to the story of capitalism itself.[43] But piracy was central to colonialism, and slavery was central to piracy. As we continue to be entertained by stories of pirate exploits and to dress up as pirates for costume parties, let us not forget the context in which they were in their prime, the horrific realities they created for countless enslaved people (even while they rescued others), or the trade that allowed for their prominence. While historical pirates are the stuff of romance and adventure, modern pirates are seen through a different lens – of terror, security threats and moral depravity. Yet there is little difference between the two. Piracy has always thrived in conditions of structural and political instability, war, exploitation and poverty.

AL

26

Boxing

Just over two hours up the M40 from London you'll find the quaint Cotswolds village of Shenington. It's a quiet place, even today – several of its country manors date back to the eleventh century, and the village is steeped in local family history. A village so small and somewhat difficult to access from cities would have been an odd choice for a championship boxing match, but on 3 December 1810 that's just what happened when English bare-knuckle fighter Tom Cribb took on American former slave Thomas Molineaux for the world championship title. Molineaux was trained for the fight by another former slave, Bill Richmond, whom historian Greg Jenner credits as being the first celebrity boxer, as well as the first Black sports celebrity.[1] 'He's known as Richmond, the Black', Jenner says. 'When they start to know him by name, he becomes a celebrity.'[2]

But the links between slavery and boxing run much deeper than Thomas Molineaux's championship match. Far away in the colonies, plantations were often secluded places, which brought together not just the enslaved people but also the overseers and authority figures who lived either on the plantations or close by. As well as the violence and degradation that was a daily feature of plantation life, isolation led to a lot of boredom, and workers would often start gambling and fighting rackets on the side with other plantations. One-on-one boxing evolved initially as a kind of entertainment, and of course as a tool for control by owners and overseers. Overseers were also aware that boxing provided a form of release for the enslaved. Fights were seen as a 'safety valve', a way to manage the rebellious spirit of the enslaved men, diverting their energies into a controlled environment and reducing the chance of resistance.[3]

We spoke to Louis Moore, a professor of history at Grand Valley State University in the US, to find out more. He revealed that 'every culture has a fighting tradition', and enslaved Africans who came to America brought a fighting tradition of their own.[4] These fighters had their own styles that blended street fighting with various martial arts. Within plantations, different types of fights would take place. There were 'Battle Royale' fights where multiple enslaved men would fight at the same time, in a sort of last-man-standing fight.[5] Unlike the version of Battle Royale that we might know from video games, the goal of real-life brawls was not a fight to the death. More importantly, Battle Royales were a way to hold boxing matches that commodified fighters while denying them the admiration or fame they might've attained as solo fighters had they been free men. And large-scale group fights were another way to control and degrade these men.

Frederick Douglass, a notable abolitionist and former slave, condemned such matches as demeaning, and just another way for slave owners to assert their dominance.[6] Slave owners relished the brutality of these matches, favouring them over any intellectual or religious activity that may have enriched the lives of enslaved people. Forcing people to box seemed to confirm the stereotype, created by European slave owners, that Africans were violent and uncivilised, whereas it was the slave owners themselves who were barbaric. Often the declared outcome of a fight was determined by how violent it was and what injuries had been inflicted. Boxing today remains notorious for head injuries, but on plantations there was no regard for the well-being of the fighters. There were frequent fatalities, and enslaved men often found themselves fighting for their lives.

Henry Bibb, a writer and campaigner for abolition who spent much of his life enslaved, gives an account of what fighting looked like on a plantation in nineteenth-century America. This is an extract from *Narrative of the Life and Adventures of Henry Bibb, An American Slave, Written by Himself*:

The Sabbath is not regarded by a large number of the slaves as a day of rest. They have no schools to go to; no moral nor religious instruction at all in many localities where there are hundreds of slaves. Hence they resort to some kind of amusement. Those who make no profession of religion, resort to the woods in large numbers on that day to gamble, fight, get drunk, and break the Sabbath. This is often encouraged by slaveholders. When they wish to have a little sport of that kind, they go among the slaves and give them whiskey, to see them dance, 'pat juber,' sing and play on the banjo. Then get them to wrestling, fighting, jumping, running foot races, and butting each other like sheep. This is urged on by giving them whiskey; making bets on them; laying chips on one slave's head, and daring another to tip it off with his hand; and if he tipped it off, it be called an insult, and cause a fight. Before fighting, the parties choose their seconds to stand by them while fighting; a ring or a circle is formed to fight in, and no one is allowed to enter the ring while they are fighting, but their seconds, and the white gentlemen. They are not allowed to fight a duel, nor to use weapons any kind. The blows are made by kicking, knocking, and butting with their heads; they grab each other by their ears, and jam their heads together like sheep. If they are likely to hurt each other very bad, their masters would rap them with their walking canes, and make them stop. After fighting, they make friends, shake hands, and take a dram together, and there is no more of it.[7]

Enslavers obviously made money on fights, and so did the enslaved fighters themselves on occasion. But there was something much more at stake: their freedom. As Louis Moore points out, Tom Molineaux, Britain's first Black celebrity sportsperson, came from a 'family of fighting slaves' whose owners would train 'their slaves in sparring and how to fight' and then would bet on the outcomes.[8] Molineaux eventually earned his freedom through a boxing match with a slave on another plantation, when both their masters bet 'an incredible sum of tobacco at that time, which was essentially currency', on the result.[9] Molineaux's owner had so much at stake that he offered the boxer his freedom if he won, which Molineaux duly did. Molineaux was granted his freedom and received a sum of 500 dollars around 1808, and by 1809 had travelled to New York and subsequently England to continue his fighting career.[10] This wasn't unusual, either, and many plantation fighters won their freedom in this way, no doubt fuelling boxing's popularity among the enslaved.

As was the case with those who were accomplished swimmers (see chapter 21, 'Swimming'), being a skilled fighter increased your value as a slave, given that, through betting, a good boxer could make more money for their owner. The same applied to enslaved people who were jockeys, as horse racing was another source of extracurricular income for slave owners.

Grimly, Louis Moore mentions an old advertisement about a search for a runaway slave, which 'says something like, "This guy's a fighter. He thinks of himself as a pugilist."'[11] This,

Moore thinks, is a way for the slave owner to let other white people know to look out for the runaway at fights and boxing matches, one of the few ways in which an escapee would have been able to support himself. We know that once he was granted freedom, Tom Molineaux went to Britain rather than stay in America. Slavery was not officially practised on British soil, and so he may have felt that he would be able to manoeuvre through society there without being regarded as a slave. Had he stayed in the US, even as a free man, the threat of slave hunters and kidnapping would have been significant: being a free man did not guarantee freedom for formerly enslaved people.

Molineaux was treated well in Britain, by and large, but he was still thought of as a thug. He dated white women, and he didn't affect to being the perfect English gentleman. Bill Richmond, conversely, worked hard to conform to social expectations, and was able to rise up in society in a way that was not possible for Molineaux. There were of course limits for Richmond, but he was in a position to work with society's elite, including teaching Lord Byron how to spar,[12] which would have been considered a high honour. But Richmond had to satisfy higher standards than did his white peers, and to be the example of a perfect human being in order to be seen as a person rather than a Black man. Molineaux was not able to achieve this because he chose to live his life authentically.

Modern Britain likes to think of itself as a tolerant country, and it had the same reputation during the age of slavery, but as Louis rightly points out, how could Britain have been a truly tolerant country while violently ruling over its colonies and participating in slavery abroad? Are we 'tolerant' when we can look you in the eye but happy to use others to mete out violence and injustice if you're at a distance, in an overseas colony? This wilful indifference is something that still infects British society. For British people living in the UK today, it is, unfortunately, all too easy to be unconcerned about British actions abroad, where abuses and scandals can be readily ignored. And when we look back at past atrocities it's surprising that things are not as different now as we might wish them to be.

RR

27

Voodoo Dolls

Voodoo dolls are everywhere, on screen and in real life: in vending machines, in shops catering to New Age spiritualism, in horror and even in Disney movies. You can read WikiHow guides on how to make a voodoo doll and buy voodoo-themed Halloween costumes on Etsy and Amazon.[1] Voodoo dolls are usually small soft figures made of fabric, which can be ripped, beaten and stabbed as a symbolic way of enacting violent revenge on your enemies without remorse or consequences. It is believed that the harm you inflict on the doll will find its way to your enemy. They are a novelty and a curiosity, a joke – but still an object of suspicion and confusion. Despite the long, complicated history of voodoo, it wasn't until the twentieth century that mainstream Western media began to pick up on the concept of the 'voodoo doll', popularising it as a symbol of mysticism, strange magic and corrupt morals.[2] Although thought to be connected to a religion called 'Voodoo' originating in the Caribbean, the doll and the belief system of which it is a part are poorly understood in the West, and are mired in racial stereotypes and assumptions.[3]

Vodou, with its roots in the Roman Catholic form of Christianity, is a monotheistic religion, worshipping Bondye, 'the good deity'.[4] The Vodou worldview advocates a belief in the existence of spirits and spiritual entities whose energy permeates everything in the universe. There is no universal set of rules or rituals, so interpretation and adaptation by each temple is encouraged, making it less hierarchical and more personal than many other religions.[5] This chapter explores how the 'voodoo doll' – which current practitioners in Haiti, Louisiana and across the British Caribbean strongly insist is of little significance in their religion – came to be such a striking and evocative symbol across cultures, one linked to a set of ideas and images about Black people.[6] This is a story with roots deeply entrenched in the cultural exchanges and entanglements of slavery.

Interestingly, the origins of the voodoo doll lie principally in medieval magical practices in Europe rather than those in Africa. The use of dolls and objects representing the human figure in ritual magic, known as 'figurative image magic', is common to almost all cultures across history.[7] Figurative objects and charms have been found in Greco-Roman, Egyptian, Byzantine and many other ancient traditions, having been buried, bathed in blood or impaled with knives that affix notes naming the demons to be conjured. In medieval Europe, the rise of Christianity and the hunting of witches encouraged such acts to be read as satanic, and eventually could be punishable with death.[8]

The notion that voodoo dolls are agents of revenge and suffering comes from a combination of ideas taken from old European magic and a misinterpretation of what West African ritual objects were actually used for, as well as the false conclusions that white people drew when observing worship among enslaved people on plantations. One such ritual object is the *nkisi nkondi*, used by the Bakongo people, a figure often pierced with nails, spikes and other sharp objects. Without other frames of reference, those from outside this culture would have interpreted such an object as 'witchcraft', based on their own folklore. In reality, Bakongo practices were vastly different from European witchcraft, in that they sought to harness psychic power and sorcery to identify and heal disease. The Bakongo believed that the cause of unexpected or early deaths of healthy people was due to evil done unto them by someone else. Ritual magic sought the individual who caused harm and caused them harm in return, not as revenge but to neutralise and destroy illness. One of the key values of the Enlightenment was to sever a belief in magic, superstition and religion from more 'rational' and 'acceptable' empirical science, medicine and governance.[9] The clashes between European and African perceptions of magic and witchcraft created misunderstandings and oversimplifications that persist even today.[10]

When traditional Christianity collided with numerous traditional African religions, the result was something new and powerful: voudou. It was a force of resilience, evidence of the enduring persistence of African cultures and traditions that managed to survive despite violent suppression, and which remained meaningful to enslaved people despite the best attempts of enslavers.[11] Different European powers had their own terms for the plethora of religions and forms of 'black magic' practised by enslaved Africans on plantations, all of which they sought to prohibit as quickly as possible.[12] It was called 'Vaudoux' or 'Vodou' in the French colonies; 'Santería' in Spanish Cuba; and 'Obeah' in the British islands.[13]

Generally, in the eighteenth and nineteenth centuries, the untrained European eye viewed them as the same religion: a vague, confusing 'mysterious cult of obscure African provenance, associated with fetishes, witchcraft, and poison, eroticism, and revenge'. But in fact Vodou and Obeah have distinct cultural roots. Obeah has Ashanti-Fanti origins (from the Gold Coast, today's Ghana), while Vaudoux originated with the Fon and Yoruba cultures in Dahomey, which today is Benin.[14] By the 1880s, the French term, an adaptation of the Dahomean word *vodu* or *vudu* meaning 'spirit' or 'light', had been widely taken up as 'voodoo' in English to refer to any Afro-Caribbean religion.[15]

The labelling of Vodou itself was designed to raise fear and scepticism among the white ruling class, to encourage them to avoid and fear physical and intellectual mingling with slaves.[16] It is possible that Vodou did pose a real threat. Nearly every slave uprising during this period across the Caribbean was said to have been started by Black religious leaders, the most famous being the Haitian Revolution in 1791, a rebellion that shaped Atlantic, and world, history.[17] In fact, some historians believe that the very *idea* of 'Obeah' grew out of British anxieties about losing control of their slaves and being overthrown from power – that the religion itself was not a violent or revolutionary one, but that the British spread this idea in order to create mistrust and division. Religious worship provided the opportunity for enslaved people to cultivate meeting places and to form an identity as well as an awareness of their own history and power away from the gaze of owners and overseers. It was this creation of an independent community where enslaved people could talk and form plans that was the greater threat, but in making the religion itself seem immoral or dangerous, something that should be restricted, suspicion and negative stereotypes of the Black population spread, along with a desire to ban religious gatherings.[18] Those found to be practising Obeah faced harsh punishment, with even electric shocks used as a form of torture after Jamaica's 1760 'Tacky's Revolt'.[19]

Obeah practitioners were genuinely feared for the power they seemed to have over people, including inciting rebellion or bringing sickness to their enemies.[20] The practice was also seen to bestow enslaved women with authority, and perpetuated the idea of Black women as impure, dangerous yet seductive, with their ritual dance.[21] It was central to medical and healing systems developed on plantation slave villages, thus also threatening the knowledge and authority of white physicians and surgeons on plantations and slave ships.[22] Strongly linked with botany and plant knowledge, Obeah itself came to be seen as a contagious disease, spreading through plantation societies, contaminating and taking hold of the minds and spirits of slaves. Fraternising with these slaves was regarded as dangerous for the integrity of British bodies and minds, as it could expose one to the threat of conversion or being cursed by a spell. It was even dealt with as an infectious illness in need of treatment and management, including quarantine.[23]

After emancipation too, in an attempt to maintain control over now free Black populations, the governments of most Caribbean islands (most of them white) introduced new laws making certain activities illegal: gambling, squatting, begging, desertion and spiritual practices. Obeah was outlawed in the British Caribbean, and punishments included imprisonment or manual labour. The result was that, even after abolition, the ruling class continued to benefit from unpaid, forced labour, and, given how easy it was to fall foul of the law, there remained many unfree people.[24]

From its initial banning by colonial governments, Vodouists began to organise themselves into secret societies, some of which still exist. These began as sites for clandestine practice, communion and discussion, for hatching plans and organising the fight for freedom and independence. Even today, the popular perception of Vodou within Black communities across the Americas is so tainted that many of those involved take vows of secrecy. Secret societies continue to provide safety and a sense of social order, justice and belonging that cannot be provided by governments.[25] Between 1980 and 2004, Obeah was finally decriminalised in the formerly British islands of Anguilla, Barbados, Trinidad and Tobago and St Lucia. Still illegal in many islands, Vodou was only officially recognised as a religion in Haiti in 2003.[26]

Voodoo has long been linked with mystery, violence, corruption and evil intent. Emphasising its connection to African spirituality over its European origins makes it seem more exotic and 'strange', especially in contrast to Christianity, even though it is really a fusion of both cultures (and far removed from the reductive image of vengefully stabbed dolls).[27] In popular form, it links Black Afro-Caribbean people with tropes of anger and irrationality, shaping and reinforcing racial stereotypes and assumptions about Europe and Africa's different beliefs and values. Obeah, or voodoo, was not 'created' by slaves purely as a means of resistance, but neither did it simply evolve out of a European desire, fuelled by ignorance, to demonise and control Africans. Rather, it was a bit of both.[28]

Voodoo, both as a real practice and as a stereotype, is an example of how migration, empire and slavery brought different groups of people into contact and caused them to share and shape one others' cultures and beliefs. Cultures never stay static, they are constantly changing, and when different peoples meet, often something new is formed. Maybe the next time you encounter a voodoo doll in a film, or bump into one on Halloween, instead of jumping to conclusions, you might think instead about the rich stories that migrations, both free and forced, have helped bring about, and that have shaped our world.

AL

28

Treadmills

Some people love the gym, some people hate it, and others are just there to take a good old-fashioned mirror selfie. Most of us have been in a gym at some stage of our life and, of course, we not only chose to be there, but we may frame that choice as a kind of personal improvement through suffering. 'Feel the burn', the adverts say, or 'no excuses', 'no pain, no gain'. We might talk about a 'punishing workout' or call a particularly hardcore exercise 'torture'. But some of our favourite machines have a dark past, which began long before the rise of gym culture in the 1980s.

The Slavery Abolition Act of 1833 made slavery illegal throughout the British colonies. But this did not mean that enslaved people were free to come and go as they pleased. Instead, they became what were known as 'apprentice labourers'. These were not like the apprenticeships we know today, where you can choose what area to work in, who you do your apprenticeship with and you can leave of your own free will. Apprenticeships for formerly enslaved people were essentially just a different type of forced labour. Yes, workers were now paid, but they did not have a choice about who they worked for, or how long, and they were unable to quit.

The most famous apprentice must surely be Ebenezer

184

Scrooge, from Charles Dickens's *A Christmas Carol*, who was Old Fezziwig's investment banking apprentice before taking over the business upon Fezziwig's death. It was Scrooge's first step to wealth and prosperity, but the apprenticeship system that formerly enslaved people were subjected to was far from aspirational. Apprenticeships can be traced back to the twelfth century but began to gain traction during the later Middle Ages, when wealthy families would send their children off to live with host families and learn from respected guildsmen.[1] As a way in which to work your way up society it was considered a noble path. However, as time went on many wealthy people became frustrated with the restrictive nature of apprenticeships – the way that apprentices were tied to their masters, and the onerous rules that employers were bound to follow. It was only during the twentieth century that apprenticeships shifted from being a mercantile vocation to a more working-class career path. The system that was used for formerly enslaved people was a derivative of the old medieval one, and made full use of the restrictions that wealthy people had grown tired of in their own apprenticeships.

We talked to Diana Paton, a historian of the Caribbean, to establish what exactly an 'apprenticeship' meant. She told us that 'apprenticeship meant that people were nominally free but they still had to stay in the same place that they had previously been enslaved, and they had to work for the people who had claimed ownership over them.'[2]

On 1 August 1834, when enslaved people were officially declared free, they were required under the apprenticeship system to serve a period of compulsory labour to their former masters. The compulsory periods were different depending on the work you did while enslaved. For example, those who worked in the fields would have to serve six years as an apprentice, whereas 'skilled' and domestic workers need only serve four.[3] Although they could be compensated, under the apprenticeship system there was no legal requirement to pay the now 'free' people for their work, which was up to forty-five hours a week. The apprentice system was supposedly designed as a transition from enslavement to freedom, but it was really to benefit plantation owners who would otherwise have to move from unpaid forced labour to paid labour, thus taking a huge hit to their wealth and profits. It's worth noting that at the same time the compensation system for plantation owners, which was set up following abolition, began making payments in 1835 – yet more government help for enslavers that left newly freed slaves out in the cold. The apprenticeship system was heavily criticised for its similarity to slavery, and there was widespread resistance from the apprentices themselves. A new class of magistrates was created, their purpose to enforce work and enact punishments if the apprentices, who might be whipped or sent to prison, refused to comply. For example, Frederick White, a magistrate, wrote in his diary that he had ordered apprentice Cecilia Henry to be imprisoned for not weaning her sixteen-month-old.[4] White also expressed frustrations that apprentices wouldn't follow his orders. These types of punishments weren't uncommon, and there were frequent instances of overseers intimidating and threatening the apprentices. The prisons they were sent to had a reputation for violence, and they also had a torturous form of punishment known as the treadwheel.

The treadmill was a large wooden wheel (or sometimes a cylinder) that turned as the person inside stepped forward. They would be tied by the wrist to a bar above the treadmill, and, as explained by Diana Paton, the punishment was intended as 'a kind of humane form of hard labour'.[5] It was thought to be more modern, and less brutal, than some of the punishments enslaved people had been subjected to previously, but in practice it caused terrible suffering. Paton points out that people were still being flogged and whipped while on the tread-mill, and that they would eventually slip, and 'end up dangling from the wrists, their lower legs being bashed over and over again by the wheel'.[6] It was, she thinks, 'at least as bad, proba-bly worse than the thing it was intended to replace'.[7]

The treadmill is an ancient invention: over 4,000 years ago a treadwheel-type machine was in use as a human-powered machine to help lift buckets of water. Later, it was adapted for grain and corn on working farms. It wasn't turned into a form of punishment until the 1800s, and was then repurposed as a form of exercise and fitness in the 1960s. It was first employed for punishment in British prisons in the 1820s, and from there it travelled to the Caribbean. The fitness machine we know is essentially the same machine that was used for Victorian pun-ishment. You have to run, walk or step indefinitely while the wheel is constantly turning, and if you don't keep up with the machine you will fall.

The apprenticeship system was eventually abolished in 1838, due to increasing resistance from apprentices and pressure from the abolitionist movement in Britain. Most apprentices saw the system for what it was – slavery by a different name – and there were concerns about its legality. Apprentices were able to buy their way out of the system by paying their former owners a fee, which was against the original Slavery Abolition Act, and many apprentices, recognising their rights under the Act, pushed back on the fees they were being charged.

Some apprentices became prominent activists in the fight to end the system. James Williams lived in the St Ann Parish of Jamaica, and was about fifteen when he was freed from slavery and forced to become an apprentice. Williams's treat-ment under apprenticeship was horrific, and included repeated prison stints, beatings and floggings. Even at a young age he became a strong voice against brutality and he made the plight of former slaves in apprenticeship visible to the British public, having moved to Britain following his emancipation, where he joined forces with leading Quaker abolitionist Joseph Sturge.

Once they had completed their apprenticeships or bought their way out, many people sought to improve their living conditions and assert their freedom in a way that apprenticeship had precluded. Many wanted to avoid work that was associated with slavery, such as field labour, and so opted instead for domestic work and trading. Fearing that slavery or the apprenticeship system might return, many people purchased their freedom in order to have peace of mind.[8] And once the apprenticeship system had been unequivocally abolished, people felt a new determination to claim and enforce their rights, and to ensure that such an oppressive system would never exist for them again.

The adoption of treadmills and fitness machines like Stair-Masters for the purpose of pleasure, for exercise and health, is just another example of how we have embraced certain technologies without understanding their history. Traces of the brutality of the slave trade are still everywhere around us – even in something as mundane as doing your morning run at the gym. As Paton points out, 'there's something kind of grotesque about the fact that this device that was invented to punish people has become something that we choose to use for our own self-improvement and our own self-discipline'.[9] Now we talk about 'punishing' ourselves in order to reach our goals – to be fitter, healthier, better able to set our destiny. But we also should think about where the technology that helps us do so came from, and the apprentices for whom this particular form of punishment was linked, not to a 'freedom to achieve', but to a continuation of the unfreedom they might have hoped they had left behind.

RR

29

Swing Low, Sweet Chariot

If you've ever seen England play a rugby match, at some point you're bound to have heard England fans singing 'Swing Low, Sweet Chariot' in the stands. Fans sing to boost the team's morale, especially when they're a few points down, and the sound of thousands of voices singing in unison lifts the energy in the stadium to show the team that the country is behind them and ready to rally. At other times it's a victory song, its choral majesty an alert to the away side (who probably have their own songs) that this is a team united, both on the field and in the stands. 'Swing Low, Sweet Chariot' is also one of those songs you'll have heard around – you probably know the basic lyrics and can join an impromptu rendition. It's taught in primary schools and sung in assemblies across the country, but what you aren't taught about the song is its history.

> Swing low, sweet chariot,
> coming for to carry me home;
> Swing low, sweet chariot,
> coming for to carry me home.
>
> I looked over Jordan and what did I see
> Coming for to carry me home

A band of angels coming after me
Coming for to carry me home

If you get there before I do
Coming for to carry me home
Tell all my friends I'm coming too
Coming for to carry me home

If I get there before you do
Coming for to carry me home
I'll cut a hole and pull you through
Coming for to carry me home

Sometimes I'm up and sometimes
I'm down
Coming for to carry me home
But still my soul feels heavenly bound
Coming for to carry me home

'Swing Low' is probably the world's most famous example of what's known as an African American spiritual. A type of song that originated among enslaved Africans, spirituals often express religious themes and emotional experiences reflecting on sorrow, hope and the spiritual beliefs of the singers. Spirituals are often characterised by improvisation or riffing, and by their poignant melodies, but they can exist in many styles. The evolution of spirituals is rooted in the experiences of enslaved Africans in America, and they are a vibrant tradition that speaks to the inventiveness and resilience of their creators.

Slave music was divided into two categories, spiritual and secular, and the spirituals have had a lasting effect on music. W. E. B. Du Bois called them the 'articulate message of the slave world'.[1] They often invoke the sorrow, suffering and longing for freedom that enslaved people felt. In contrast to other types of historical records that we use to learn about slavery, African American folk music is something you can experience today, whether in person or at the click of a button online. As is common with all kinds of folk music, there have been many variations to the lyrics to 'Swing Low, Sweet Chariot' over the centuries. Wallace and Minerva Willis, former enslaved people in Oklahoma, have been credited with writing the song in the nineteenth century.[2] However, due to the lack of reliable information from the time and the shifting, collaborative nature of folk music, it's unclear whether they originally composed the song or if they were simply the first be to credited for recording a version, having heard it from others or on plantations.

Many of the song's most poignant images are rooted in religion: 'Swing Low, Sweet Chariot/coming for to carry me home' references Elijah in 2 Kings in the Old Testament, which describes the prophet Elijah being taken up to heaven by a chariot.[3] Religious imagery of salvation was common in spirituals: it's been suggested that the Jordan River in 'Swing Low' is a stand-in for the Red River, which bordered the plantation where Willis was forced to work, and the Jordan was a common image in later blues songs such as 'I Got To Cross That River Jordan' by Blind Willie McTell.[4] Another interpretation of 'Swing Low' is that it is about the Underground Railroad, and that it was sung to signify that help was on the way.

The song speaks of a chariot coming to take the singer home, a powerful metaphor for hope and a longing for the end of suffering. In *The Souls of Black Folk*, W. E. B. Du Bois refers to this song as a 'cradle song of death'.[5] A cradle song lulls a child to sleep; a cradle song of death would imply a haunting opposite. 'Swing Low, Sweet Chariot' is a fascinating piece of history in itself, but the song also expresses a collective memory and the spiritual resilience of the African American community. It's perhaps ironic, then, that this song of Black resilience and hope has been adopted by England rugby fans and the sport as a whole, considering that a 2022 report by the Rugby Football Union found systemic racism endemic at every level of elite rugby.[6]

Enslaved Africans used music and dance as a form of expression. Retaining the musical traditions from their home cultures would've been a powerful form of resilience amid the hostile life of plantation work. Traditional African music makes heavy use of drums, call-and-response singing and rhythmic patterns. In the aggressive new environments of American slave society, enslaved people adapted these traditions to rally themselves and to hold onto their culture. As well as being a form of resistance, music was used to motivate one another on the plantations. Another common kind of spiritual, the work song, was used to coordinate labourers' efforts in the fields, and keeping time with a song helped maintain a pace and rhythm when ploughing a field or harvesting crops. There was often a call-and-response element to the songs and rich harmonies that involved dozens of singers, and as they were sung in workplaces or fields, work songs rarely had any musical accompaniment. A shared set of songs, which combined music from home with an expression of what life was really like in the New World, was a powerful way for enslaved people to uplift their spirits and build a sense of community. Lyrics would often be adapted to reflect specific tasks or labour, for example in the 'corn song' called 'Sold Off to Georgy':

Farewell, fel-lo -sarvants!
O -ho! O -ho! I'm gwine to leabe you;
O -ho! O -ho! I'm gwine to leabe de ole coun-try;
O -ho! O -ho! I'm sold off to Geor-gy!

Swing Low, Sweet Chariot

Farewell, ole plantation, (O -ho! O -ho!)
farewell, de ole quarter, (Oho! O -ho!)
Un daddy, un manmy, (O-ho! O-ho!)
Un marster, un missus (O -ho! O -ho!)

My dear wife un one chile, (O -ho! O -ho!)
My poor heart is breaking, (O -ho! O -ho!)
No more shall I see you, (O -ho! O -ho!)
Oh! no more foreber! (O -ho! O -ho!)[7]

The song describes the pain and sorrow of a slave being separated from their loved ones and home. The lyrics express feelings of forlornness, as the singer lists the people they are saying farewell to – their parents, their children and wives, even their former 'master' and 'missus'. It highlights the emotional turmoil that came with being sold and separated from a familiar place and reflects the callousness of slavery that denied Black people their autonomy and possessions. Enslavers could treat people like property, but they couldn't take away their songs, or the memories and the feelings that singing together could conjure. Although work songs were designed to rally the workers, they often told the truth about what was happening in the lives of the enslaved. Often, they had a great sense of fun, like the more upbeat corn song 'Roun de Corn, Sally':

Hoo-ray, Hoo-ray, Ho!
Roun de corn, Sally!
Hoo-ray for all the lubbly ladies
Roun de corn, Sally!

Dislub's er thing dat's sure to hab you,
Roun de corn, Sally!
He hole you tight, when once he grab you!

Roun de corn, Sally!

Un ole'un ugly,
Young'un pritty
Roun de corn, Sally!
You need'un try when once he git you,
Roun de corn, Sally![8]

The rhythm was probably meant to coordinate work for enslaved people loading cotton, and 'Roun' de Corn, Sally' was later adopted by the sailors as a sea chanty where it became 'Round the Corner, Sally', to keep time while working on a ship. Interactions between different singing communities often led to the creation of new songs or new renditions, which is why 'Swing Low, Sweet Chariot' has ended up being sung in such a different context to its spiritual origins.

Another form of slave music was dance music, which was played at social gatherings and was all about recreation and enjoyment, and was often accompanied by music in contrast to singer-led work songs. Dance music was an integral part of community life, characterised by lively rhythms and played with drums, which were often made from whatever enslaved people could find, like the bottoms of tubs and barrels. Banjos were a common instrument for enslaved musicians, and the banjo itself is believed to have come from Africa. Sundays were often the only day that enslaved people had for themselves, and so that was when most of the social gatherings would take place. The sound of banjos could always be heard on a Sunday in the slave quarters of a plantation, along with fiddles and other string instruments that were also a staple in dance music.

Slave music was a new genre that evolved into an honest reflection of the struggles of enslaved Africans – as well as a powerful source of joy in dancing and the invention of new

musical styles. Though it was heavily based on African traditions of rhythmic beats and communal singing, the music of
enslaved people became an entirely new form as it crossed the
Atlantic, where European influences were adopted, reshaping
those traditions in turn. In this way, like the voodoo religion in
the Caribbean, slave music and spirituals are some of the oldest
forms of African cultural expression in the Americas: a blend
of influences that fundamentally reshaped world culture.

But how did a song with deep routes within slavery come
to be the song of England rugby? An oft-repeated story was
that the song became a stand favourite in 1987, when Martin
Offiah – whose nickname was Chariots – took to the field.[9] But
in a 1966 article for *Tatler*, Ivor Turnbull writes that 'Sooner or
later some group would start to sing Swing Low, Sweet Chariot
and, in a minute or so, the several hundred beer-charged customers, already packed shoulder to shoulder, would sway as
one man.'[10] 'Sweet Chariot' must have been a rugby song for
much longer than that, then. While the origins of the song
within English rugby are still a mystery, the conversation of
whether it is an appropriate choice, given England's history as
a proponent of the slave trade, is still ongoing. In 2020, then
prime minister Boris Johnson made his view clear. The song
shouldn't be dropped and can serve as an opportunity to teach
people its history.[11] I'm not sure it's possible to teach history
while enjoying a rugby match, but what is clear is that the
song's ubiquity in popular culture does give us a chance to get
conversations started.

RR

30

Quilts

Quilts are synonymous with cosiness: small wonder we call them comforters. Keeping us warm, adorning the bedroom and even offering an outlet for creativity, the quilt is not an item you would expect to have a grim past. But there was a time when they provided more than just warmth. For thousands of enslaved people, quilts could be a form of rebellion and a way to organise within their communities.

It's difficult to ascertain when quilting as a practice began – undoubtedly, the art of piecing together multiple layers of padded fabric to make a blanket dates back to the earliest human societies. Quilting generally involves three layers: the top layer, featuring a decorative design, a middle layer, for insulation, and a final third layer as backing. Quilts have long been used as a form of artistic expression, with their various patterns and designs a vibrant representation of the designer's culture, their personal histories or even their political beliefs. It has always been primarily a women's art, an activity that brings people together, and a collaborative practice that invites multiple makers to stitch together a shared understanding of their lives and times.

When the first English and Dutch settlers came to North America, the quilts they brought with them would have been strictly utilitarian – there was little time for ornamentation or artistic expression. Over time, however, quilting became a sophisticated practice in colonial America, and, inevitably, these techniques were taught or forced upon enslaved people on plantations, who, alienated from their own cultural traditions, had to adopt European styles of needlework and design. Nevertheless, quilting became a way for enslaved women to create practical items and to meet socially. Quilting parties, known as 'frolics', were social gatherings that gave women a chance to get together to sew, share stories and relax without the usual surveillance they experienced on plantations.[1] Communities were formed during these gatherings, where women shared recycled cloth scraps and used them in their designs – quilting has always been about making something beautiful from discarded materials. Quilting also gave enslaved women a rare chance to demonstrate their creative flair and personalities.

Quilts made by enslaved women were also a way to generate extra money that could (eventually) be used to buy freedom. The more skilled your needlework, the more valuable your quilts could be and, if they held value, often they were sold. But sometimes quilts could be used by enslaved people as collateral for a loan from a sympathetic white ally. Elizabeth Hobbs Keckley was a Black woman who was born into slavery in Virginia in 1807.[2] She became known across Virginia for her needlework, and used her quilts as collateral for a loan of $1,200 from some white patrons who supported her work in St Louis. This was a substantial amount, around $43,000 in today's money. Keckley used this loan to buy her freedom and that of her son, after which she used her sewing skills to support her family and moved to Washington DC, sometime around 1860. In DC, Keckley served as dressmaker to Mary Todd Lincoln, the wife of President Abraham Lincoln. Later in life, Keckley worked as a sewing instructor and Director of

Domestic Arts at the historically Black Wilberforce University, becoming a prominent figure among her contemporaries and an inspiration for successive generations of Black women.

It was also said that quilts in the American South were used to send secret messages, involving patterns and symbols that conveyed information about the Underground Railroad, a network of secret routes and safe houses that were used during the nineteenth century. These routes, which required the assistance of abolitionists and allies, both Black and white, helped enslaved people escape to safe states in the North and in Canada. The routes even extended to the Caribbean once the islands became a safe haven following Britain's Slavery Abolition Act in 1833.

The legend of 'quilt codes' is an oral history passed down within African American families that started with their enslaved ancestors. Although there's debate among historians about whether such codes really existed, the story was that certain patterns could indicate safe routes or could point runaways to safe houses. A bow tie meant that you should dress in disguise in order to appear of a higher status, and thus be less likely to be questioned. A bear paw meant that you should follow an animal trail through the mountains to find water and food, and a log cabin that you should seek shelter now, and that the people here were safe to speak with. A safe house also may have been indicated by a quilt hanging from a clothesline or windowsill. A monkey wrench square warned that you should get ready to escape. If that was followed by a wagon wheel square, it meant that a wagon or safe travel was on the way.

Tracey Vaughan-Manley, a Black Studies professor at Northwestern University, believes that the myth of quilt codes is just that – a myth. She says 'there is no evidence at all' that they really existed as a secret language on the Underground Railroad.[3] And while it is known that enslaved women created quilts from scraps of material given to them, there is nothing in the archives to support the theory of secret coding: 'No letters, no notes, nothing that would signify that quilts were used as codes.'[4]

Many myths surround the Underground Railroad, and historians have spent their careers trying to figure out what is true. What we do know is that the records and sources we have from the slavery era were usually told from the viewpoint of slave owners, rather than by enslaved people themselves. American slavery ended in 1865 when Congress passed the 13th Amendment, and even though no contemporaneous sources mention quilt codes there's a good chance that the oral histories passed down in families contain some truth. We'll never know definitively – after all, the point of the Underground Railroad was that it was a secret network, and writing down secrets wasn't a good idea. Nevertheless, quilting was a proud African American art form, one that continues to this day, and its history as a kind of defiant upcycling and as an early form of networking and solidarity for enslaved people is an important part of the story of slavery in America. An example of this tradition that has persisted from slavery until today is a community in Gee's Bend, Alabama, known for quilts in vivid colours, with improvisational designs and the personal stories and heritage within them. Quilters in Gee's Bend see their art as an important connection to their history, a thread that connects the legacy of slavery in the South to the fight for civil rights and the persistence of community bonds that were formed through quilting circles. In recent years, the Gee's Bend quilts have gained significant recognition in the art world, which has helped to highlight the contribution of African American women to mainstream arts and culture.

RR

31

Wisbech Chest

In 2020, the National Trust shared a thread on Twitter that detailed locations and objects in their care linked with the slave trade. This caused outrage among some of the National Trust's members, who vowed to cancel their memberships. A few days later the BBC's Last Night of the Proms decided that the lyrics to 'Rule, Britannia!' would not be sung. The reason they gave was the COVID-19 pandemic and the spread of germs, but centrist and right-wing figures saw this as 'Wokeism gone mad'. Cat Lewis, an executive TV producer behind otherwise inoffensive programme such as *Songs of Praise*, tweeted at the time:

> Do those Brits ... believe it's ok to sing an 18th Century song about never being enslaved, written when the UK was enslaving and killing millions of innocents ...[1]

To which the BBC's former political editor and presenter Andrew Neil replied:

> If Britannia had not ruled the waves there would never have been a Royal Navy strong enough to abolish the slave trade, intercepting 1,600 ships and freeing 150,000 Africans while

sustaining major casualties. Guess it's too late to delete your tweet ...[2]

During my time at secondary school, Britain's role in the transatlantic slave trade was taught through the lens of abolition. The hundreds of years during which Britain participated in capturing and enslaving people for profit were always left out. Were it not for the fact that I am descended from enslaved people, I would have been unaware (like many Britons), of the country's full involvement in slavery. But I always knew there was more to the story than what we covered in school – I just didn't have the details. But I knew that Britain was not the hero, as so many often believe.

About twenty-five miles east of Peterborough is the Wisbech and Fenland Museum, the home of Thomas Clarkson's Campaign Chest. The chest, a heavy wooden box with dark metal hinges and various compartments and boxes inside, once contained items that demonstrated the riches from Africa and the colonies that did not involve the enslavement of people. Wood, ivory, seeds, spices and gum were all held in the box, items which promised opportunity. On the lower level of the chest, iron chains, knives and sandals represented the enslaved people and the brutality they experienced. The British Abolition movement is usually presented as a moral crusade, a story of how the nation was so disgusted with the inhumanity of the slave trade that Britain fought tooth and nail for the best interests of enslaved people to make them free. It's true that many abolitionists and people in Britain were disgusted by slavery and worked tirelessly to stop the injustice for good. Still, the reality was that the country was extremely split on abolition, because a lot of those in power had become extraordinarily wealthy through the forced labour of enslaved people. Abolitionists had to find other ways to convince them that abolition could be a good thing, which is what Clarkson tried to do with his chest.

Thomas Clarkson was born in Wisbech, Cambridgeshire in 1760.[3] He had a humble upbringing, as the son of a clergyman, and taught at a local grammar school before attending the University of Cambridge in 1779. During his time there, Clarkson won a Latin essay competition for a piece of writing about whether it was lawful or not to enslave people against their will. In it, Clarkson outlined the most common causes of slavery and its injustices. He divided slavery into two categories, voluntary and involuntary; an example of involuntary slaves were 'Prisoners of War', those captured during wars and battles. Clarkson wrote:

> The law, by which prisoners of war were said to be sentenced to servitude, was the law of nations. ... It had two points in view, the persons of the captured, and their effects; both of which it immediately sentenced, without any of the usual forms of law, to be the property of the captors.[4]

It was assumed that for every ten Africans captured, hundreds would have died during these battles. 'Convicts' were also enslaved, and often their sentence of servitude as unfree labourers would be proportionate to their crime. Clarkson wrote in detail about the kidnapping that took place to capture people to enslave. Sailors would dock their ships and hide in the thickets to kidnap unsuspecting shepherds and farmers when they encountered them alone. Once the kidnappers had forced the captured people aboard their ships they would sail them to foreign markets for sale, in countries where they lacked the language or the connections to defend themselves or escape. When slave hunters weren't collecting a direct fee for ambushing people and forcing them into slavery, sometimes the captured Africans would be bartered with European merchants for goods. Slave hunters were independent contractors who sought opportunities to make money from the slave trade. Clarkson even mentions an African prince who made a deal with a slave merchant to trade a group of captured people into slavery in exchange for liquor. The prince attacked his own village in the dead of night to capture the people to trade with the slave merchant, surrounding their settlement and setting fire to the buildings to drive the people out and into the clutches of the kidnappers.[5]

Clarkson also makes several cases for why slavery is not compatible with British values and is morally wrong. He states

> Slavery is contrary to the principles of law and government, the dictates of reason, the common maxims of equity, the laws of nature, the admonitions of conscience, and the whole doctrine of natural religion ... The practice of slavery is considered impious and wicked as it goes against the principles of Christianity, justice, and nature.[6]

In 1785, while travelling from Cambridge to London, Clarkson could not stop thinking about the brutality of slavery and knew that he had to do something to stop it. From then on, claiming that he had had a spiritual revelation from God, Clarkson spent the remaining years of his life fighting for abolition. He worked tirelessly to gather evidence against the trade, conducting investigations and interviews with enslaved people and sympathetic seamen to gather first-person evidence of the dark realities of the business. He then compiled his findings in a report that was presented to Parliament, after which he began a nationwide campaign giving lectures to expose the evils of slavery. One example of the horrific conditions Clarkson cited was that of a nineteen-year-old boy in Barbados who was found completely stripped naked with an iron collar around his neck that contained five long spikes that tore into his skin. The boy's body was covered in gaping wounds, his belly and thighs dripping with ulcers, and he was unable to sit down due to his injuries. This incident had been reported to General Tottenham, a military officer in Bridgetown in 1780.[7] The story was used to demonstrate the mistreatment and the extreme cruelty that enslaved people often endured at the hands of their owners.

In Clarkson's evidence to Parliament, he rebutted the argument that Africans were barbaric compared to people in Britain and the West by demonstrating that African customs were the same as some of those in ancient Britain. The idea that Africans were 'uncivilised' was commonly advanced to justify the 'naturalness' of slavery, and to reassure slave owners that the people they abused were not their equals. Indeed, Clarkson showed that much-touted stories of African barbarism were no different to what British people were doing in the colonies. A story that was regularly put forward was that of an African boy put to death for running away from his African master, which pro-slavery advocates used to show the violence of Africans towards their own. But on further examination, Clarkson found that the master had in fact been motivated by money. Every time the boy ran away the master had to pay his total value in order to get him back, and so after the third runaway attempt the master decided he could no longer shoulder the economic burden and killed the boy instead. Putting an enslaved person to death was not uncommon in the British West Indies, so the story did not demonstrate that Africans were more bloodthirsty than the British; if anything, it proved that slave owners of all backgrounds were equally barbaric.

In working for abolition Clarkson faced many personal attacks, and even criticism from the sons of William Wilberforce, who was an MP and a leading figure in the abolition movement. Wilberforce's sons believed that Clarkson had tried to suppress Wilberforce's abolition work while advancing his own. But Wilberforce and Clarkson actually worked together in the fight to end transatlantic slavery, with Clarkson providing Wilberforce with evidence through his detailed reports on the realities of the trade, while Wilberforce used his sway in Parliament and political influence to champion the cause. Together, their efforts were crucial to raising the public's awareness of the inhumanity of the slave trade.

In 1807 the trade of enslaved people from Africa in the British Empire was abolished. It would be a further twenty-five years before the 1833 Slavery Abolition Act was passed, finally putting an end to slavery in all British colonies. It wasn't enough to just present the atrocities; after all, a lot of white British people did not believe that enslaved Africans felt pain or understood the world in the same way that they did. The abolitionists had to present alternative reasons to end slavery, including economic imperatives that would benefit future former enslavers and those who benefited from the trade. Britain's abolition story is not as straightforward as we are often led to believe, and it certainly wasn't as simple as the nation having a change of heart and sending in the Royal Navy, as suggested by bickering tweeters in 2020. It took decades of work by abolitionists to change the tide of public opinion, and before politicians and capitalists began to look for other ways to squeeze profit from their colonies and investments. The contents of the Wisbech chest were part of this. It was a display intended to show that there were alternatives to brutalising and enslaving Black people, that other goods could be traded that didn't rely on forced labour. Abolition wasn't a decision made for the greater good or one made entirely for the benefit of those enslaved, it was a decision made because more efficient ways to exploit Africa and its people presented themselves.

RR

32

Maps

Most of us can picture a map of the world in our mind's eye. We know at least roughly the shapes and sizes of the continents and their coastlines. But what you might not know is that the map of the world you are so used to seeing is not actually a scientific or objective bird's-eye view of the earth. It's the creation of one cartographer hundreds of years ago, a product of how he saw the world, and what he saw as the purpose of the map. This map, the one in use most widely today, is called the Mercator Projection Map, and was created in 1569 by Dutch cartographer Gerardus Mercator.

The map was originally intended for maritime navigation and charting weather, and so it stretches the land in order to create straight lines that could be followed by boats. As a result of the distortion, the shapes and sizes of many places appear bigger and smaller than they actually are.[1] Intentionally or not, the Mercator Projection makes Europe and North America look much larger than in reality, and warps and shrinks other places such as the African continent, which is shown as similar in size to Greenland when it is in fact fourteen times bigger.[2] For a number of reasons, including its use on colonial voyages and expeditions, over the next 300 years this specialised map became the dominant commercial map in atlases and in schools, despite its blatant unsuitability for that purpose.[3] So used are we to seeing the world in this way that many of us now unquestioningly picture the globe as Mercator drew it and, as a consequence, we subconsciously think of the Global North as imposing and powerful and the Global South as less so. Until you have a look at the Gall–Peters projection map, which gained popularity in the 1980s and was explicitly presented in opposition to the Mercator as a more true representation of the globe, you may not appreciate just how central maps are in ingraining our sense of the world, and our place in it.[4] Take a look, if you haven't already. You might be surprised by what you see.

Maps have been around for millennia, and many cultures have their own ways of representing space. But the European, two-dimensional, bird's-eye view is the one that now governs our mental image of the globe. The first such world maps showed unknown lands decorated with strange, mythical creatures: elephants, Cyclops and barbarians, reflecting the mysteriousness of such places, and begging the question: were its inhabitants human?

Over time maps began depicting trade routes, links and networks, perhaps the threats of nature and natives. By the nineteenth century, imperial maps were about territory, settlement and the availability of natural resources. They divided up places into colours corresponding to the European empires that claimed dominion over a territory, to indicate religious or linguistic groups, or according to a region's status on a scale of civilised to savage. They allowed people to visualise the world beyond their town or village for the first time. Today, maps show us the evolution of imperial ambitions.[5] Historian of geography and exploration, Ed Armston-Sheret, takes us on a fascinating journey through Africa to understand how, and why, we got here, and why map-making and slavery were two sides of the same coin.

Armston-Sheret explains that 'exploration was integral to empire. What made imperialism global was that it kept expanding, and explorers were leading that expansion.' Without it, empire and slavery would not have developed as they did. He says, 'Maps were central to this process, because maps are often about control. To incorporate land into an empire, you need to know what's there, who's there, and where they are. Cartography becomes a key way of establishing colonial power, and of controlling the populations that live within those states.'[6]

As Britain struggled to establish sovereignty over indigenous land, maps provided the illusion of order and control in the Americas. Caribbean maps, for example, shift over time from mysterious, strange and fantastical in the early modern era – depicting exotic natives, animals, and mythical creatures like mermaids – to something more familiar and domesticated. The Caribbean was soon shown as ordered, agricultural and productive, with neatly bordered plantations. Those earlier symbols get phased out and replaced by ports and shipping routes in eighteenth-century maps. An untravelled British observer of both maps would come away with two very different ideas of the region, who lived there, and what it had to offer.[7]

We see something of this approach in Africa, too. Unexplored by Europe, the African interior had been mapped by Arabic explorers in the late Middle Ages, who filled their maps with rich information. But, as Armston-Sheret remarks, 'you don't see many of these features on British early-nineteenth-century maps'. Despite the evidence of the Arabic maps, the British 'suddenly decided that the map – the interior of Africa – was actually blank. They made it blank. They chose to discount all this oral information.' They created the fiction that Africa was largely uninhabited, or that its people were so uncivilised that they were essentially animals who could be disregarded when trying to take over the land – ignoring the reality that it was occupied by many major city-states and kingdoms.[8]

This reflected a fundamental shift in attitude during this period about what was or was not a valid source of information, which complicates an idea that we take for granted in our modern-day lives – that science is constantly improving and advancing in a clear upward trajectory. Maps should, by this reckoning, only get fuller, clearer and more accurate over time, not less so. Yet looking at a nineteenth-century map of Africa wouldn't tell you very much about the continent, though it would reveal much about the aims and intentions of the person who made the map. As Armston-Sheret points out, what we consider to be definitive knowledge is never stable, and will continue to change over time.[9]

Forced to give up the wealth created by slavery as a consequence of abolition, Britain sought new markets and places to control, a reorientation known as the 'Imperial Meridian'.[10] Instead of just sticking to its coastlines for slave trading, Britain began to explore Africa's interiors for potential profit, and was particularly keen to map its long rivers. 'On one level that sounds quite neutral. You just want to know where a river goes – that doesn't seem controversial.' But, as Armston-Sheret explains, charting Africa's waterways was intertwined with empire and slavery, as British explorers knew that understanding how to travel by river and access the centre of Africa would expand the empire and provide solutions to the problems caused by the end of slavery.[11]

Mungo Park (1771–1806), a Scottish MP and a most celebrated explorer of the late eighteenth century, attempted to find and map the Niger river. On his second mission in 1805, two years before the abolition of the slave trade, he and his last remaining soldiers disappeared and were never heard of again. His vanishing haunted British society. Other adventurers set out to find him, and the Niger, to no avail.[12] Inspired by Park's endeavour, James MacQueen (1778–1870), a Scottish slave owner on the Caribbean island of Grenada, interrogated the slaves on his plantation, some of whom were Mandingos from the Upper Niger, about their memories of their homeland and the Niger's location.[13] MacQueen used the memories of a young boy, under the age of ten, to make the claim that he had discovered and proved the whereabouts of the Niger – which he had never visited or seen. He was an armchair geographer, someone who makes maps of places without travelling there, a very common activity until the early twentieth century. MacQueen relied on the 'captive knowledge' of enslaved people who had been violently removed from their homelands, memories that probably caused them great pain. He was strongly anti-abolition, and believed that mapping the Niger could prevent future economic disaster, advocating for slavery's 'slow abolition' in Africa even if it had to be abolished immediately in the Caribbean. He thought that colonising the African continent would require exploiting Africans for unpaid slave labour, at least at first.[14]

British explorers such as David Livingstone, Richard Burton and John Speke continued to trace Africa's river networks after abolition, particularly in East Africa, throughout the rest of the nineteenth century. Spanning Arab and Muslim states, India, Europe and Zanzibar's Omani Empire, the East African slave trade was massive, complex, transnational and transoceanic. Small numbers of enslaved East Africans were shipped to the Americas from there, while other kingdoms became so dependent on European cloth, guns and other commodities that participation in the slave trade was a necessary evil.[15] Naturally, opportunistic Brits saw no issue with becoming embroiled too.[16] But, 'by the 1860s and 1870s, the British Empire [had] totally pivoted' towards suppressing global slavery, justifying increased involvement in Africa through the need to protect it from 'ruthless' Arabs and Muslims. Armston-Sheret says, 'it reminds me a lot of current rhetoric around humanitarian intervention, the West "saving" people from evil in other places, while not exactly being saints themselves.'[17]

Huge expeditions from Zanzibar into the African interior (along slave-trading routes) comprised perhaps a couple of British explorers to a hundred African porters or soldiers providing assistance. Many on these expeditions were either enslaved or formerly enslaved people.[18] For linguistic reasons alone, geographical surveying expeditions relied extensively upon indigenous assistants, guides and local informants.[19] These 'headsmen' were crucial to the day-to-day functioning and gritty work of the expeditions.[20] Armston-Sheret says that it's hard to find these stories because the explorers had to be cautious in writing about having illegal slaves for fear of being discredited in Britain (alongside their general unwillingness to value or credit Black contributions). Mentions of these informants are rare, and when they are present they are usually disparaging and critical, thick with racism. Explorers struggled to trust oral information from some Africans, believing that Europeans remained the arbiters of truth and authority.[21] In ignoring or denying the help of their assistants, Armston-Sheret believes that British explorers hoped to diminish their importance to an expedition's success, and to appear heroic and independent. Yet many of the resulting maps are confusing, unclear about their sources and mired by egotism.[22]

When press-ganged into an expedition, African porters were vulnerable, cut off from their social, cultural and familial networks. Armston-Sheret has detailed incredible violence and exploitation used by British explorers against these people, either as an exercise of power, or because they didn't care how discipline was maintained as long as an expedition was successful. The extreme abuse suffered was condemned by many even at the time.[23] Child assistants, certainly non-consensual, were common too. With their strong linguistic abilities, children would be 'purchased' from a local slave owner, then either trained at missionary school or immediately brought on expeditions.[24] Speke showcased a young boy named George Tembo to audiences as 'proof' that his maps were correct.[25] As Armston-Sheret says, 'There's a lot of really quite disturbing, horrible stories, when you think these children are stripped from their families and sent across the world. This is in the 1890s – not that long ago.'[26]

We cannot underestimate the importance of Black bodies and minds to modern map-making.[27] Explorers like Mungo Park projected masculine strength and bravery, but ultimately their lives were in the hands of the native people who determined their fates. Native guides were relied upon for food, fodder, resources, and information not just about the geography but also about the climate, what was safe to eat and which routes were safe to travel: 'communities that refused to cooperate could and did seriously impede progress'.[28] One small error, misunderstanding or white lie could have fatal consequences. The causes of Mungo Park's and David Livingstone's deaths are unclear, but many speculate that it could have been animal attacks, drowning, starvation, climate (the natural world they sought to control) or murder (the people they sought to control).[29]

Armston-Sheret concludes that 'maps are not neutral: they are always made with some agenda'. He asks us to compare maps of the same places with different dates or authors. 'They'll show quite different features.'[30] Thinking historically about labour is important too: 'Particularly with our reliance now on things like Google Earth, we rarely consider how large, coordinated and painstaking these operations needed to be, how many were literally there to carry the surveying equipment or to cook the food.'[31] The entanglements of slavery and maps are manifold: the geographic imagination of the Caribbean and Africa was important to the Atlantic slave system, stabilising, entrenching and normalising slavery. Geography was important to maintaining slavery through both surveying and surveilling, for it required the control of land, plants, animals and people. Not understanding the whereabouts of runaways, Maroons and rebels could prove catastrophic for the system. Crucially, though, the enslaved themselves were often the greatest carriers and producers of geographical knowledge.[32]

The British, through their maps and surveys, created the illusion of objective and authoritative knowledge, while appropriating that of others. Fundamentally, it is impossible to represent a 3D object in a 2D form in a perfectly accurate way. The reality is that we will never achieve full or complete geographical knowledge, nor will geography remain the same eternally. [33] Maps cannot accurately capture the disorder and messiness of the human-made world in its entirety. Maps maintain their discrepancies with the land, they fail to capture full stories. Though if you look closely enough, you can often find the shadows of other, untold stories, and bring them into focus.

AL

33

The *Guardian*

Growing up, I was always sceptical of the news. I grew up on the outskirts of London and remember the news being overwhelmingly about Black boys stabbing each other. For a while, as a child, I genuinely thought that if you went into central London you'd be stabbed. There was rarely any positive example of Black people in the media. If we were on a television show the Black person was the antagonist. Black men specifically would portray robbers, domestic abusers, rapists, murderers and generally the bad people of society. This is all we had in terms of representation. There were some high points, like *Desmond's*, the Channel 4 sitcom that ran from 1989 to 1994, about a barbershop in Peckham. The lead actors were all Black and all beloved members of their communities, and they represented normal Black folks that most of us could relate to. Of course, we had access to American sitcoms like *The Cosby Show* and my mum used to watch *LA Law* religiously, which was where I saw my first Black lawyer, Blair Underwood's character Jonathan Rollins. But the news never provided respite.

Black journalists have long seen a problem with representation in the newsroom. In 2023, the Ethical Journalism Network released the report 'Structural Racism in UK Newsrooms'.

Although the report was published with the aim of providing a pathway to a better future and working practices, it was damning about the current conditions for Black journalists. Considering the direct experiences of Black journalists within the UK, the report stated that 'Black journalists are undermined, harassed and excluded from newsroom processes and content.'[1] The report talks about how Black journalists are often pigeonholed into covering certain stories and beats, how they're often believed to lack objectivity when addressing certain topics and are often obstructed from progressing their careers. Although I'm not a journalist, I have spent my career working in media and pigeonholing is something I've experienced often, especially when running my production company Broccoli Productions. It can be frustrating when you see your white counterparts able to work on projects across a variety of subjects and you are restricted to what people assume is related to your Black identity. The report, however, does recognise the *Guardian*'s progressive approach to the newsroom and journalism. In the words its authors:

> There was a unanimously positive response to the creation of roles such as community affairs and race correspondents at a number of media organisations, including the *Guardian*, the *Independent* and ITN. These roles were seen as integral to ensuring that the issues of structural racism in society are critically analysed for audiences.[2]

The *Guardian* is known for championing diversity, and well before the reckonings of 2020 it had been at the forefront in holding organisations accountable about their pasts, specifically when addressing links to the transatlantic slave trade. So it was only a matter of time before the paper began to look inwards and investigate its own beginnings. In 2020, the Scott

Trust, which owns the *Guardian*, commissioned an academic review into the founders of the *Manchester Guardian*.

The *Manchester Guardian* was founded in the aftermath of the Peterloo Massacre in 1819.[3] On 16 August, over 50,000 people gathered at St Peter's Field in Manchester to protest for the right to vote. Before the Reform Act of 1832, the county of Lancashire was represented by only two MPs, and only around 11,000 people – all of them men – were eligible to vote out of a population of nearly a million. The people had gathered to hear a speech on parliamentary reform by Henry Hunt but as soon as Hunt began speaking the authorities gave the order to shut it down. There was an attempt to arrest Hunt, which created chaos among the crowd. Soldiers on horseback then charged the people gathered, which resulted in the deaths of up to twenty people and more than four hundred more injured.[4] After witnessing the events, John Edward Taylor sent reports to be published in *The Times*. After following up with more reports on the injuries and deaths he decided to found a new independent newspaper to 'zealously enforce the principles of civil and religious Liberty'.[5] Taylor needed financial backing to start a new paper, and was able to raise £1,100 in loans from eleven backers, just over £133,000 in today's money.[6] With their support, the *Manchester Guardian* published its first edition on 5 May 1821.

Although the difference between those who profited from slavery directly (such as plantation owners and slave traders) and those who benefited indirectly from the wealth it created is frequently affirmed, assessing the ill-gotten gains of slavery remains a crucial part of understanding how the trade made modern Britain. It's important to recognise that many more people profited from the slave trade through investments and secondary trades involving goods produced by enslaved people. Despite the *Manchester Guardian*'s liberal credentials, John

Edward Taylor was a beneficiary of the slave trade, through the investments of his financial backers and particularly via his partnerships with cotton manufacturing firm Oakden & Taylor and with the cotton merchant firm Shuttleworth, Taylor & Co.[7]

Taylor was born on 11 September 1791 in Somerset, the son of an Anglican reverend originally from Stand in Greater Manchester.[8] Taylor attended the same school as his father before leaving at the age of fourteen to begin an apprenticeship at an Oldham cotton manufacturer, Benjamin Oakden. Taylor worked with Oakden for five years before rising through the company to become a partner at just twenty-one.[9] During their partnership, Oakden and Taylor conducted deals with cotton merchants and they also exported finished textiles to slave societies in the Americas. The raw cotton that the company imported most likely came from the southern states of America, as well as from Brazil and the Caribbean. Oakden and Taylor's partnership was dissolved in 1815, after three years of trading, after which time Taylor look over sole ownership of the cotton merchants.[10]

Following the dissolution of his partnership with Oakden, Taylor partnered with a business contact, John Shuttleworth, to form Shuttleworth, Taylor & Co. in 1815.[11] Two of the *Manchester Guardian*'s eleven investors were also involved in this new partnership, Robert Philips and George William Wood. Through his mother's second marriage Robert Phillips was related to the Hibbert family, who had multiple direct links to slavery. Philips's mother, Elizabeth Hibbert, had married Nathanial Hibbert, who was the son of notorious slave and plantation owner George Hibbert.[12] George William Wood, meanwhile, was a prominent figure among Manchester's social elite as well as the MP for Kendal from 1837 to 1843, and was involved in several cotton companies besides Shuttleworth, Taylor & Co.

Shuttleworth, Taylor & Co. did significant business with the Strutt family, another family of cotton traders, for whom Shuttleworth, Taylor & Co. acted as agents selling the Strutts' goods for a commission. Between 1817 to 1824, Shuttleworth, Taylor & Co. received £2,300 in sales commission from the Strutts, just over £316,000 today.[13] Shuttleworth, Taylor & Co. received significant amounts of raw cotton from the Sea Islands, a group of over a hundred tidal and barrier islands along the south-eastern coast of the United States, which were known for the production of 'Sea Island Cotton' and home to multiple plantations.

As the cotton capital of Britain, Manchester was awash with wealthy investors involved in the textile industry and, inevitably, the slave trade. It was through Shuttleworth, Taylor & Co. and the cotton trade that John Edward Taylor was able to meet the other *Manchester Guardian* investors, including Sir George Philips, who was the cousin of Robert Philips at Shuttleworth, Taylor & Co.[14] Out of the eleven investors, nine had links with the transatlantic slave trade beyond those involved in Shuttleworth, Taylor & Co. Two more investors, Edward Baxter and William Duckworth (who was also Robert Philips's son-in-law) were cotton merchants like Taylor and the others who worked with Shuttleworth, Taylor & Co. A further two investors, Sir Thomas and Richard Potter, had a warehouse in Manchester where the cotton goods they manufactured and sold were stored. Samuel Pullein was a director and trustee of the Manchester Fire and Life Assurance Company, many of the directors and trustees of which were involved in cotton trading and most likely utilised Pullein's talents as a risk assessor in deciding what cotton trades to make. Thomas B. W. Sanderson was another cotton merchant, and manufacturer of Sanderson T. B. W. & Co., who would have met Taylor through Manchester's business elite.

The remaining two investors in the *Manchester Guardian*, Thomas Jenkins and Thomas Wilkins, have not been found to have had any links to slavery. This doesn't mean those links don't exist – it's not possible to determine specific details of their businesses and investments because of the commonness of their names, and the often tangled and unreliable nature of archives from the time. Both men are listed in the *Manchester Guardian* loan agreements as merchants, with Thomas Wilkins listed as a cotton merchant, but beyond that it is not possible to know for certain whether their wealth was derived from the slave trade.

Through his partnerships, John Edward Taylor was able not only to make significant amounts of money through trading enslaved-produced goods but also to network with some of Manchester's elite. It's a mark of just how far-reaching the legacy of slavery is in modern Britain that one of our most liberal national newspapers could only have been founded from the profits of enforced labour. Its benefits are often stripped down to financial gain, but slavery didn't just enrich investors and company directors. It shaped communities, and directly reshaped the social structures we live within now. Today's *Guardian* and *Observer* newspapers are often praised for their forward-thinking and diverse reporting, but there is still a lack of Black leaders within the organisation and across news media in general within the UK. Whatever the lofty mission statements or founding principles of these organisations profess, the structural institutions built during slavery can't be equitable for all if the system was biased from the start.

RR

34

Peabody Trust

Walk around London or the home counties and it won't take long before you come across a Peabody building. I live in a Peabody property and a few of my friends do too. The row of early Edwardian houses and flats where I live in Walthamstow are all Peabody Trust properties, some of which are housing association and some of which are leasehold.

Housing associations are private non-profit organisations that provide low-cost social housing.[1] Although private, and separate from the social housing offered by local councils and the government, they are still state-regulated and often receive public funding for new developments. Housing associations are major providers of new housing for rent, and they also participate in affordable housing schemes like shared ownership, where people who qualify (usually based on a salary cap) can buy a share of a newly built property owned or managed by housing associations.

Founded in 1862 by George Peabody, the Peabody Trust was part of a wider movement of philanthropy that sprang up in the late nineteenth century among wealthy capitalists who, as part of a broader Christian morality, felt they owed something to the millions of working people who still lived in slum conditions while they themselves had grown rich amid the rapid industrialisation of the Victorian age. Today the Peabody Trust has over 100,000 properties in and around London.[2] George Peabody set up the Peabody Donation Fund (as it was originally called) to provide homes for what was then known as the 'artisans and labouring poor of London', inspired by George's recognition of social injustice and, in the words of the Trust, his desire to 'tackle the poverty he saw around him': 'George's vision and sense of social justice has shaped us and made Peabody the organisation it is today.'[3]

George Peabody's vision for housing in London was a noble one, and the Trust are rightly proud of his philanthropic efforts – but his ambitious, capitalist past with the slave trade has barely been acknowledged. Following the global race reckoning of 2020, companies and organisations worldwide commissioned research into the histories of their businesses or founders. In the US, the Peabody Institute were no different, and their research revealed George Peabody's direct and indirect links to the slave trade. The UK-based Peabody Trust, however, has not been so forthcoming. This could be because most of George Peabody's wealth was acquired through businesses and relationships in the US, where slavery wasn't abolished until 1865, thirty-two years after the UK. Even after abolition within the British Empire, there was money to be made from the trade and its associated industries in the US and George Peabody was someone who profited greatly from its long shadow.

George Peabody was born in Danvers, Massachusetts in 1795.[4] The southern part of Danvers, originally South Danvers, has since been renamed Peabody. After a childhood beset by poverty, he moved to Washington DC and then on to Baltimore, where he lived between 1815 and 1837.[5] From a young age Peabody had a hunger to earn money and to make a profit from international trade, including from goods produced by enslaved people. Contemporary sources show that he had been involved in the cotton trade as early as 1812, beginning work as an independent proprietor in Georgetown advertising the sale of cotton fabrics produced in England that he imported via New York.[6] Tax records show that Peabody paid personal property tax on $400 (equivalent to $9,400 in 2021) of non-real estate property in July 1812.[7] Although records of this kind rarely defined the personal property involved, the George Peabody and Slavery research report speculates that 'this $400 might have been Peabody's dry goods company materials, a horse, or enslaved people.'[8]

Later that year Peabody served as an artillery soldier during the War of 1812 between the United States and its allies against the United Kingdom. During the war, he met Elisha Riggs, an experienced merchant and financier. They went on to form Riggs, Peabody and Co. in 1815, a business that specialised in importing and selling cotton goods.[9] Soon RP&C were taking out adverts in the *Baltimore Patriot* that they had received and were selling 'clothes, blankets, velvet, baizes [wool], and other textiles from Liverpool'.[10]

Liverpool was the centre of the British cotton industry. The majority of the raw cotton received at the Liverpool docks was harvested by enslaved people in the southern United States. Mill workers in Lancashire then treated the raw cotton and manufactured it into textiles, which were exported back across the Atlantic to merchants like Riggs, Peabody and Co. This company also traded other goods harvested by enslaved people, such as tea, coffee and tobacco, all the while enriching themselves and growing the industries that made slavery so profitable. Often the goods they traded would travel on the same ships used to transport enslaved people. The ship HMS *Franklin*, from which Riggs, Peabody and Co. received goods in September 1818, transported forty-six enslaved people from Baltimore to New Orleans in 1819.[11]

When Peabody went on his first trip to England in 1827, he drafted a will that showed a significant rise in the wealth he had amassed while working with Riggs. The will indicated that Peabody had assets totalling $85,000, which today would be worth just under $2.7 million – somewhat higher than the humble $400 in assets he had a mere fifteen years before.[12] Although Peabody remained an active partner in Riggs, Peabody and Co. until 1843, he permanently left Baltimore for England in 1837, by which time his assets had increased to £322,000, just over £45 million in today's value. The business was incredibly lucrative for both Peabody and Riggs.[13] Peabody remained with the business until 1845, by which point he had been living in London for seven years.

In London, Peabody traded as a merchant banker, and in 1851 formally incorporated under the name George Peabody & Co.[14] In 1854, Peabody made J. S. Morgan, an American banker living in London with whom he'd become close, a partner in the firm, which was then renamed Peabody, Morgan & Co. Following Peabody's retirement in 1864 the firm became J. S. Morgan & Co.[15] The modern-day banks JPMorgan Chase and Chase Bank are its descendants.

Much of the UK's international trade at this time was based upon chattel slavery, whether through the direct ownership of colony-based plantations, investment in plantations owned by others, the import and export of goods produced by enslaved people, or in the factories which turned raw materials into saleable products. In his 1855 book *Cotton is King*, the American anti-abolitionist and apologist for slavery David Christy proclaimed that 'slavery is not an isolated system, but is so mingled with the business of the world, that it derives facilities from the most innocent transactions'.[16] This was especially true of the business done by bankers and financiers like Peabody.

Even in England, the greater portion of Peabody's business

dealings involved transatlantic slavery. Through his bank, Peabody provided credit to southern plantation owners and invested in plantation banks, which were a type of bank that emerged in Louisiana in the early 1820s to serve plantation owners and enslavers. The plantation banks extended credit to people looking to purchase enslaved people, build new plantations or to expand existing ones. Enslaved people were used as collateral against the loans, and historian Bonnie Martin estimates that 88 per cent of loans secured with mortgages in Louisiana at the time used enslaved people as collateral.[17] These banks were private, but they had the backing of their states, which acted as guarantors and significantly reduced the investment risks for enslavers. Peabody also invested heavily in New Orleans, which was then the centre of the domestic slave trade in America. At least two of the banks Peabody invested in owned enslaved people directly, making Peabody a partial owner of enslaved people himself.

Between 1831 and 1865, JP Morgan Chase's predecessor banks, Citizens' Bank and Canal Bank, both of which George Peabody had invested in, accepted around 21,000 enslaved people as collateral.[18] The banks also assumed ownership over 1,200 enslaved people due to foreclosures and debt. Again, Peabody became a partial owner of these enslaved people via his investments.

In 2005, JP Morgan Chase admitted the role they had played in chattel slavery and issued an apology letter to their employees signed by then chief executive William Harrison:

> We apologise to the African-American community, particularly those who are descendants of slaves, and to the rest of the American public for the role that Citizens' Bank and Canal Bank played. The slavery era was a tragic time in US history and in our company's history.[19]

Throughout his trading and banking career, George Peabody profited twice over from enslaved people's labour – first as an importer and exporter of slave-made commodities, and secondly as a partial owner of slaves through his investments, earning interest from loans given to plantation owners and enslavers. It's a common story that wealthy people who've made their money in less than savoury ways turn to philanthropy, as much to launder their reputations as out of a genuine desire to help people. Peabody is no different; he has sometimes been called the 'father' of modern philanthropy, alongside figures like Andrew Carnegie and Johns Hopkins. In 1857 he founded the Peabody Institute, which in 1977 became affiliated with Johns Hopkins University; it is now a dance and music conservatory and prep school in Baltimore. Seventeen of the twenty-four founding trustees of the Peabody Institute owned enslaved people in the same decade as the Institute's opening – and all of them were handpicked by Peabody himself.

In 1869 a statue of a seated George Peabody was unveiled in the Royal Exchange commemorating all the work he had done for London housing. It was the first statue in London of an American:[20] the next such statue, of Abraham Lincoln in Parliament Square, would not be unveiled until 1920.[21] What George Peabody did for affordable housing in London is not something to be downplayed but the Peabody Trust should recognise the true origins of its founder's wealth in the same way that its US counterparts have acknowledged Peabody's past. As a social landlord, Peabody Trust has faced criticism in recent years for rent increases amid the cost of living crisis, as well as backlash from tenants for the Trust's plans to evict them and demolish social housing as part of regeneration projects. At the Thamesmead Estate in South-east London, some tenants have described their Peabody estate as 'a battleground against social cleansing'.[22] The Trust might benefit from a review of their founder, and a clearer focus on which of George Peabody's principles they want to carry forward in the present day. The rights we do at the end of our lives don't negate the wrongs that lurk in our darker histories.

RR

35

The Metropolitan Police and the Conservative Party

If you have ever watched a UK-based crime drama, there's a good chance that at some point you'll have seen a shot of a revolving rectangular sign that reads 'New Scotland Yard'. The building on Victoria Embankment was formerly Whitehall Police Station and is now the headquarters of London's Metropolitan Police, the most famous legacy of Home Secretary Sir Robert Peel, who founded it in 1829.[1]

The Metropolitan Police have a complicated history, plagued with institutional racism since its inception and in recent years by a rising number of current and former officers who have been convicted of serious sexual assaults. The Met has, for the most part, lost the trust of the citizens it is meant to protect – and that's before we examine the connections between its founder and the slave trade.

Sir Robert Peel was a British statesman who is best known for forming the Metropolitan Police in 1829. In 1822, he was appointed Home Secretary and became involved in penal reform.[2] Peel wanted to establish a professional and unified police force to deal with the rising crime rates among London's fast-expanding population. It's thanks to Peel that the police are sometimes called bobbies or peelers.

I talked to Sami Pinarbasi, a historian of slavery and abolition, to find out more. He started with Peel's inheritance from his father of £140,000, a significant fortune in 1830.[3] 'Robert Peel's father was one of ten millionaires at the turn of the nineteenth century. Peel Senior and Junior both employed around 15,000 men, women and children to work in the cotton manufacturing industry in Britain.'[4] Peel also inherited forty mill refineries and warehouses throughout Lancashire and Staffordshire, making him the inheritor of a significant stake in slavery through his involvement in the cotton trade – wealth derived, Pinarbasi reminds us, from 'cotton picked by enslaved people throughout the thirteen colonies'.[5] As a wealthy man with many investments, Peel came to see maintaining law and order as the most important job for the government – 'This idea of order and industry really permeates the political career and business career of Peel', Pinarbasi tells us.[6]

Robert Peel joined the government, becoming an MP in 1809 after being elected to the seat of Cashel in Tipperary, although some believe that he had in fact bought his way in.[7] At the time this was perfectly possible because of the existence of so-called 'rotten boroughs' – seats in parliament where the area of the constituency was owned by one landowner who could influence the votes of the tenants on the land. This meant that 'people like Robert Peel could pay the landowner, to purchase a seat and go into parliament'.[8] It's worth noting too that the seat was in Ireland, despite Peel himself being 'rabidly anti-Irish, anti-Catholic'.[9]

When Peel started in politics he was a member of the Tory Party, which would eventually become the Conservative Party of today (we still refer to them as 'the Tories'). In 1834, Peel became prime minister, but his term was short-lived due to political instability, and his party faced internal divisions as well as having difficulty passing key legislation.[10] During the election campaign at the end of that year, however, Peel had delivered the Tamworth Manifesto, which outlined many of the key principles that laid the foundations for the modern Conservative Party. But despite his role in founding one of the country's two most significant political parties, the Metropolitan Police is Peel's lasting legacy.

Before the Metropolitan Police were formed, law and order were maintained at a local level, with volunteer parish constables charged with keeping the peace – often haphazardly, as their training and authority varied enormously from role to role. Many cities also employed 'watchmen', who were responsible for patrolling the streets during the night in order to deter crime and served as an alert system to authorities in emergencies. In growing cities, the small number of watchmen in charge of larger and larger populations often had their effectiveness questioned.[11] In 1798, the Thames River Police had been established as an organised unit to combat smuggling and theft, but the force only patrolled the river.[12] In addition to the limited police presence, local magistrates had some powers to maintain order and could call on local constables and militia for assistance. These magistrates, known as 'justices of the peace', were probably among the least effective crime deterrents.[13] Clearly, a more organised approach to law enforcement was needed in London, and it was Peel's responsibility as Home Secretary to devise a new system.

When creating the Met, Peel set out nine principles that should guide the police force. These principles have been adapted and adopted by forces across the world and even used during training for certain law enforcement agencies across America. The first 'Peelian' principle states that the police are there 'To prevent crime and disorder, as an alternative to their repression by military force and severity of legal punishment.'[14] The second is 'To recognise always that the power of the police to fulfil their functions and duties is dependent on public approval of their existence, actions and behaviour, and on their ability to secure and maintain public respect.'[15] Broadly, they lay out a plan for police action that rests on fairness and the use of force only as a last resort, when other methods of 'persuasion, advice and warning are found to be insufficient to obtain public co-operation to an extent necessary to secure observance of the law or to restore order'.[16]

But the Met wasn't the first police force that Peel was involved in. As Pinarbasi tells us, Peel 'had a belief in despotic government and authoritarianism, and so, he first established a police force in Cashel in Tipperary in Ireland'. In Ireland, Peel's approach to policing had an emphasis on community cooperation and the prevention of crime rather than responding to crime after it happened. These philosophies led to the formation of the Royal Irish Constabulary in 1836, which was modelled on the Metropolitan Police. The Royal Irish Constabulary was created to maintain order in Ireland, particularly during significant political and social unrest, and in the later nineteenth and twentieth century the RIC became an infamous tool of British repression. Despite the common consent advocated by the Peelian principles, the modern police force came into being in a colonial territory – Ireland – and was therefore always associated, in Pinarbasi's words, with the way that colonialism was 'administered through brute force and brutality and exploitation and violence'.[17]

Indeed, the civilian-style model that Peel used for the Met was not the approach taken by police forces across the empire. Colonial policing varied from place to place and often combined different theories of law enforcement, with many colonies following the style of the Met while other police forces were more military-adjacent, akin to the heavily armed police seen across the US.[18]

Peel was an authoritarian, and a pro-slavery politician, but by the standards of his day he was seen as a liberal. His approach to policing was pragmatic and sensitive to the needs of communities – at least in Great Britain – and recognised that crime deterrence and avoidance was a better focus than punishing criminals who'd already offended. Nonetheless, it is also the case that Peel gained his power and wealth through the slave trade, in helping his father to build their business empire on the backs of enslaved people and the goods they produced, and in his role advocating for heavy-handed policing in Ireland and other places colonised by the British.

Today, Sir Robert Peel is still commemorated as the humble son of a textile manufacturer who became a politician who went on to achieve greatness. We have a habit of humbling the stories of the most extravagant, well-connected people, ignoring their privileges and perhaps over-emphasising their struggles, and it's that very refusal to look directly at the reality of the past that allows Britain to avoid dealing with its systemic social inequalities today. This attitude was prevalent in Peel's own lifetime, and Peel distanced himself from the landed gentry and 'old money' in his self-portrayal as a self-made capitalist, a 'man of the people' – a tactic that politicians often use. During the 2024 Conservative Party leadership contest, frontrunner Kemi Badenoch claimed that although she had grown up middle class she had 'become' working class when she worked at McDonalds.[19] Obviously, we know that this is not how class works, but the importance of finding ways to connect with working-class people is a necessity, whether the connection is real or fabricated.

When we look at the headlines today and see stories of abuse and reports of failings in the Metropolitan Police, and

other forces founded in its likeness, it's clear that law enforcement has lost its way and steered away from the original Peelian
principles. Politicians are constantly pushing for more powers
and equipment for the police, as though communities (and
especially Black and global majority ethnic communities) are
potential troublemakers who need to be managed rather than
citizens who the police should work with. We may be moving
towards a more militarised presence, which seems to be the
opposite of Peel's original intentions – although we shouldn't
forget that Peel and others were involved in the colonial policing
of Ireland and the rest of the empire. Like many figures linked
with the slave trade, Peel has a complicated legacy that is often
viewed through rose-coloured lenses that serve to blur out the
parts of his story that are not as clean as people would like.
As the Conservative Party and the Met Police seek to restore
their damaged reputations, we – and they – need to understand
their origins, and remember the principles on which they were
founded.

RR

36

Athletics

The day before the men's 100-metre sprint at the London 2012 Olympic Games, Channel 4 released a documentary entitled *Survival of the Fastest*, narrated by African American Olympic sprinter Michael Johnson. The documentary's investigation into why Black men seem to make excellent runners concluded that it must be due to a form of historical slavery-induced natural selection, in which the intensity and high mortality of the plantation system led to the survival only of the strongest and fittest enslaved people. It suggested, controversially, that the DNA of Black descendants of the enslaved could have been altered by a condensed and accelerated form of Darwinian natural selection, making them stronger, faster and more muscular: ideal for sprinting. This theory was heavily discussed by the media and in Olympics coverage in the days following.[1] All reputable academic research, however, flatly refutes the theory. In reality, these ideas are based on little more than disturbing stereotypes about Black people (particularly Black men) as threatening and animalistic, and who, in contrast to white people, are unable to embody characteristics such as beauty, elegance or intelligence. Below, we debunk these theories and emphasise how flawed, and ultimately racist, it is to connect the physical capacities of Black bodies with the history of slavery. The deeply rooted racist myths that make this theory even possible are the actual legacy of slavery in this story.[2]

How did this idea begin? Black bodies and Black athletes have always been subject to discrimination based on assumptions and stereotypes that create fear about their violent capabilities and brute physical force. In the early twentieth century Black athletes, from Jack Johnson, heavyweight boxing champion of the world in 1908, to Jesse Owens, who dominated the 1936 Berlin Olympic Games in sprinting, shocked the world.[3] White audiences were forced to reconsider the assumptions that had justified slavery: Black people's natural, innate physical and mental inferiority. These unexpected victories could only be rationalised by white audiences by diminishing athletes to 'black brutes', 'physically strong but mentally weak'. Placed in opposition to 'white brains', 'black brawn' was seen as primitive, closer to nature.[4] Black athletes, rather than praised for their abilities and dedication, were seen as exceptions to the rule, as it was a scary prospect to consider that Black people might have the ability to overtake them.[5] Brilliant white athletes were trained, coveted and betted on as the next 'great white hopes' for defeating looming, unacceptable Black competition, transforming the boxing ring and racetrack into racial battlegrounds.[6] Animal-like physical strength and a propensity for violence became a way in which Blackness was seen in wider society.[7]

We still see this attitude in our media today. Scholars Matthew Hughey and Devon Goss, experts in the field, analyse mainstream media reports on twenty-first-century athletics events and find that, indeed, white sporting success is more often attributed to intelligence, hard work and discipline. Conversely, non-white success is generally described as the outcome of natural ability and speed, and genetic factors such as long limbs and muscle mass, believed to be innate genetic predispositions of Black athletes.[8]

The opening lines of the trailer for *Survival of the Fastest* reveal a dynamic of white fear, vulnerability and victimhood at the hands of Black men: 'It's been over thirty years since the last white man won the Olympic hundred-metre sprint. But the fastest men on earth are not just Black. There is a deeper, and more controversial truth.' It ends with the claim that, through the investigation, the four times Black Olympian Michael Johnson will find out whether the 'secret of his success' is the fact that he is descended from slaves (read: not his talent and dedication).[9]

The theory proposes, by way of unconfirmed historical 'facts', that natural selection occurred on American and Caribbean plantations, producing a physically stronger than average population, and that there were two factors involved: first, that high mortality rates meant that the weakest (genetically speaking) must have been the first to die; and second, that enslaved people were widely 'bred' by slave owners, who selected men and women and forced them to reproduce as part of a long-term plan to create more chattel slaves 'for free'. Many were probably selected for 'positive' attributes that made them ideal workers, such as physical strength, good health and a hard-working but docile attitude. In contrast, physically weak, 'lazy', or rebellious people would not have been chosen.[10] It is argued that this led to their descendants having physiognomies and inherited traits that lend themselves to sprinting, such as fast muscle twitch in the ACTN3 gene, which would thus have been intensified in the population.[11]

This relies on a multitude of incorrect assumptions about race and slavery. Beyond the notion that the conditions of slavery were capable of promoting natural selection, it requires us to believe that 'races' are biologically distinct categories possessing unique genetic traits. It further implies that nature is always more important than nurture, and that your biology dictates your destiny: that is, that no one can change their fate through hard work, and that people are not influenced in their choices and achievements by the social and cultural environments in which they are raised.[12] This narrative has been so widespread and convincing that it has been promoted by spokespeople both white and Black.[13]

But there is absolutely no biological, genetic or scientific truth behind it, and most scholars strongly refute the idea. Statistics show that, even in a laboratory, it would take approximately 1,500 years, or fifty generations, to create a strong enough genetic shift to produce a genuinely higher proportion of strong runners. In short, 'the Western system of chattel slavery failed to possess enough time, constant social conditions, or the amount of singularly forced African heredity (there was slave rape and sexual coercion [perpetrated by white people] that introduced different genetic heritages into the "gene pool") for a genetic selection process to occur'.[14]

The idea that Black success in sport needs genetic explanation is in itself deeply racist, implying as it does that Black people should not be in elite sports, and that their success is so shocking it requires some kind of justification. No one has ever thought to investigate why white people are good at tennis or golf, or writing novels or computer science, because no one would ever imagine that they couldn't be. The white population is understood as varied enough that it's expected for people to be good at different things. Investigating a link between Blackness and running suggests that all Black people are the same, and must have the same physical strengths and weakness, with no variation. It ignores an individual's hard work, commitment to training and dedication to being the best. In short, it denies Black athletes agency in creating their own success.[15]

What is not considered here is why certain sports attract certain ethnic groups. This is a social question rather than a biological one.[16] Sports such as tennis, golf or swimming, for example, require access to specialist equipment, coaching and training facilities that are expensive and possibly time-consuming, while other sports have lower barriers to access as they can be enjoyed for free or played for fun on the streets. These sports are more likely to be taken up by less privileged, lower-income communities.[17] This might be part of the reason that athletics has been such a successful sport in parts of the Caribbean. The Jamaican-American historian and sociologist Orlando Patterson looks to history rather than genetics for clues. Assessing Jamaican history from the colonial period onwards, he notes the success of a 1920s public health programme in post-emancipation Jamaica that coincided with government promotion of athletics and sports as a form of community development. The programme focused on a range of things, including hygiene, education and clean water, in order to improve both quality of life and life expectancy, and ensured that local communities and their leaders were strongly involved in the decision-making.[18] Competitive sport and exercise were promoted as part of this through interscholastic games in the same style as in British public schools that were introduced from the late nineteenth century. The programme was a huge success, and life expectancy had risen to seventy years by the 1970s. Jamaica became a pioneer across the Caribbean and was used as a model for social development by the British colonial government. Running, being practically free, was popular. Besides, running and walking in mountainous terrain was already a normal part of Jamaican life in many areas just to get to school.[19]

The increasing popularity of running in Jamaica is likely to have led to a concentration of resources for it, and, in such a small country, it may have become the obvious choice for young people who enjoyed sport, leading to an oversubscribed but rich talent pool from which to draw. Norman Manley, Jamaica's founding father, was himself an avid runner, raising the status of the sport. As head of the government from 1955 to 1962, Manley, as Patterson tells us, 'tirelessly promoted track and field as part of his de-colonising and nationalist agenda', encouraging the building of community centres, athletics facilities, and the national stadium in 1962, despite limited funds. Jamaica's affinity for athletics became a self-sustaining, self-fulfilling prophecy.[20] This is an example of how seeing aspirational role models from your own communities in a sport, with training sympathetic to their needs, inspires more people from that background to take it up.[21]

Sports sociologists explain that even if there is a small biological advantage (indeed small, given that the ubiquity of the ACTN3 mutation needed for sprinting is only 98 per cent in Black and 82 per cent in white athletes), it is only advantageous in conjunction with social factors such as class, access to coaching and facilities, representation and role models, and the undeniable persistence of institutionalised discrimination and biases – and one's own commitment to success.[22]

While white athletes are usually seen as individuals, examples of excellence that stand outside wider social and cultural forces, Black athletes are still entangled in dubious biological narratives that flatten their stories and achievements. Some see Black athletic and physical prowess as a response to an emasculation born of long-term historical oppression and discrimination, the construction of alternative forms of masculinity and strength.[23] Black men are often depicted in mainstream media as hyper-masculine, and as possessing innate and threatening physical strength and power, thus furthering one-dimensional stereotypes and promoting racial difference.[24] Jack Johnson was primarily known for his

physical strength and brutality; Muhammad Ali for his rebel-
liousness and militancy.[25] Serena Williams is consistently cast
as too powerful, too masculine, and not feminine or sexually
appealing enough – she is cast in the familiar stereotype of the
angry Black woman, and has even been likened to a gorilla.
There are countless other examples of Black athletes who face
relentless negative attention, their success belittled and attributed to their genetics.[26] Individual Black athletes often become
symbols or spokespeople for entire communities, 'saviours' of
the downtrodden. But one wrong move and they can just as
quickly become scapegoats or be labelled aggressive.[27]

The impact of this racism can be devastating for the mental
and physical health of athletes, who are not only frequently
harassed and denigrated but also face immense pressure to
perform well on behalf of their communities, facing racist
backlash when a sportsperson of their ethnicity is considered
to have let their team or country down.[28] As we have seen, discrimination creates biases and structural barriers, both real
and perceived, that prevent athletes of colour from accessing
certain sports and from getting the high-quality training and
attention they need to succeed, and can prevent them from
being chosen or permitted to progress into elite categories.[29]

Sport is often seen as a space in which race does not matter:
a level playing field where each athlete has an equal chance,
regardless of origin. Raw talent, strength, hard work and
resolve ought to be the only factors determining victory. As
such, many laud sport as colour-blind and prejudice-free, a
field that promotes racial harmony.[30] It is a space in which economic and social problems play no role, and a demonstration
of the individual's innate strength and ability: the Olympics are
the ultimate, fairest play-off between nations.[31] But you don't
have to look far to see that sport is far from apolitical. The
nations that top the Olympic medal charts are almost always

'developed' Western countries. Sports matches have long provided the arena for larger political contests between coloniser and colonised, or the opportunity to sanction or shun countries whose governments commit apartheids and genocides.[32] While Black dominance in running does not actually have its roots in slavery, the fact that many people believe the two to be connected is itself rooted in those racial tropes that once helped slavery to thrive. Though slavery has ended, many of the beliefs and attitudes it created continue to linger. Until we challenge and shed these beliefs, sport will continue to be mired in racism and inequality, and it will always be political.

AL

37

Trains

There's something innately British about getting the train, and rightly so: the British railways are world-famous and have cultivated a self-consciously warm and fuzzy image. In 2023 and 2024 Great Western Railway ran an advertising campaign that featured a family from the 1940s rushing through town to catch a train. It's distinctly British and a throwback to a time when life seemed simpler (or at least easy for us to romanticise). But where did the trains come from – and is their history really as cosy as the rail companies would have it?

We spoke with Dr Oliver Betts, the research lead at the National Railway Museum in York. He told us that while we tend to think of the railways as a Victorian invention they are actually an eighteenth-century innovation. Much like the slave trade itself, he said, they are 'rooted in an eighteenth-century experience and system of capitalism'.[1]

And, if you follow the money, the links between slavery and the railways are clear. It's estimated that around £5 million was invested in railway projects by 175 individuals who owned slaves.[2] These combined investments accounted for a staggering £800 million in today's money. Multiple railway projects ran the length and breadth of the UK and Ireland, and, while not all projects were made a reality, a large number of those that were completed became the core of the modern rail network. The table below shows the estimated costs of building a railway in the early nineteenth century, and it's easy to see how attractive investments from slave owners would have been to get such projects off the ground.[3] Although slavery was abolished by the time many of these railways were opened, many rail investors continued to profit from the practice for far longer than that, and a substantial portion of their investment money came from the compensation that slave and plantation owners received from the British government.

TABLE 3

Project	Year Opened	Estimated Cost
Liverpool & Manchester Railway	1830	£0.82m
Leeds & Selby Railway	1834	£0.3m
Grand Junction Railway	1837	£1.6m
London & Birmingham Railway	1838	£5.5m
London & Southampton Railway	1840	£1.6m
Great Western Railway	1841	£6.5m

The total cost for these projects (as shown in the table here) was £16.32 million, and the investment from slave owners therefore accounts for over a third of the total cost of the railways. One of the investors was a banker from Liverpool named John Moss, who invested around £60,400: in today's money that's nearly £9 million, a significant investment by any measure.[4] Moss owned a plantation with his brother Henry in Guyana, where, at its peak in 1830, the brothers owned eight hundred enslaved people. Following abolition, each Moss brother received £40,343 in compensation.[5] John Moss became a key figure in the birth of Britain's railways, assuming the roles of Deputy Chair of the Liverpool & Manchester Railway and Chair of the Grand Junction Railway, although his involvement was more critical than that.[6] Many believe that without Moss and his investments, the railways would never have been built.[7]

The Great Western Railway was Britain's most expensive network to build and operate, having been designed by Isambard Kingdom Brunel and employing a broad track gauge that both allowed for faster running trains and ramped up construction costs.[8] The GWR received its Enabling Act of Parliament in 1835 and ran its first train in 1838, officially opening in 1841.[9] Between the late 1830s and the mid-1840s, there was a period known as 'Railway Mania' because of the intense and speculative rush to promote, invest in and construct railways across the country.[10] Railway companies were authorised by Parliament to raise around £35 million to construct nearly 15,000 miles of railway lines.[11] The mania was accompanied by a lack of government regulation – anyone with significant wealth could form a railway company and then seek parliamentary approval for their projects. Following the perceived successes of the early railway investors, the manias that followed gave people who had missed the opportunity to invest originally the chance to throw their hats in the ring and experience the new gold rush. After abolition, those who'd profited from the trade and its associated industries were keen to find alternative investment opportunities.

As Oliver Betts pointed out, 'we're talking about enormous amounts of money', but while re-investment of profits provides is a clear-cut connection it was not the only thing that linked the railways to slavery.[12] The early railways were about freight rather than passenger transport, especially the transport of coal, which powered the Industrial Revolution, but also the moving of goods from major ports like Liverpool, many of which would have come from the empire. Betts continued: 'People who had an interest in the slavery system were often big owners of shipping and heavily invested in maritime trade.

So it's not a weird thing for them to shift into another mode of transport.'[13] And while we tend to think of the railways as a solid and immutable part of the British landscape, when they were first in the offing they were seen by many as risky investments. As Betts told us: 'there were a lot of jitters early on, about whether [the railways] are going to be something that sticks around. So it's going to appeal to people who've already got experience of working with high risk and experience of investing in transport capital. And both of those tend to be the same sort of people who are invested in the slave trade.'[14]

Even when former slave owners weren't coming to railway mania through the shipping connection, the high-risk, high-reward nature of the early railway seemed to have been a perfect proposition for those who'd made a fortune from enslaved people. Investors needed to have an appetite for risk to succeed in rail – and plantation owners had plenty of experience with high-risk investment during the slave trade. Enslaved people were indeed 'human resources'; they could become sick, run away, die or rebel. And plantations themselves were little safer: any farmer knows that the yield of a crop is not always guaranteed, especially when you are running the land under dangerous conditions and with forced labour.

When we're rushing about busy with our day-to-day activities or heading away on a trip it's easy to disregard the histories of the tracks beneath us. But taking a train to Bristol or Liverpool and thinking about how these routes once carried the spoils of slavery across the country can help us to keep this knowledge alive. In the UK, all of us benefit every day from the profits of slavery. Britain's elite built up enormous wealth that we know helped not just to build the railways but also to influence governments, found the police, and create the institutions and news organisations that shape everything we do. It's something that we would prefer to write off as having happened 'ages ago' or even not think about at all. But we need to remember these brutal histories and how fundamental they are to modern Britain so that we have a chance of not making the same mistakes.

RR

38

Surnames

I've always found my last name, Richardson, annoying. It's too long, and three syllables are a bit much. It has always made work email addresses fiddly, especially when I have to spell it out over the phone. I hadn't thought much about the origins of my surname; I knew it was the same as my father's and his father's and so on, but I didn't give much thought to why we were all Richardsons. That was until I saw an interview with Kwame Kwei-Armah, who portrayed paramedic Finlay Newton on the BBC medical drama *Casualty*, and later read a piece in the *Guardian* by him for the bicentenary of abolition in the UK. In the piece, Kwei-Armah discussed why he had changed his name from Ian Roberts:

> It was when I was 19 and reading the autobiography of Malcolm X that I decided I could no longer carry the name of someone who once owned my family.[1]

I'm not quite sure when I realised that my name was a 'slave name'. It was probably during school – there would have been an off-the-cuff comment of some kind by a white student. I can't recall a specific incident, but there were so many racist moments that they all rolled into one. Even though I had a rough idea about my name, it wasn't until the interview with Kwei-Armah that I realised that there was a whole part of my identity missing, something that people from other cultures and ethnicities might never have to even think about, simply because their ancestors had not been ripped from one continent and shipped to another thereby having every ounce of who they were taken from them. A large proportion of Caribbeans like me are unsure of their ancestral origins before slavery. And taking a DNA test will not always help as the results are often unreliable. The databases that most DNA testing companies use are largely based on the genes of people with European ancestry, and the gaps in their records are biggest when it comes to people with sub-Saharan African heritage. In 2018, one of the largest genome and biotechnology companies, 23andMe, could only match people to three large regions in Sub-Saharan Africa.[2]

While many descendants of slaves are proud to be who they are, whether they're African American, Caribbean or Brazilian, it is hard not to feel hopeless when you look at how other cultures have been able to keep hold of their rich traditions. Kwei-Armah said it best, calling the loss of our history 'the true legacy of slavery: the deculturalisation of a people and the perpetual perception of inferiority thereafter.'[3]

The names we carry around have no real meaning in terms of who we are or where we're from. We are walking reminders of an unresolved history. Following slavery's abolition we had to start from scratch to learn our histories and our place in the world, as so many of our customs and traditions became westernised or lost to time. Many of us have never stepped foot on the African continent. But the names we do have can tell us a little more about how enslavers enacted control over enslaved people, and about what our ancestors' day-to-day lives were actually like.

In 'Slave Naming Practices', Professor Trevor Burnard, Director of the Wilberforce Institute for the Study of Slavery and Emancipation at the University of Hull, examines the naming practices of individuals in Jamaica, and discusses how different naming conventions were used to enforce separateness between white people and the enslaved.

White people typically had three or more names: a first name, a surname and at least one middle name. Children were often named after relatives such as grandparents, but white families usually allowed for necronymic naming, which is to say that it wasn't unusual to name children after a deceased sibling. Between 1722 and 1758, twenty-five names accounted for just over 87 per cent of boys baptised in the Kingston parish of Jamaica. The top four first names were John, William, Thomas and James.[4]

In contrast, enslaved people would usually have only one name, and might also be known by an identifier; for example, their name could be followed by their age, their job or race. Only 0.5 per cent of slaves inventoried in 1753 had a first name and a surname, and although some African names did survive, they were stripped of their original meanings, badly transliterated and thus became associated solely with slavery: names such as 'Sambo', 'Quashie' and 'Cuffee'.[5] These names were often derivatives of local slang and patois – Quashie from the Jamaican patois Kwesiada, which meant Sunday; and Cuffee, a variant of Kofi.[6] Some of these names became derogatory insults for modern-day Black people. 'Sambo' became a common slur targeted at Black people, insinuating that they were slaves or less than other people.

Another important factor was that denying enslaved people multiple names meant that they were denied cultural significance. Although white Jamaicans recycled names across generations, they were still able to honour their roots in Europe and link themselves to family history. White people used more standard English names for themselves, from the small number of names to choose from, in contrast to those they gave enslaved people, which were sometimes diminutive forms taken from biblical, classical or African sources. It was just another way to highlight the difference in status between the enslaved and their oppressors, and for white Jamaicans to reassure themselves of their supposed superiority.

For white slave owners, giving the people they enslaved just a single name was a form of degradation. They sometimes used explicitly demeaning names for enslaved people, like 'Monkey' and 'Villain'. Other names such as 'Time' and 'Chance' were less obviously insulting but still served to objectify the person by naming them after an action or a moment – another kind of dehumanisation.[7]

Following abolition, many formerly enslaved people in Jamaica opted to change their names, not only to distance themselves from their enslavement but as a way to reclaim some form of identity. Some freed slaves chose to distance themselves from their African and slave legacy by favouring European names, out of a desire to associate themselves with the prestige that white people still had as landowners with money and connections. This attitude, of wanting to deny one's Blackness as a way to 'fit in' with white society, is something that Kwei-Armah talks about in his *Guardian* piece, recalling a conversation with his teenage son and his friends about which girls were considered attractive at school. At the bottom of the list were the girls who looked most like his son's own family, Black girls. When Kwei-Armah challenged the teenagers about this he was accused of being racist for bringing race into the conversation. Kwei-Armah added that it 'became evident why 50 per cent of African Caribbean men are in relationships outside of their community and cannot connect that to a bigger picture'.[8]

This conversation, unfortunately, is consistent with the fact that Black women receive the fewest matches on dating apps. When these apps were first gaining traction, in 2014, OkCupid released data confirming that Black women were the 'least favourite' online.[9] And things haven't improved much over the last decade. A 2024 Nimble study found that, although dating app usage is fairly equal across different ethnicities, Asian women had higher response rates from white, Latino and Black men compared to women of other races. Black women found Black men most desirable, Black men desired Black women the least.[10]

Under slavery, Black people were subjected to abuse that diminished their worth and their humanity. Given this trauma, it was inevitable that, even after abolition, that way of thinking – that white people were superior, lived better, and had more to offer – would affect the way formerly enslaved people thought about themselves. It's a sad fact that internalised racism has trickled down through generations, making white and European beauty standards the ones to aspire to even in Black communities. In Jamaican manumission records – the documents that record who was freed from slavery and when – a substantial number of freed people retained their slave names, though many adopted to mark their new 'free' status by choosing new, more English names, like Mary and John.[11] There was also a significant rise in the number of people with a surname. The percentage of formerly enslaved people with surnames rose from just over 21 per cent in 1775 to over 31 per cent towards the end of the century.[12] It was apparent that no former enslaved person chose to adopt an African or slave-based last name.

When choosing their names, it's clear that former enslaved people wanted to erase as much of that part of their past as they could and to build a free life away from painful memories.

To many, choosing 'white' names achieved this. But this need to distance themselves from slavery meant assimilating even further into white society, despite what they knew about that society's capacity for brutality and its indifference to suffering.

I had always assumed that my last name was a result of a slave owner forcing it upon my ancestors, and I think that's what many descendants of enslaved people assume. To learn that many formerly enslaved people had the option to choose their own names upon freedom changed everything for me. Knowing that my ancestors may have *chosen* European names, either because they had converted to Christianity or because they wanted to distance themselves from their former lives, helps me to understand the complexity of the trauma involved in the forging of a new identity in an unequal place. They would have associated their rich African heritage with the horror, death and barbarity of slavery, and breaking away from that legacy meant divorcing themselves from their former culture. This is heartbreaking. As late as the early 2000s, African children in British schools were being teased for being African because their identity was still, well over a hundred years later, associated with inferiority. The idea that Caribbean people had willingly distanced themselves from their African brothers and sisters also created tension within the diaspora. Sometimes, those from the Caribbean feel they are being patronised, and that African people consider themselves to be superior to both Caribbeans and African Americans because their ancestors were never enslaved. This prejudice is still passed on today. Thankfully, it's something that is fading with the rise of African-centric culture, which is now entering the mainstream, but such tensions do remain under the surface.

Every day there are online battles about Black men and women favouring white people and culture over Black culture. Interracial couples, where a Black man or woman has a white partner, are called out for turning their backs on Black people. Black activists with white partners are often seen as hypocrites who are somehow unable to be pro-Black. Yet at the same time, Black beauty traits suddenly become desirable when they're adopted by white people, and celebrities like the Kardashian-Jenner family and Ariana Grande have in fact been accused of Black-phishing in the past. These modern frictions are rooted in the different ways that formerly enslaved people tried to distance themselves from their time as slaves. For hundreds of years, Black people were told they were inferior, ugly, barbaric and not worthy of a free life. It's no wonder that Black people, having been subjected to mental degradation for decades, across multiple generations and all across the world, have had their self-image profoundly damaged, and that some of that trauma abides in the very names we go by.

RR

39

Holiday Resorts

Jamaica's Tryall Club is a swish private beach club, complete with villas and a golf course overlooking the Caribbean Sea, decorated in crisp blues and whites that mirror the sea and sand. A large estate, it centres on a seventeenth-century fort from the days of Oliver Cromwell's first Caribbean conquests that sits atop what was once a settlement and burial ground of the indigenous Arawaks, who were subjected to a geno-cide at the hands of incoming Europeans. Later, it served as a sugar-cane plantation, where enslaved Africans and their descendants would have lived, worked, suffered, celebrated and died.[1] In an interview with the online news platform 'Business View Caribbean' in 2017, the Tryall Club's director of sales promotes the resort's stunningly undisturbed hiking trails, from the top of which 'you will see the forest environment that Columbus would have seen when he first set sight on Jamaica'. With its deep and well-preserved history, the club is, he claims, both authentically and inherently Jamaican.[2]

This is just one of countless hotels and resorts across the Anglophone Caribbean that have links to transatlantic slavery through their names, owners or the sites on which they are built. The Great House in Antigua, honeymoon pick of Prin-cess Margaret and writing retreat of former prime minister

Sir Anthony Eden, is a one-time plantation dating back to 1670. Its website boasts of the 'Cotswolds stone' shipped over hundreds of years ago for its building, a stark contrast with its interior Chippendale mahogany furniture (see chapter 17, 'Mahogany').[3] Meanwhile, St Lucia's uber-elite Sugar Beach Resort occupies the land of the old eighteenth-century sugar-producing Jalousie Plantation, in the shadow of the Piton mountains. Now, it is frequented by the likes of Hollywood celebrities Gwyneth Paltrow and Matt Damon.[4] On Nevis, the Montpelier Plantation & Beach, famed for its 'romantic charm' that transports you to 'another era'[5] received visits from Sir Hans Sloane in 1687 (see chapter 13, 'Hans Sloane'), and provided a wedding location for Horatio Nelson, its website proudly boasting the plantation's high status and wealth.[6]

The Caribbean, the Deep South of the US, and other regions with similarly troubled pasts all abound with hotels and wedding venues built upon the sites of old plantations on which unfree labourers were held against their wills. Their advertising materials often flaunt their long histories, yet make no mention of the slave labour that was once the reason for their existence. This chapter explores how and why these sites of trauma and horror became those of fantasy, luxury and unforgettable memories.

Today, there is hardly a country with a stretch of sand and an airport or ferry terminal that does not have a resort or two run by an international hotel chain. But lying on a sun-soaked beach was not always the pinnacle of rest and rejuvenation.[7] Beach resorts began in eighteenth-century England and quickly caught on around the world. English physicians and medical practitioners began promoting the healing properties of sea water and salty air. This was a new belief that formed at a time when the medical field was expanding and evolving, with new ideologies about what caused illness and preserved wellness.

Historian Robert C. Ritchie writes that 'resorts emerged right at the beginning of this movement because they provided needed services such as housing, meals, and entertainment to anyone who sought the comfort of seawater'.[8] Leisure sites shifted from inland Roman spa towns such as Bath to the coast, firstly for the elite and then for the masses, no doubt helped by the steady expansion of the railways. As it became possible for more people to take paid leave from work, resorts grew more commercial, and began to provide lively entertainment programmes for visitors. Today, resorts are a worldwide phenomenon that attracts floods of tourists, but often this comes at the expense not only of the natural environment but of local people and their communities, which must rapidly adapt to deal with tourist demands.[9]

Having spread across Europe, the resort concept eventually made its way to 'exotic' locations at a point when empire would no longer be fuelled by slavery and was looking for alternative ways to capitalise on what the tropics had to offer.[10] Until the late nineteenth century the Caribbean was not seen as 'paradise', or even as a safe tourist destination. Instead, the region was regarded by Europeans as an economically important but dangerous zone, a place of disease, and one that an unaccustomed European body would be lucky to survive.[11] Its Black inhabitants seemed immune to malaria and yellow fever, which we understand now to be the result of previous exposure in their originating countries, something that medicine at the time could not explain. The people, therefore, were seen as part of the threat – mysterious, potentially magical, possibly ill-intentioned and violent.[12] After the abolition of slavery, fearing declining fortunes from the Caribbean's sugar plantations, concerned colonial administrators and local white elites sought alternative ways to make the islands lucrative and attractive. As a certain scepticism about the region persisted, colonists sought to transform the image of the islands into that of a pleasure ground for leisure and health, drawing on developments in science and medicine that were used to promote the sea, and a relaxing lifestyle, as good for the health.[13]

In the 1880s, American and British hoteliers in Jamaica and the Bahamas set out to 'refashion the islands as picturesque tropical paradises'.[14] This was a massive operation, involving tidying up the island's unruly vegetation to make it look orderly, clean and picturesque, images of which were then displayed through new photography and advertising technologies. It was also necessary to transform the conception of the island's peoples themselves, from the stereotype of barely human, violent African slaves into hospitality workers who were caring and unproblematic – cheerful, accommodating staff who would ensure you had everything you needed for a pleasant stay.[15]

These colonial officials made the landscape look, and mean, something completely different.[16] The sprawling sites of former slave plantations made perfect locations for romantic, opulent and secluded tropical retreats. The focus of the islands moved from the inland agricultural plantation to the coastlines, with new emphasis placed on the beauty of the landscape and the climate.[17] As we saw in chapter 12, 'Gardening', the value of the Caribbean to colonisers before abolition lay in the profitable resources that could be extracted from its natural landscape. Under slavery it had been the products from the region that had provided pleasure and enjoyment to Europeans – in Europe.[18] But now, the islands' value came to lie in how they could be marketed as somewhere to visit, luxurious and pleasure-giving, in and of themselves.[19]

As mass tourism developed at pace from the 1950s, the economy of many Caribbean islands became increasingly dependent upon the industry.[20] According to the Caribbean

Tourism Organisation, 32.2 million tourists visited the Caribbean in 2023.[21] On several Caribbean islands, the majority of accommodation options for tourists lie within gated all-inclusive resorts.[22] Between 75 and 80 per cent of tourist expenditure goes to tour operators, airlines and hotels, all owned by global corporations that have their headquarters abroad, meaning that very little profit reaches the islands or the people who live there.[23] Cruise ships can be even worse for the local economy as (in addition to their environmental impact) cruise-organised tours, on-board entertainment and all-inclusive buffets discourage people from spending money at local restaurants and businesses.[24]

In a resort or on a cruise ship the tourist is in seclusion, where they do not have to see any of the realities of life, particularly poverty and underdevelopment. But this can produce the anxiety it is designed to allay, as sleeping and sunbathing behind gates with constant security creates the impression that the threat of violence from the local population is real. This is likely to make tourists even more afraid or tentative about the world outside their resort, and it also contributes to racial stereotyping.[25]

The white family who owned a Caribbean plantation in the era of slavery would lead a life of leisure, doing very little work. And they could do so because there was a gang of labourers, sometimes hundreds of them, forced to do back-breaking, life-threatening work on the fields and industrial workshops for no pay. Spending the bare minimum on accommodation, food, clothing and healthcare for their workers, and with no expenditure on wages, slave owners could keep the majority of profits for themselves. While it is of course incomparable to slave labour, Afro-Caribbean descendants of enslaved workers who are employed in the tourism industry today also work long hours for low wages as they provide a service for (mostly white) guests in search of freedom and recreation. The plantation and the resort are enclosed spaces in which one group's leisure depends on another group's labour, in both cases based on a racial hierarchy of power. And while tourists may pay large sums of money for their pleasure, we know that very little of that money reaches local people.

Many historians have drawn parallels between plantations and holiday resorts.[26] For example, Caribbean economies continue to be dependent on foreign investments and transnational companies that manage and control tourist sites and hotels from abroad and take the profits with them. This is a region that repeatedly finds itself with an economy centred on an extractive industry that exploits its natural resources. The Caribbean tourist industry, and its economies as a whole, end up beholden to the whims of a seasonal industry that is constantly influenced by new trends.[27] While it is self-evident that the Caribbean today has an agency and freedom absent during the era of plantation slavery, the resorts remain a troubling reminder of the economic hold that Western countries still retain. Ritchie refers to this as a 'new form of colonialism', suggesting that there was never really a tangible break from the colonial relationship, only a restructuring. The region's economic survival largely depends upon it being able to fulfil a fantasy of luxury and leisure.[28]

It's not just a financial legacy but one that touches every aspect of society. Most of the jobs available to the Black population are in poorly paid manual labour, with few Afro-Caribbeans progressing to senior or managerial roles. In a facsimile of the era of slavery, those in positions of authority are usually white foreigners, while the Black population must do the hardest work for the lowest reward, and in an attitude of subservience. Studies into the experiences of Black staff at Jamaican hotels from the 1960s onwards reveal colourism and racial hierarchies in hiring practices and hotel cultures, with the most senior jobs largely reserved for white or mixed-race people, or the lightest skinned Afro-Caribbeans, as well as vast pay disparities and little room for upward mobility.[29] Unofficial boundaries, such as fences around gated developments, membership fees and high prices, as well as the threat of racism, keep tourists and locals apart. Such boundaries are often only crossed by staff, entertainers, tour guides, sellers and escorts.[30]

As more land is taken up by resorts there is less available land and coastline for the agriculture and fishing that form many people's livelihoods, or for public beaches providing community-building, recreation, leisure and exercise spaces.[31] In Barbados and Cuba for instance, locals are actually prohibited from entering luxury resorts and exclusive golf courses unless they are staff, or membership fees are so high above local incomes that it is effectively a ban.[32] All but nineteen of Jamaica's 488 miles of coastline had been privatised by 1992, meaning that even Jamaicans living close to the sea have no access to it.[33] This exclusion from land and beaches, as well as pollution – another side effect of mass tourism, the plastic waste from which washes ashore and chokes marine life – have been huge points of contention, sparking protests and conflict.[34]

The rebranding of the Caribbean as a tropical paradise must by necessity exclude its more complex and traumatic history, which would be unpleasant and uncomfortable for guests who just want to have a good time. Much of the marketing material contains photographs of white sand, sunbeds and palm trees, images that could be from any number of places. There is nothing specific in terms of people, culture or history that identifies where you are. The Caribbean, represented through this dreamlike advertising, is shown as one vast stretch of empty beach. It creates the idea that the islands are uninhabited and untouched.[35]

The islands are shown as wild and just tropical enough to provide an exotic experience and a true escape to a different world – but not *so* different that they're frightening or unsettling. The Caribbean has been represented like this ever since the first European artists and writers went there and sent home their impressions to those who would never be able to visit such faraway lands. For hundreds of years, then, the islands have been considered places that provide both financial and mental happiness.[36] And the African-descended people who live there, from the enslaved people to hotel staff, have been the ones to facilitate that leisure so that foreigners can relax and enjoy the benefits.[37]

Today, a wealth of vibrant Caribbean literature and poetry responds to tourism's colonial echoes, entreating us to enjoy our holidays in a more ethical, reciprocal and thoughtful manner.[38] Visiting a Caribbean beach resort might make for a lifelong memory of sun, sea and pleasure, but we should not forget these darker histories, and the ways in which our presence impacts both the lives of those who live there and the environment.[39]

Made from natural resources like wattle, daub and thatch, plantation slave quarters have mostly disintegrated and decomposed back into the land they came from, leaving no obvious trace of the crimes against humanity committed within them.[40] In contrast, the planters' Great Houses stand secure and tall, now comprising or incorporated into luxury holiday locations, some trendy, some professing old-world charm and authenticity. All have been glossily painted, obscuring their disturbing origins. Yet they continue to haunt us.

AL

Notes

Introduction

1 Equal Justice Initiative, 'The Transatlantic Slave Trade', 2022.

2 Ibid.

3 Ibid.

4 Freedom Quilts, based on a compilation of works by Professor Lynda Colgan of Queen's University, Ontario, 30 January 2008, https://www.dpcdsb.org/Documents/Freedom%20Quilts.pd

5 Louis Evan Grivetti and Howard-Yana Shapiro (eds), *Chocolate, History, Culture and Heritage*, John Wiley & Sons, 2009.

6 Ibid.

7 Padraic X. Scanlon, *Slave Empire: How Slavery Built Modern Britain*, Robinson, 2020.

8 'Slavery and the British Industrial Revolution', Stephan Heblich, Stephen J. Redding and Hans-Joachim Voth, National Bureau of Economic Research, Working Paper, Working Paper Series 30451, 2022, doi:10.3386/w30451, http://www.nber.org/papers/w30451

9 Stephan Heblich, Stephen J. Redding and Hans-Joachim Voth, 'Slavery and the British Industrial Revolution', National Bureau of Economic Research Working Paper 30451, 17 August 2023.

10 Louis Evan Grivetti and Howard-Yana Shapiro (eds), *Chocolate, History, Culture and Heritage*.

11 Scanlon, *Slave Empire: How Slavery Built Modern Britain*.

12 Equal Justice Initiative, 'The Transatlantic Slave Trade Report'.

13 *The Interesting Narrative of the Life of Olaudah Equiano or Gustava Vassa, The African by Himself*, 1789, third edition, pp. 47–48, https://equianosworld.org/assets/files/3rd%20Edition%20-%20The%20Interesting%20Narrative.pdf

14 Sidney W. Mintz, *Sweetness and Power: The Place of Sugar in Modern History*, Penguin Books, 1986.

15 Equal Justice Initiative, 'The Transatlantic Slave Trade Report'.

16 Niamh McIntyre, Nazia Parveen and Tobi Thomas, 'Exclusion rates
   five times higher for black Caribbean pupils in parts of England',
   Guardian, 24 March 2021, https://www.theguardian.com/
   education/2021/mar/24/exclusion-rates-black-caribbean-pupils-england
17 Feyisa Demie and Christabel McLean, 'Black Caribbean
   Underachievement in Schools in England', Schools', Research and
   Statistics Unit, Lambeth Education and Learning, 2017.
18 Children's Commissioner, 'Strip searching of children in England and
   Wales: First complete dataset for 2018–2023, including new data July
   2022–June 2023', 19 August 2024, https://www.childrenscommissioner.
   gov.uk/resource/
   strip-searching-of-children-in-england-and-wales-first-complete-
   dataset-for-2018-2023-including-new-data-july-2022-june-2023/
19 Scanlon, *Slave Empire: How Slavery Built Modern Britain*.
20 Ibid.
21 Ibid.
22 *Human Resources* (podcast), season 1, episode 2, 'The Tree of Life', 19
   May 2021, Broccoli Productions.

1. Accounting
1 *Human Resources* (podcast), season 1, episode 9, 'Dirty Money', 7 July
   2021, Broccoli Productions.
2 Caitlin Rosenthal, recorded interview, 24 March 2024.
3 Ibid.
4 Caitlin Rosenthal, *Accounting for Slavery: Masters and Management*,
   Harvard University Press, 2018.
5 Church Commissioners for England, 'Church Commissioners' Research
   into Historic Links to Transatlantic Chattel Slavery', 2023, https://
   www.churchofengland.org/sites/default/files/2023-01/church-
   commissioners-for-england-research-into-historic-links-to-
   transatlantic-chattel-slavery-report.pdf
6 Jan Richard Heier, 'A Content Comparison of Antebellum Plantation
   Records and Thomas Affleck's Accounting Principles', *Accounting
   Historians Journal*, vol. 15, no. 2, 1988.
7 Rosenthal, interview.
8 Ibid.
9 Ibid.
10 Josselyn Andrea Garcia Quijano, 'Workplace Discrimination and
   Undocumented First-Generation Latinx Immigrants', 2020, https://
   knowledge.uchicago.edu/record/7306?v=pdf
11 Ibid.

Notes

12 Ibid.

2. Gunpowder

1 Nicholas Radburn, recorded interview, 8 March 2024.
2 Ibid.
3 Ibid.
4 Ibid.
5 Nicholas Radburn, 'The British Gunpowder Industry and the Transatlantic Slave Trade', *Business History Review*, vol. 97, no. 2, 2023, pp. 363–84.
6 Radburn, interview.
7 Ibid.
8 Radburn, 'The British Gunpowder Industry'.
9 Radburn, interview.
10 Ibid.
11 Priya Satia, *Empire of Guns: The Violent Making of the Industrial Revolution*, Prelude Books, 2018; Priya Satia, 'What Guns Meant in Eighteenth-Century Britain', *Palgrave Communications*, vol. 5, no. 1 2019, pp. 1–6.
12 Radburn, 'The British Gunpowder Industry'.
13 Ibid.; Warren C. Whatley, 'The Gun-Slave Hypothesis and the 18th Century British Slave Trade', *Explorations in Economic History*, vol. 67 (2018), pp. 80–104.
14 Whatley, 'The Gun-Slave Hypothesis'.
15 Radburn, interview.
16 Radburn, interview; Nathan Nunn, 'The Long-term Effects of Africa's Slave Trades', *The Quarterly Journal of Economics*, vol. 123, no. 1, 2008, pp. 139–76; 'History of Slavery: West Africa', National Museums Liverpool. https://www.liverpoolmuseums.org.uk/history-of-slavery/west-africa
17 Ibid.
18 Ibid.
19 Ibid.
20 Nonso Obikili, 'The Impact of the Slave Trade on Literacy in West Africa: Evidence from the Colonial Era', *Journal of African Economies*, vol. 25, no. 1, 2016, pp. 1–27; James Fenske and Namrata Kala, 'Climate and the Slave Trade', *Journal of Development Economics,* vol. 112 (2015), pp. 19–32; Nathan Nunn and Diego Puga. 'Ruggedness: The Blessing of Bad Geography in Africa', *Review of Economics and Statistics*, vol. 94, no. 1, 2012, pp. 20–36.
21 Toby Green, *A Fistful of Shells: West Africa from the Rise of the Slave*

Trade to the Age of Revolution, Penguin, 2019; Whatley, 'The Gun-Slave Hypothesis'.

22 Radburn, 'The British Gunpowder Industry.'
23 Radburn, interview.
24 Radburn, interview.
25 Priya Satia, 'Guns and the British Empire', Aeon, 2021, https://aeon.co/essays/is-the-gun-the-basis-of-modern-anglo-civilisation.
26 Radburn, interview.
27 Ibid.

3. The British Monarchy

1 Amelia Gentleman, Maya Wolfe-Robinson and Kate Chappell, 'Prince William speaks of "profound sorrow" for slavery in address to Jamaica PM', *Guardian*, 24 March 2022, https://www.theguardian.com/uk-news/2022/mar/23/jamaicas-pm-tells-kate-and-william-his-country-is-moving-on
2 Charles Lintner Killinger, 'The Royal African Company Slave Trade to Virginia 1689–1713' (1969), W&M ScholarWorks, Dissertations, Theses, and Masters Projects, Paper 1539624680, https://dx.doi.org/doi:10.21220/s2-92be-5k39
3 'Slavery and the Bank', exhibition, Bank of England, 2022.
4 Alicia Marie Bertrand, 'The Downfall of the Royal African Company of the Atlantic African Coast in the 1720s', Trent University, Peterborough, Ontario, 2011.
5 'Does the royal family pay inheritance tax?', inheritance-tax.co.uk, 10 January 2024, https://inheritance-tax.co.uk/royal-family-pay-inheritance-tax/
6 Church Commissioners for England, 'Church Commissioners' Research into Historic Links to Transatlantic Chattel Slavery', 2023.

4. The Church of England

1 The Archbishop of Canterbury, Anglican Communion, https://www.archbishopofcanterbury.org/about/anglican-communion
2 The Church of England, The Church Commissioners of England, https://www.churchofengland.org/about/leadership-and-governance/church-commissioners
3 Church Commissioners for England, 'Church Commissioners' Research into Historic Links to Transatlantic Chattel Slavery', 2023.
4 Historic Royal Palaces, 'Queen Anne', hrp.org.uk, https://www.hrp.org.uk/kensington-palace/history-and-stories/queen-anne

5 Church Commissioners for England, 'Church Commissioners' Research into Historic Links to Transatlantic Chattel Slavery', 2023.

6 Louis Evan Grivetti and Howard-Yana Shapiro, *Chocolate: History, Culture and Heritage*, John Wiley & Sons, 2009.

7 Church Commissioners for England, 'Church Commissioners' Research into Historic Links to Transatlantic Chattel Slavery', 2023.

8 Ibid.

9 Ibid.

10 Dr Helen Paul, recorded interview, 5 March 2024.

11 Church Commissioners for England, 'Church Commissioners' Research into Historic Links to Transatlantic Chattel Slavery', 2023.

12 Church Commissioners for England, 'Church Commissioners' Links to African Chattel Enslavement', https://www.churchofengland.org/historic-links-to-enslavement

13 Ibid.

5. The Colour Indigo

1 Helena Neimann Erikstrup, recorded interview, 15 March 2024.

2 Ibid.

3 Ibid.

4 'Slavery and the History of the Collections We Care For', Slavery and the Natural World, Natural History Museum, 2018, https://www.nhm.ac.uk/discover/slavery-and-the-natural-world.html

5 David L. Coon, 'Eliza Lucas Pinckney and the Reintroduction of Indigo Culture in South Carolina', *The Journal of Southern History*, vol. 42, no. 1, 1976, pp. 61–76.

6 Ibid.

7 Denise Lee, 'Jamaica's Sad Connection to the Blue Jeans Industry', Jamaicans.com, 2020, https://jamaicans.com/jamaicas-sad-connection-to-the-blue-jeans-industry/

8 Frederick Knight, 'In an Ocean of Blue: West African Indigo Workers in the Atlantic World to 1800', in *Diasporic Africa: A Reader*, Michael A. Gomez (ed.), New York University Press, 2006, pp. 28–44.

9 Willem van Schendel, 'The Social Locations of Colonial Knowledge: Indigo in Bengal, Java and Senegal', in *Across Colonial Lines*, Devyani Gupta and Purba Hossain (eds), Bloomsbury Publishing, 2023.

10 Knight, 'In an Ocean of Blue'.

11 Tiffany Lethabo King, *The Black Shoals: Offshore Formations of Black and Native Studies*, Duke University Press, 2019.

12 Knight, 'In an Ocean of Blue'.

13 Lee, 'Jamaica's Sad Connection to the Blue Jeans Industry'.

14 Knight, 'In an Ocean of Blue'.
15 van Schendel, 'The Social Locations of Colonial Knowledge'. Read the chapter on denim to learn how indigo still underpins one of your most worn garments today: a pair of jeans.
16 Ibid.
17 Ibid.
18 Jordanna Bailkin, 'Indian Yellow: Making and Breaking the Imperial Palette', *Journal of Material Culture*, vol. 10, no. 2, 2005, pp. 197–214.
19 Slavery and the Natural World, Natural History Museum; Adrian Masters, 'Europe, Slavery and the Colour Black', Talking Humanities, 2021, https://talkinghumanities.blogs.sas.ac.uk/2021/05/11/europe-slavery-and-the-colour-black/
20 'The Science of Color', Smithsonian Libraries, https://library.si.edu/exhibition/color-in-a-new-light/science
21 James Delbourgo, 'The Newtonian Slave Body: Racial Enlightenment in the Atlantic World', *Atlantic Studies*, vol. 9, no. 2, 2012, pp. 185–207.
22 Mechthild Fend, 'Introduction', in *Fleshing Out Surfaces: Skin in French Art and Medicine, 1650–1850*, Manchester University Press, 2016.
23 Fend, *Fleshing out Surfaces*.
24 Keith Piper in Jack Ashby, *Black Atlantic: Power, People, Resistance*, Jake Subryan Richards and Victoria Avery (eds), Bloomsbury (exhibition catalogue), 2023.
25 Bailkin, 'Indian Yellow'.
26 Ashby, *Black Atlantic: Power, People, Resistance*; Bailkin, 'Indian Yellow'.
27 Piper in Ashby, *Black Atlantic: Power, People, Resistance*.
28 Fend, *Fleshing out Surfaces*.
29 Neimann Erikstrup, interview.

6. Denim/Blue Jeans

1 Jenny Balfour-Paul, 'Indigo: From Bengal to Blue Jeans', *MARG: A Magazine Of The Arts*, vol. 73, no. 4, 2022, pp. 94–101.
2 Balfour-Paul, 'Indigo: From Bengal to Blue Jeans'; David L. Coon, 'Eliza Lucas Pinckney and the Reintroduction of Indigo Culture in South Carolina', *The Journal of Southern History*, vol. 42, no. 1, 1976, pp. 61–76; Sonia Dahl, 'America's Indigo Obsession: From Colonial Plantations to Contemporary DIY Ethos', Crosscurrents: Land, Labor, and the Port. Textile Society of America's 15th Biennial Symposium (19–23 October 2016), p. 63, https://digitalcommons.unl.edu/tsaconf/960/

Notes

3   Anna Arabindan-Kesson, *Black Bodies, White Gold: Art, Cotton, and Commerce in the Atlantic World*, Duke University Press, 2021.
4   James B. Salazar, 'Fashioning the Historical Body: The Political Economy of Denim', *Social Semiotics*, vol. 20, no. 3, 2010; Frederick Knight, 'In an Ocean of Blue: West African Indigo Workers in the Atlantic World to 1800', in *Diasporic Africa: A Reader*, Michael A. Gomez (ed.), New York University Press, 2006, pp. 28–44.
5   Amy Leverton, 'Denim and Slavery: Are You Uncomfortable yet?' Denim Dudes, https://denimdudes.co/denim-and-slavery-are-you-uncomfortable-yet/
6   Maxine Bédat, *Unraveled: The Life and Death of a Garment*, Portfolio, 2021.
7   Kazuo Kobayashi, 'The British Atlantic Slave Trade and Indian Cotton Textiles: The Case of Thomas Lumley & Co.', in *Modern Global Trade and the Asian Regional Economy*, Tomoko Shiroyama (ed.), Springer, 2018, pp. 59–85; Ronald Bailey, 'The Other Side of Slavery: Black Labor, Cotton, and Textile Industrialization in Great Britain and the United States', *Agricultural History*, vol. 68, no. 2, 1994, pp. 35–50.
8   Kobayashi, 'The British Atlantic Slave Trade and Indian Cotton Textiles'.
9   Joseph E. Inikori, 'Slavery and the Revolution in Cotton Textile Production in England', *Social Science History*, vol. 13, no. 4, 1989, pp. 343–79; Emma Slocombe, 'Industrialisation and the Import of Cotton', in Sally-Anne Huxtable, Corinne Fowler, Christo Kefalas and Emma Slocombe (eds), 'Interim Report on the Connections between Colonialism and Properties now in the care of the National Trust, including Links with Historic Slavery', National Trust, 2020.
10 Inikori, 'Slavery and the Revolution'; Slocombe, 'Industrialisation and the Import of Cotton'.
11 Giorgio Riello, *Cotton: The Fabric that Made the Modern World*, Cambridge University Press, 2013.
12 Slocombe, 'Industrialisation and the Import of Cotton'.
13 Bailey, 'The Other Side of Slavery'.
14 Ibid.
15 Inikori, 'Slavery and the Revolution;' Riello, *Cotton: The Fabric that Made the Modern World*.
16 Slocombe, 'Industrialisation and the Import of Cotton'.
17 Bailey, 'The Other Side of Slavery'; Slocombe, 'Industrialisation and the Import of Cotton'.
18 Bédat, *Unraveled: The Life and Death of a Garment*.
19 Slocombe, 'Industrialisation and the Import of Cotton'.

20 Ibid.

21 Bailey, 'The Other Side of Slavery'.

22 Dominic Green, 'The turbulent reign of King Cotton: The dark history of one of the world's most important commodities', *Spectator*, 15 January 2015, https://www.spectator.co.uk/article/the-turbulent-reign-of-king-cotton-the-dark-history-of-one-of-the-world-s-most-important-commodities

23 S. G. Annapoorani, 'Introduction to Denim', in *Sustainability in Denim*, Subramanian Senthilkannan Muthu (ed.), Woodhead Publishing, 2017, pp. 1–26.

24 Ibid.

25 Balfour-Paul, 'Indigo: From Bengal to Blue Jeans'.

26 Ibid.

27 Prakash Kumar, *Indigo Plantations and Science in Colonial India*, Cambridge University Press, 2012.

28 Daniel Miller, 'Denim', *Consumption Markets & Culture*, vol. 18, no. 4, 2015, pp. 298–300.

29 Balfour-Paul, 'Indigo: From Bengal to Blue Jeans'.

7. Wool and Linen

1 Learning Links International, 'From Sheep to Sugar', 2019, http://www.welshplains.cymru/

2 Haptic & Hue, podcast episode no. 39, 'A Sliver of Deep Blue Cloth', 2024, https://hapticandhue.com/episode-39-sliver-of-deep-blue-cloth/

3 Chris Evans, *Slave Wales: The Welsh and Atlantic Slavery, 1660–1850*, University of Wales Press, 2010.

4 Marian Gwyn, 'Merioneth Wool and the Atlantic Slave Trade', *Journal of the Merioneth Historical and Record Society*, vol. 18, no. 3, 2020, pp. 284–98.

5 Haptic & Hue, 'A Sliver of Deep Blue Cloth'.

6 Liz Millman in *Woven Histories of Welsh Wool and Slavery*, Charlotte Hammond and Laura Moseley (eds), trans. Elin Meek, Common Threads Press, E-book, 2023, https://pure.southwales.ac.uk/ws/portalfiles/portal/17338700/Woven_Histories_of_Welsh_Wool_and_Slavery_CTP.pdf

7 Ibid.

8 Evans, *Slave Wales*.

9 Sally Tuckett and Christopher A. Whatley. 'Textiles in Transition. Linen, Jute, and the Dundee Region's Transnational Networks, c. 1740–c. 1880', in *Scotland's Transnational Heritage: Legacies of Empire*

and Slavery, Emma Bond and Michael Morris (eds), Edinburgh University Press, 2023, pp. 38–54.

10 Ibid.

11 Haptic & Hue, 'A Sliver of Deep Blue Cloth'.

12 Tuckett and Whatley, 'Textiles in Transition'.

13 Ibid.

14 'Dundee's shame: Historian reveals city linen was used to clothe American and Caribbean slaves', *Courier*, 12 June 2020, https://www.thecourier.co.uk/fp/news/dundee/1370288/dundees-shame-historian-reveals-city-linen-was-used-to-clothe-american-and-caribbean-slaves/.

15 Tuckett and Whatley, 'Textiles in Transition'.

16 *Courier*, 'Dundee's shame'.

17 Severin Carrell, 'V&A Dundee exposes Scottish design icons' Slavery Links', *Guardian*, 27 August 2020, https://amp.theguardian.com/artanddesign/2020/aug/27/va-dundee-exposes-scottish-design-icons-slavery-links?CMP=Share_iOSApp_Other&__twitter_impression=true

18 Tuckett and Whatley, 'Textiles in Transition'; Teleica Kirkland, 'Tartan: Its Journey through the African Diaspora', in *Scotland's Transnational Heritage: Legacies of Empire and Slavery*, Emma Bond and Michael Morris (eds), Edinburgh University Press, 2023, pp. 23–37.

19 Iain Whyte, *Scotland and the Abolition of Black Slavery, 1756–1838*, Edinburgh University Press, 2006.

20 Sati Fwatshak, 'Notes on the Role of Cloths in the Atlantic Slave Trade', University of Jos, Nigeria, https://www.welshplains.cymru/index.asp?pageid=713823

21 Evans, *Slave Wales*.

22 Fwatshak, 'Notes on the Role of Cloths in the Atlantic Slave Trade'; Hammond and Moseley, *Woven Histories of Welsh Wool*; Gwyn, 'Merioneth Wool and the Atlantic Slave Trade'.

23 Fwatshak, 'Notes on the Role of Cloths in the Atlantic Slave Trade'.

24 Hammond and Moseley, *Woven Histories of Welsh Wool*.

25 Ibid.

26 Ibid.

27 Haptic & Hue, 'A Sliver of Deep Blue Cloth'.

28 Danielle C. Skeehan, 'Caribbean Women, Creole Fashioning and the Fabric of Black Atlantic Writing', *The Eighteenth Century*, vol. 56, no. 1, 2015; Kirkland, 'Tartan: Its Journey through the African Diaspora'; Steeve Buckridge, *The Language of Dress: Resistance and*

Accommodation in Jamaica, 1750–1890, University of West Indies Press, 2004.
29 Skeehan, 'Caribbean Women, Creole Fashioning'.
30 Gwyn, 'Merioneth Wool and the Atlantic Slave Trade'; Fwatshak, 'Notes on the Role of Cloths in the Atlantic Slave Trade'. See chapter 19, 'Salt Fish' for more on markets.
31 Buckridge, *The Language of Dress*.
32 Kirkland, 'Tartan: Its Journey through the African Diaspora'.
33 Skeehan, 'Caribbean Women, Creole Fashioning'; Buckridge, *The Language of Dress*.
34 Ibid.
35 Haptic & Hue, 'A Sliver of Deep Blue Cloth'.
36 Evans, *Slave Wales*.
37 Gwyn, 'Merioneth Wool and the Atlantic Slave Trade'.

8. Sugar
1 Tom Sasse and Sophie Metcalfe, 'Sugar Tax' explainer, 14 November 2022, The Institute for Government, https://www.instituteforgovernment.org.uk/explainer/sugar-tax
2 Laura Gozzi, 'Jamie Oliver: Sugar tax could fund school meals', 27 December 2022, BBC News, https://www.bbc.co.uk/news/education-64101304
3 Ulbe Bosma, *The World of Sugar: How the Sweet Stuff Transformed our Politics, Health and Environment over 2,000 Years*, Belknap Press, 2023.
4 Mimi Goodall, 'Sugar in the British Atlantic World 1650–1720', PhD, University of Oxford, 2022, https://ora.ox.ac.uk/objects/uuid:3f9fa73b-7fdf-4e68-b92a-02938b328dc3
5 Ibid.
6 Ibid.
7 Eric Williams, 'Laissez Faire, Sugar and Slavery' (1943), Faculty Reprints, Paper 218, http://dh.howard.edu/reprints/218
8 Ibid.
9 Ibid.

9. Lloyds of London
1 'The Transatlantic Slave Trade', Lloyds.com, 2023, https://www.lloyds.com/about-lloyds/history/the-trans-atlantic-slave-trade
2 Ibid.
3 Ibid.

Notes

4 'Links to Slavery of the 1771 Founders of New Lloyd's Coffee House', Lloyds.com, https://www.lloyds.com/1771founders

5 Ibid.

6 Ibid.

7 Robin Pearson and David Richardson, 'Insuring the Transatlantic Slave Trade', *The Journal of Economic History*, vol. 79, no. 2, 2019, pp. 417–46, doi:10.1017/S0022050719000068

8 Lloyd's List 1749–1750, digitised by Google, original from University of Michigan, https://babel.hathitrust.org/cgi/pt?id=mdp.39015028378936&seq=344

9 Centre for the Study of the Legacies of British Slavery, UCL database, https://www.ucl.ac.uk/lbs/person/view/2146642495

10 'Links to Slavery of the 1771 Founders of New Lloyd's Coffee House'.

11 Ibid.

12 Centre for the Study of the Legacies of British Slavery, UCL database.

13 'Links to Slavery of the 1771 Founders of New Lloyd's Coffee House'.

14 'Gist Settlement: It took nearly 200 years', 27 February 2018, *News Journal*, Wilmington, https://www.wnewsj.com/2018/02/27/gist-settlement-it-took-nearly-200-years/

15 'Inclusive Futures', Lloyds.com, https://www.lloyds.com/about-lloyds/culture/lloyds-market/diversity-and-inclusion/inclusive-futures/

16 Jessica Elgot, 'Diane Abbott more abused than any other female MP during election', *Guardian*, 5 September 2017, https://www.theguardian.com/politics/2017/sep/05/diane-abbott-more-abused-than-any-other-mps-during-election

10. Bank of England

1 Jasper Jolly, 'Bank of England owned 599 Slaves in 1770s, new exhibition reveals', *Guardian*, 15 April 2022, https://www.theguardian.com/world/2022/apr/15/bank-of-england-owned-599-slaves-in-1770s-new-exhibition-reveals

2 Dr Michael Bennett, Research Associate, University of Manchester, 'A Story of Archival Discovery: The Bank of England and the Grenada Plantations', Bank of England Museum, 30 September 2022, https://www.bankofengland.co.uk/museum/online-collections/blog/a-story-of-archival-discovery

3 Centre for the Study of the Legacies of British Slavery, UCL database, https://www.ucl.ac.uk/lbs/person/view/2146649829

4 Ibid.

5 Caitlin Rosenthal, *Accounting for Slavery: Masters and Management*, Harvard University Press, 2018.

6   Helen Paul, 'The South Sea Bubble and the Erasure of Slavery and Impressment', *English Studies*, vol. 102, no. 7, 2021.
7   'Slavery and the Bank', exhibition, Bank of England, 2022.
8   Ibid.
9   Ibid.
10 Ibid.
11 Ibid.
12 Ibid.
13 Ibid.
14 Ibid.
15 Ibid.
16 Ibid.
17 Alicia Marie Bertrand, 'The Downfall of the Royal African Company on the Atlantic African Coast 1720s', 2011, Trent University, Peterborough, Ontario.
18 Ibid.
19 Craig Simpson 'Grenada demands Bank of England pay slavery reparations', 31 May 2024, *Telegraph*, https://www.telegraph.co.uk/news/2024/05/31/grenada-demands-bank-of-england-pay-slavery-reparations/
20 Sinai Fleary 'Grenada demands Bank of England pay reparations for its ownership of slave plantations' 7 June 2024, *Voice*, https://www.voice-online.co.uk/news/world-news/2024/06/07/grenada-demands-bank-of-england-pay-reparations-for-its-ownership-of-slave-plantations

11. Chocolate

1   *Human Resources* (podcast), season 1, episode 4, 'A Sour Taste', 2 June 2021, Broccoli Productions.
2   Ibid.
3   Louis Evan Grivetti and Howard-Yanna Shapiro (eds), *Chocolate: History, Culture and Heritage*, John Wiley & Sons, 2009.
4   Ibid.
5   Ibid.
6   Ibid.
7   'Chocolate Market Size, Share & Trends Analysis Report by Product (Traditional, Artificial), by Distribution Channel (Supermarket & Hypermarket, Convenience Store, Online), by Region, and Segment Forecasts, 2024–2030', Grand View Research, https://www.grandviewresearch.com/industry-analysis/chocolate-market
8   'Child Labor and Slavery in the Chocolate Industry', Food

Notes

Empowerment Project, January 2022, https://foodispower.org/human-labor-slavery/slavery-chocolate/

9 'Not So Sweet: The Dark History of Chocolate and Slavery', Cocoa Runners, https://cocoarunners.com/chocopedia/the-dark-history-of-chocolate-slavery

12. Gardening

1 Roderick Floud, 'The Hidden Face of British Gardening', lecture given at Gresham College, 2011, https://www.gresham.ac.uk/watch-now/hidden-face-british-gardening

2 Carlos Offenbach, 'The Orchids of John Henry Lance (1793–1878)', https://www.redalyc.org/journal/443/44369099008/html/

3 'Bitter fruits: On the anniversary of the abolition of the slave trade, Emma Townshend considers how this dark chapter of our history influenced the world's plant life', 25 March 2007, https://www.independent.co.uk/property/gardening/bitter-fruits-on-the-anniversary-of-the-abolition-of-the-slave-trade-emma-townshend-considers-how-this-dark-chapter-of-our-history-influenced-the-world-s-plant-life-5337253.html

4 Kent Mensah, 'Mimosa, the sensitive plant that spied on slave hunters for Africans', Face2Face Africa, 7 October 2019, https://face2faceafrica.com/article/mimosa-the-sensitive-plant-that-spied-on-slave-hunters-for-africans

5 Mary Kuhn, *The Garden Politic: Global Plants and Botanical Nationalism in Nineteenth-Century America*, New York University Press, 2023.

6 National Trust, 'A Potted History of Houseplants', https://www.nationaltrust.org.uk/discover/history/gardens-landscapes/a-potted-history-of-houseplants.

7 Kuhn, *The Garden Politic*.

8 Floud, 'The Hidden Face of British Gardening'.

9 Victoria Perry, *A Bittersweet Heritage: Slavery, Architecture and the British Landscape*, Hurst Publishers, 2022.

10 National Trust, 'A Potted History of Houseplants'.

11 Kuhn, *The Garden Politic*.

12 National Trust, 'A Potted History of Houseplants'.

13 Kuhn, *The Garden Politic*.

14 Jim Endersby, 'The Role of Kew and Colonial Botanic Gardens', lecture given at Gresham College, 2019, https://www.gresham.ac.uk/watch-now/gardens-empire

15 Kuhn, *The Garden Politic*.

16 Duncan Taylor, 'Botanical Gardens and their Role in the Political Economy of Empire: Jamaica (1846–86)', *Rural History*, vol. 28, no. 1, 2017, pp. 47–68; J'Nese Williams, 'Plantation Botany: Slavery and the Infrastructure of Government Science in the St. Vincent Botanic Garden, 1765–1820s', *Berichte zur Wissenschaftsgeschichte*, vol. 44, no. 2, 2021, pp.137–58.

17 Londa L. Schiebinger, *Plants and Empire: Colonial Bioprospecting In the Atlantic World*, Harvard University Press, E-book, 2004.

18 Williams, 'Plantation Botany'.

19 Ibid.

20 Christina Welch, 'Unearthing Indigenous Caribbean Contributions to Western Botanical Knowledge', University of Winchester, https://www.winchester.ac.uk/research/Our-impactful-research/Research-in-Humanities-and-Social-Sciences/Research-projects/Unearthing-Indigenous-Caribbean-contributions-to-western-botanical-knowledge-/

21 Ibid.

22 Williams, 'Plantation Botany'.

23 Ibid. See also chapter 19, 'Salt Fish'.

24 Ibid.

25 Kuhn, *The Garden Politic*; Schiebinger, *Plants and Empire*.

26 Kuhn, *The Garden Politic*.

27 Williams, 'Plantation Botany'.

28 Ibid.

29 Schiebinger, *Plants and Empire*.

30 Schiebinger, *Plants and Empire*; Pratik Chakrabarti, 'Medical Botany in Jamaican Plantations', in *Materials and Medicine: Trade, Conquest and Therapeutics in the Eighteenth Century*', Manchester University Press, 2017, pp. 143–70. See also chapter 13, 'Hans Sloane'.

31 Kathleen S. Murphy, 'Collecting Slave Traders: James Petiver, Natural History, and the British Slave Trade', *William and Mary Quarterly*, vol. 70, no. 4, 2013, pp. 637–70. Hear Kate Murphy speak in our *Human Resources* podcast, season 1, episode 2, 'The Tree of Life', 19 May 2021, Broccoli Productions.

32 Ibid.

33 Heather V. Vermeulen, 'Thomas Thistlewood's Libidinal Linnaean Project: Slavery, Ecology, and Knowledge Production', *Small Axe: A Caribbean Journal of Criticism*, vol. 22, no. 1, 2018, pp. 18–38.

34 James Delbourgo, 'Gardens of Life and Death', *British Journal for the History of Science*, vol. 43, no. 1, 2010, pp. 113–18, https://doi.org/10.1017/S0007087410000245

35 Judith Carney, *In the Shadow of Slavery: Africa's Botanical Legacy in the Atlantic World*, University of California Press, 2010.

36 Judith Carney, 'Seeds of Memory: Botanical Legacies of the African Diaspora', in *African Ethnobotany in the Americas*, Robert Voeks and John Rashford (eds), 2013, pp. 13–33.

37 Murphy, 'Collecting Slave Traders'; Carney, *In the Shadow of Slavery*. See chapter 19, 'Salt Fish'.

38 'Transfer of Knowledge', Slavery and the Natural World, Natural History Museum, 2018, https://www.nhm.ac.uk/content/dam/nhmwww/discover/slavery-natural-world/chapter-9-transfer-of-knowledge.pdf

39 'John Edmonstone: The Man Who Taught Darwin Taxidermy', Natural History Museum, 2020, https://www.nhm.ac.uk/discover/john-edmonstone-the-man-who-taught-darwin-taxidermy.html

40 Jay Sullivan, 'Hidden Figures: Forgotten Contributions to Natural History,' Natural History Museum, 2020, https://www.nhm.ac.uk/discover/hidden-figures-forgotten-contributions-to-natural-history.html

41 James Poskett, *Horizons: A Global History of Science*, Penguin, 2022.

42 Delbourgo, 'Gardens of Life and Death'.

43 Schiebinger, *Plants and Empire*.

44 Ibid.

13. Hans Sloane

1 Katie Pavid, 'Hans Sloane: Physician, Collector and Botanist', Natural history Museum, https://www.nhm.ac.uk/discover/hans-sloane-physician-collector-botanist.html

2 Stanley A. Hawkins, 'Sir Hans Sloane (1660–1735): His Life and Legacy', *Ulster Med Journal*, vol. 79, no. 1, 2010, pp. 25–29.

3 Tony Rice, *Voyages of Discovery: A Visual Celebration of Ten of the Greatest Natural History Expeditions*, Natural History Museum, 2017.

4 Ibid.

5 Hawkins, 'Sir Hans Sloane (1660–1735): His Life and Legacy'.

6 Ibid.

7 Pavid, 'Hans Sloane: Physician, Collector and Botanist'.

8 'People and the Slave Trade', Slavery and the Natural World, Natural History Museum, 2018, https://www.nhm.ac.uk/discover/slavery-and-the-natural-world.html

9 'Sir Hans Sloane', British Museum, https://www.britishmuseum.org/about-us/british-museum-story/sir-hans-sloane

10 Ibid.

11 Ibid.

12 Ibid.
13 'The Museum Podcast Special: Sir Hans Sloane', British Museum, August 2020, https://www.britishmuseum.org/the-british-museum-podcast#hans-sloane-special

14. Isaac Newton/Gravity

1   Quoted in Nicholas Dew, 'Vers la ligne: Circulating Measurements Around the French Atlantic', in *Science and Empire in the Atlantic World*, James Delbourgo and Nicholas Dew (eds), Routledge, 2008.
2   'Francis Williams – a Portrait of a Writer' Victoria and Albert Museum, https://www.vam.ac.uk/articles/francis-williams-a-portrait-of-a-writer.
3   James Poskett, 'Enhancing Diversity in UK Astronomy from a Historical Perspective', Evidence Submitted to the 'UK Astronomy' Parliamentary Committee Inquiry, 12 October 2023, https://committees.parliament.uk/writtenevidence/125435/pdf/
4   'Francis Williams – a Portrait of a Writer'.
5   Ibid.
6   James Poskett, *Horizons: A Global History of Science*, Penguin, 2022.
7   Ibid.
8   Simon Schaffer, 'Newton on the Beach: The Information Order of Principia Mathematica', *History of Science*, vol. 47, no. 3, 2009, pp. 243–76. Hear Simon Schaffer speak about his research on our *Human Resources* podcast, season 1, episode 2, 'The Tree of Life', 19 May 2021, Broccoli Productions.
9   Poskett, *Horizons*.
10 Ibid.
11 Schaffer, 'Newton on the Beach'.
12 Ibid.
13 Ibid.
14 Poskett, *Horizons*.
15 Ibid.
16 Schaffer, 'Newton on the Beach'.
17 Poskett, *Horizons*; Peter Broughton, 'Arthur Storer of Maryland: His Astronomical Work and his Family Ties with Newton', *Journal for the History of Astronomy*, vol. 19, no. 2, 1988, pp. 77–96.
18 Schaffer, 'Newton on the Beach'.
19 Simon Schaffer, 'Golden Means: Assay Instruments and the Geography of Precision in the Guinea Trade', in *Instruments, Travel and Science: Itineraries of Precision from the Seventeenth to the Twentieth Century*, Marie-Noëlle Bourguet, Christian Licoppe and H. Otto Sibum (eds), Routledge, 2002, pp. 20–50.

20 Schaffer, 'Golden Means'.

21 Poskett, *Horizons*.

22 Ibid.

23 Eric Herschthal, *The Science of Abolition: How Slaveholders Became the Enemies of Progress*, Yale University Press, 2021.

24 Jenny Bulstrode, 'Black Metallurgists and the Making of the Industrial Revolution', *History and Technology*, vol. 39, no. 1, 2023, pp. 1–41.

25 James Delbourgo, 'The Newtonian Slave Body: Racial Enlightenment in the Atlantic World', *Atlantic Studies*, vol. 9, no. 2, 2012, pp. 185–207.

26 Poskett, Horizons.

27 Hear Simon Schaffer and Kate Murphy discuss these legacies on our *Human Resources* podcast, season 1, episode 2, 'The Tree of Life', 19 May 2021.

15. Gynaecology

1   'UK Maternal Mortality 2020–2022 Report', MBRRACE-UK, https://www.npeu.ox.ac.uk/mbrrace-uk/data-brief/maternal-mortality-2020-2022

2   P. R. Lockhart, 'New York just removed the statue of a surgeon who experimented on enslaved Women', *Vox*, 18 April 2018.

3   Maia A. Hill, 'The Stain of Slavery on the Black Women's Body and the Development of Gynecology: Historical Trauma of a Black Women's Body', *Macksey Journal*, vol. 1, no. 1, 2020.

4   'The Legacy of Henrietta Lacks: Honoring Henrietta', Johns Hopkins Medicine, https://www.hopkinsmedicine.org/henrietta-lacks

5   Ibid.

6   Ibid.

7   *Human Resources* (podcast), season 1, episode 2, 'The Tree of Life', 19 May 2021, Broccoli Productions.

8   Dr Annabel Sowemimo, recorded interview for *Human Resources* podcast, 28 September 2021, Broccoli Productions.

9   Ibid.

10 Ibid.

11 Ibid.

12 Hill, 'The Stain of Slavery on the Black Women's Body and the Development of Gynecology'.

13 Britannica, 'Sarah Baartman, Khoekhoe Woman', https://www.britannica.com/biography/Sarah-Baartman

14 Hill, 'The Stain of Slavery on the Black Woman's Body and the Development of Gynacology'.

15 Dr Annabel Sowemimo, *Human Resources* podcast interview.

16 Hill, 'The Stain of Slavery on the Black Women's Body and the Development of Gynaecology'.
17 Du Bois, *The Souls of Black Folk*.
18 Thomas Clarkson, *An Essay on the Slavery and Commerce of the Human Species*, 1786, https://oll.libertyfund.org/titles/clarkson-an-essay-on-the-slavery-and-commerce-of-the-human-species
19 Ibid.
20 Cary Funk, 'Black American's Views of and Engagement with Science', report, Pew Research Center, 7 April 2022.
21 Dr Annabel Sowemimo, *Human Resources* podcast interview.

16. Blood Pressure Monitoring
1   High Blood Pressure, NHS website, https://www.nhs.uk/conditions/high-blood-pressure/
2   D. Fraser Harris, 'Stephen Hales, The Pioneer in the Hygiene of Ventilation', *Scientific Monthly*, vol. 3, no. 5, November 1916.
3   Jaime Wisniak, 'Stephen Hales', *Revista CENIC Ciencias Biológicas*, vol. 43, no. 3, 2012.
4   Fraser Harris, 'Stephen Hales, The Pioneer in the Hygiene of Ventilation'.
5   Ibid.
6   I. B Smith, 'The Impact of Stephen Hales on Medicine', *Journal of the Royal Society of Medicine*, vol. 86, June 1993, pp. 349–52.
7   Jaime Wisniak, 'Stephen Hales'.
8   *The Interesting Narrative of the Life of Olaudah Equiano or Gustava Vassa, The African by Himself*, 1789.
9   Ibid.
10 *Human Resources* (podcast), season 1, episode 2 'The Tree of Life', 19 May 2021, Broccoli Productions.

17. Mahogany
1   'Crafting Elegance: Mahogany's Enduring Legacy in American and British Woodworking', Heritage Woodwork Consultancy, https://heritagewoodworkconsultancy.com/blogs/crafting-elegance-mahoganys-enduring-legacy-in-american-and-british-woodworking/
2   Justin Abraham Linds, 'Fermentation, Rot, and Power in the Early Modern Atlantic', *Edge Effects*, 11 August 2020, https://edgeeffects.net/fermentation-rot-and-power/
3   Paul Newton Jackson, 'Mahogany, Ivory, and Tortoiseshell: Towards a Political Ecology of Eighteenth-Century Keyboard Instruments', IASH,

Notes

https://www.iash.ed.ac.uk/profile/dr-paul-newton-jackson; Craig
Stephen Revels, 'Timber, Trade, and Transformation: A Historical
Geography of Mahogany in Honduras', Louisiana State University and
Agricultural & Mechanical College, 2002, https://repository.lsu.edu/
gradschool_dissertations/1285/

4   Desha Osborne, 'Facing Our Past: The Difficult History of Mahogany',
National Trust for Scotland, 2022, https://www.nts.org.uk/stories/
facing-our-past-the-difficult-history-of-mahogany

5   Jennifer L. Anderson, *Mahogany: The Costs of Luxury in Early
America*, Harvard University Press, 2012.

6   Osborne, 'Facing Our Past'.

7   Anderson, *Mahogany: The Costs of Luxury in Early America*; Jennifer
L. Anderson, 'Nature's Currency: The Atlantic Mahogany Trade and
the Commodification of Nature in the Eighteenth Century', *Early
American Studies*, vol. 2, no. 1, 2004, pp. 47–80.

8   Anderson, *Mahogany: The Costs of Luxury in Early America*.

9   James Walvin, *Slavery in Small Things: Slavery and Modern Cultural
Habits*, John Wiley & Sons, 2017.

10 Anderson, *Nature's Currency*.

11 Anderson, *Mahogany: The Costs of Luxury in Early America*; Walvin,
Slavery in Small Things.

12 Anderson, *Mahogany: The Costs of Luxury in Early America*.

13 Walvin, *Slavery in Small Things*.

14 Christine Horn, 'Picturing the Plantation as a Site of Displacement in
Sarawak', *Edge Effects*, 2020. https://edgeeffects.net/
picturing-the-plantation-as-a-site-of-displacement/

15 Walvin, *Slavery in Small Things*.

16 Anderson, *Mahogany: The Costs of Luxury in Early America*.

17 Elaine Freedgood, 'Souvenirs of Sadism: Mahogany Furniture,
Deforestation, and Slavery in Jane Eyre', in *The Ideas in Things:
Fugitive Meaning in the Victorian Novel*, University of Chicago Press,
2006, pp. 30–54.

18 Osborne, 'Facing Our Past'.

19 Alyce Perry Englund, 'Tracing the Rise of Thomas Chippendale, From
Hometown Hero to London Lion', The Metropolitan Museum of Art,
2018, https://www.metmuseum.org/articles/thomas-chippendale-
director-home-town-hero-london-lion; Walvin, *Slavery in Small Things*.

20 Anderson, 'Nature's Currency'; Osborne, 'Facing Our Past'.

21 Anderson, *Mahogany: The Costs of Luxury in Early America*; Walvin,
Slavery in Small Things.

22 Walvin, *Slavery in Small Things*.

23 Daniel R. Finamore, 'Sailors and Slaves on the Wood-Cutting Frontier: Archaeology of the British Bay Settlement, Belize', Boston University, 1994, https://search.worldcat.org/title/Sailors-and-slaves-on-the-wood-cutting-frontier-:-archaeology-of-the-British-Bay-settlement-Belize/oclc/333382653; Revels, 'Timber, Trade, and Transformation'; See also chapter 5, 'The Colour Indigo', for more on British involvement in deforestation and slavery in this region.

24 Hannah Cusworth, 'Mahogany, Enslaved Africans, and Miskito Indigenous Peoples at Chiswick House, Kenwood and Marble Hill, London', lecture given at 'New Approaches to Material Culture in Historic Houses: Miskito Indigenous Cultures, Mahogany and Environmental Futures', Institute of Historical Research, 2022, https://www.history.ac.uk/podcasts/new-approaches-material-culture-historic-houses-miskito-indigenous-cultures-mahogany-and.; Sara Thomas, 'Shona Jackson on Decolonizing Labor in the Caribbean', *Edge Effects*, 28 January 2020, https://edgeeffects.net/shona-jackson/

25 Anderson, *Mahogany: The Costs of Luxury in Early America*.

26 Ibid.

27 'Greenpeace Curbs Mahogany Logging in Brazil, 1999–2004', Global Nonviolent Action Database, https://web.archive.org/web/20181122164606/https://nvdatabase.swarthmore.edu/content/greenpeace-curbs-mahogany-logging-brazil-1999-2004

28 Lizabeth Paravisini-Gebert, 'Extinctions: Chronicles of Vanishing Fauna in the Colonial and Postcolonial Caribbean', in *The Oxford Handbook of Ecocriticism*, Greg Garrard (ed.), Oxford University Press, 2014.

29 Paravisini-Gebert, 'Extinctions'.

30 Ibid.

31 Freedgood, 'Souvenirs of Sadism'.

32 Marie Widengård, 'Saving the Forest to Secure the Mine in Jamaica's Cockpit Country', *Edge Effects*, 2 April 2024, https://edgeeffects.net/cockpit-country-mining-conservation/

33 Horn, 'Picturing the Plantation'.

34 Anderson, *Mahogany: The Costs of Luxury in Early America*.

18. Tobacco Merchant's House, Glasgow

1 Chris Jones, 'Jamaica Street', 27 February 2010, glasgowhistory.com, https://www.glasgowhistory.com/jamaica-street.html

2 'The Tobacco Merchant's House at 42 Miller Street', 'Legacies of Slavery in Glasgow Museums and Collections', 5 August 2019, https://

glasgowmuseumsslavery.co.uk/2019/08/05/
the-tobacco-merchants-house-at-42-miller-street/
3   Ibid.
4   Ibid.
5   Ibid.
6   Charles Lintner Killinger, 'The Royal African Company Slave Trade to
    Virginia 1689–1713', (1969), W&M ScholarWorks, Dissertations,
    Theses, and Masters Projects, Paper 1539624680, https://dx.doi.org/
    doi:10.21220/s2-92be-5k39
7   Ibid.
8   University of Strathclyde, 'Historical Links to Slavery Report', October
    2023, https://www.strath.ac.uk/
    historicallinkstoslaveryreport/#:~:text=Strathclyde's
9   'Tobacco Slave', documentary film by Ray Maconachie and Simon
    Wharf, University of Bath, 2023, https://youtu.be/BuqA2xAusso
10 'Tobacco Lords, Industry and Urban Expansion', It Wisnae Us, 2024,
    https://it.wisnae.us/tobacco-lords-industry-and-urban-
    expansion/
11 University of Strathclyde, 'Historical Links to Slavery Report'.
12 Centre for the Study of the Legacies of British Slavery, UCL database,
    https://www.ucl.ac.uk/lbs/person/view/2146667231
13 Centre for the Study of the Legacies of British Slavery, UCL database,
    https://www.ucl.ac.uk/lbs/person/view/46072
14 Centre for the Study of the Legacies of British Slavery, UCL database,
    https://www.ucl.ac.uk/lbs/person/view/46073
15 Centre for the Study of the Legacies of British Slavery, UCL database,
    https://www.ucl.ac.uk/lbs/person/view/43409
16 Centre for the Study of the Legacies of British Slavery, UCL database,
    https://www.ucl.ac.uk/lbs/person/view/16019
17 B. W. E. Alford, *W. D. and H. O. Wills and the Development of the UK
    Tobacco Industry 1786–1965*, Routledge, 1973, https://doi.
    org/10.4324/9781315019215
18 Ibid.
19 Ibid.
20 Ibid.
21 Ibid.
22 'The Wills Family', University of Bristol website, https://www.bristol.
    ac.uk/university/anti-racism-at-bristol/university-slavery/wills-family/
23 Ibid.
24 Dan Glaister, 'Ghosts of Bristol's shameful slave past haunt its graceful
    landmarks', *Guardian*, 2 April 2017, https://www.theguardian.com/

uk-news/2017/apr/02/bristol-slave-trade-
ties-wills-building-colston-hall-rename-petition

25 Professor Evelyn Welch, Vice-Chancellor's blog, University of Bristol,
28 November 2023, https://vice-chancellor.blogs.bristol.
ac.uk/2023/11/28/university-of-bristol-pledges-10-million-to-
address-racial-inequalities-following-consultation-into-building-names/

26 Ibid.

27 Reparative Futures Programme, University of Bristol, https://www.
bristol.ac.uk/university/anti-racism-at-bristol/reparative-
futures-programme/

19. Salt Fish

1 David Alston, *Slaves and Highlanders: Silenced Histories of Scotland
and the Caribbean*, Edinburgh Scholarship Online, 2022, https://
academic.oup.com/edinburgh-scholarship-online/book/42207

2 Alison Campsie, 'How Scots fishing towns boomed from sale of salted
herring to slave plantations', *Scotsman*, 8 August 2020, https://www.
scotsman.com/heritage-and-retro/heritage/
how-scots-fishing-towns-boomed-from-sale-of-salted-herring-to-slave-
plantations-2936978

3 Campsie, 'How Scots fishing towns boomed from sale of salted herring
to slave plantations'; Donald S. Murray, *Herring Tales: How the Silver
Darlings Shaped Human Taste and History*, Bloomsbury Publishing,
2016.

4 David Alston, Juanita Cox-Westmaas and Rod Westmaas, *Slaves and
Highlanders: Silenced Histories of Scotland and the Caribbean*,
Edinburgh Scholarship Online, 2022, https://doi.org/10.3366/
edinburgh/9781474427302.001.0001

5 Kate Davies Designs, 'Learning From Loch Fyne', KDD & Co, 13 April
2023, https://kddandco.com/2023/04/13/learning-from-loch-fyne/.

6 Ibid.

7 Alston, *Slaves and Highlanders*.

8 Bertie Mandelblatt, 'A Transatlantic Commodity: Irish Salt Beef in the
French Atlantic World', *History Workshop Journal*, vol. 63, no. 1, 2007,
pp. 18–47.

9 Ibid.

10 Ibid.

11 Ibid.

12 Ibid.

13 Ibid.

14 Shrinagar I. Francis, 'From "Slave" to "Poor People" to "Traditional"

Food: The Journey of Saltfish across the Atlantic to the West Indies and
its Movement through the Culinary Landscape of Trinidad and
Tobago', Dublin Gastronomy Symposium, 2022, https://arrow.tudublin.
ie/dgs/2022/colonialism/3/

15 Jenna Karina Hershberger, 'Virginia House Painters 1750–1840/Shad,
    Herring, and Slavery in the Chesapeake Bay and Albemarle Sound',
    W&M ScholarWorks, Dissertations, Theses, and Masters Projects,
    2020, https://scholarworks.wm.edu/etd/1616444455/; Murray, *Herring
    Tales*.

16 Francis, From "Slave" to "Poor People" to "Traditional" Food.

17 Ibid.

18 Ibid.

19 James E. Candow, 'A Reassessment of the Provision of Food to Enslaved
    Persons, with Special Reference to Salted Cod in Barbados', *Journal of
    Caribbean History*, vol. 43, no. 2, 2009.

20 Diane Wallman and Sandrine Grouard, 'Enslaved Laborer and
    Sharecropper Fishing Practices in 18th–19th Century Martinique: A
    Zooarchaeological and Ethnozoohistorical Study', *Journal of
    Ethnobiology* 37, no. 3, 2017, pp. 398–420.

21 Peggy Brunache, 'Mainstreaming African Diasporic Foodways When
    Academia is Not Enough', *Transforming Anthropology*, vol. 27, no. 2,
    2019, pp. 149–63.

22 Brunache, 'Mainstreaming African Diasporic Foodways'; Francis, 'From
    "Slave" to "Poor People" to "Traditional" Food; Wallman and Grouard,
    'Enslaved Laborer and Sharecropper Fishing Practices'.

23 Brunache, 'Mainstreaming African Diasporic Foodways'.

24 Sarah Lawson Welsh, *Food, Text and Culture in the Anglophone
    Caribbean*, Rowman & Littlefield, 2019. Read chapter 12, 'Gardening'
    to learn more about the African seeds and plants that were subversively
    brought across the ocean by the enslaved, and lovingly cultivated on
    plantation plots, maintaining nostalgic cultural links and knowledge
    that still survive today.

25 See discussion of breadfruit in chapter 12, 'Gardening'.

26 Candow, 'A Reassessment of the Provision of Food'.

27 Wallman and Grouard, 'Enslaved Laborer and Sharecropper Fishing
    Practices'. See discussion of slave markets in chapter 7, 'Wool and
    Linen'.

28 Candow, 'A Reassessment of the Provision of Food'; Wallman and
    Grouard, 'Enslaved Laborer and Sharecropper Fishing Practices'.

29 Kelley Fanto Deetz, 'Stolen Bodies, Edible Memories: The Influence and
    Function of West African Foodways in the Early British Atlantic', in

The Routledge History of Food, Carol Helstosky (ed.), Routledge, pp. 113–30, 2014; Brunache, 'Mainstreaming African Diasporic Foodways'.

30 Alston, *Slaves and Highlanders*.
31 Yvonne Singh, 'The Forgotten World: How Scotland Erased Guyana from its Past', *Adda*, Commonwealth Foundation, 21 March 2019, https://www.addastories.org/the-forgotten-world/
32 Listen to our Human Resources episodes about Scotland and the Highlands to learn more about how Scotland has been simultaneously oppressed and an oppressor, one that has participated and deepened the impacts of slavery and colonialism around the world.
33 Candow, 'A Reassessment of the Provision of Food'; 'The Origins of 'Slave Food': Callaloo, Dumplings and Saltfish', Black History Month, 2016, https://www.blackhistorymonth.org.uk/article/section/history-of-slavery/origins-slave-food-callaloo-dumplings-saltfish/; Francis, From "Slave" to "Poor People" to "Traditional" Food.

20. Cromarty

1 National Museums Liverpool, International Slavery Museum Expansion, https://www.liverpoolmuseums.org.uk/ism-expansion
2 'England Local Authorities: Population, Land area and Density', Demographia, http://www.demographia.com/db-engla.htm
3 'Why Guyana is part of the Caribbean', blog at The Caribbean Reunion Club, https://www.flycrc.com/blog/guyana_caribbean
4 David Alston, Juanita Cox-Westmaas and Rod Westmaas, *Slaves and Highlanders: Silenced Histories of Scotland and the Caribbean*, Edinburgh Scholarship Online, 2022, https://doi.org/10.3366/edinburgh/9781474427302.001.0001
5 Centre for the Study of the Legacies of British Slavery, UCL database, https://www.ucl.ac.uk/lbs/estate/view/7334
6 Alston, *Slaves and Highlanders*.
7 Centre for the Study of the Legacies of British Slavery, UCL database, https://www.ucl.ac.uk/lbs/person/view/2146633105
8 David Alston, recorded interview, 22 January 2024.
9 Ibid.
10 Ibid.
11 Ibid.
12 *Human Resources* (podcast), season 1 episode 4, 'A Sour Taste', 2 June 2021, Broccoli Productions.
13 For more on the Scottish presence in the Caribbean you can listen to the *Human Resources* podcast, season 2, episodes 8, 9 and 10: 'Taking the

High Ground' (8 March 2022); 'Bairns' (15 March 2022); and 'Winners and Losers' (22 March 2022), Broccoli Productions.

21. Swimming

1 Rhiannon Batton, '"Today is a magic moment": Bath's 207-year-old lido reopens after four decades of neglect, *Guardian*, 30 September 2022, https://www.theguardian.com/travel/2022/sep/30/bath-cleveland-pools-lido-reopens

2 Centre of the Study of the legacies of British Slavery, UCL database, https://www.ucl.ac.uk/lbs/person/view/4843

3 Naomi Fowler, 'Britain's Slave Owner Compensation Loan, reparations and tax havenry', Tax Justice Network, 9 June 2020, https://taxjustice.net/2020/06/09/slavery-compensation-uk-questions/

4 'Sport for All', 27 January 2020, Sport England, https://www.sportengland.org/news/sport-for-all

5 Kevin Dawson, recorded interview, 30 January 2024.

6 Ibid.

7 Ibid.

8 Ibid.

9 Ibid.

10 Ibid.

11 Ibid.

12 Ibid.

13 Ibid.

14 Ibid.

15 Ibid.

16 Ibid.

22. Football: Liverpool and Everton

1 Joe Mulhern, 'Everton's new Bramley-Moore stadium Is a stark reminder of Liverpool's historic Entanglement with slavery in Brazil', LSE Latin America and Caribbean blog, 24 February 2021, https://blogs.lse.ac.uk/latamcaribbean/2021/02/24/evertons-new-bramley-moore-stadium-is-a-stark-reminder-of-liverpools-historic-entanglement-with-slavery-in-brazil/

2 David Kennedy, 'Merseyside Football and the Slave Trade', *Soccer & Society*, vol. 24, no. 6, 2023, pp. 883–95.

3 Ibid.; Petra Kendall-Raynor, 'Exclusive: Everton to acknowledge Bramley-Moore Dock's history of slavery at new stadium site', *LiverpoolWorld*, 20 August 2021, https://www.liverpoolworld.uk/news/

exclusive-everton-to-acknowledge-the-history-of-slavery-at-new-stadium-site-3353888.

4   The Story, 'Football and the State of the Nation', podcast, *The Times*, 16 July 2021, https://www.boomplay.com/episode/6815849.; Kennedy, 'Merseyside football and the slave trade'.

5   Joe Mulhern, recorded interview, 12 April 2024.

6   Ibid.

7   Ibid.

8   Ibid.

9   Mulhern, interview; J. G. Kelly, 'The Problem of Anti-Slavery in the Age of Capital, c. 1830–1888', PhD thesis, University of Liverpool, 2017, https://livrepository.liverpool.ac.uk/3019963/; see chapter 6, 'Denim/Blue Jeans' for more on cotton.

10 Mulhern, interview.

11 Joseph Martin Mulhern, 'After 1833: British Entanglement with Brazilian Slavery', doctoral thesis, Durham University, 2018, available at Durham E-Theses Online, http://etheses.dur.ac.uk/13071/

12 Ibid.

13 Ibid.

14 Ibid.

15 Bradley Cates, 'The Origins of St. Domingo', EFC Statto, 2017, https://www.efcstatto.com/stories/the-origins-of-st-domingo/.

16 Kennedy, 'Merseyside football and the slave trade'.

17 Tony Collins, *How Football Began: A Global History of How the World's Football Codes were Born*, Routledge, 2018; Alan McDougall, *Contested Fields: A Global History of Modern Football*, University of Toronto Press, 2020.

18 David Kennedy and Peter Kennedy, 'Merseyside Football's Earliest Patrons and the Slave Trade Connection', The Open University blog, 2023, https://www5.open.ac.uk/research-centres/herc/blog/merseyside-football%E2%80%99s-earliest-patrons-and-slave-trade-connection.

19 McDougall, *Contested Fields*.

20 Kennedy, 'Merseyside football and the slave trade'.

21 Ibid.

22 Ibid.

23 Ibid.

24 Ibid.

25 Ibid.

26 Ibid. (See also chapter 2, 'Gunpowder').

27 Ibid.

Notes

28 Ibid.
29 Kennedy and Kennedy, 'Merseyside Football's Earliest Patrons'.
30 Ibid.
31 Mulhern, interview.
32 Ibid.
33 Ibid.
34 Ibid.
35 *Human Resources* (podcast), season 1, episode 6, 'A City with a Slaving Past', 16 June 2021, Broccoli Productions.
36 The Story, 'Football and the State of the Nation'.
37 Dominic Bliss and Jarek Zaba, 'The Remarkable Story of Andrew Watson', *Broadway to Brazil*, podcast, 21 September 2021, https://podcasts.apple.com/gb/podcast/the-remarkable-story-of-andrew-watson/id1300239356?i=1000536108298.
38 Bliss and Zaba, 'The Remarkable Story of Andrew Watson'; 'The "most influential" black footballer for decades lost to history', BBC Sport, 12 October 2021, https://www.bbc.co.uk/sport/football/58841184; Simao Valente, 'The debate over Brazilian football's British origins', University Of Oxford News Blog, 4 August 2014, https://www.ox.ac.uk/news/arts-blog/debate-over-brazilian-footballs-british-origins
39 Tusdiq Din, '"We Looked Identical": one man's discovery of slavery, family and football', *Guardian*, 24 December 2020, https://amp.theguardian.com/football/2020/dec/24/slavery-family-and-football-malik-al-nasir-andrew-watson-first-black-international-footballer; Malik Al Nasir, as told to Ed Thomas, 'Searching for my slave roots', BBC News, July 2020, https://www.bbc.co.uk/news/extra/3k9u8lh178/Searching_for_my_slave_roots.
40 Ibid.
41 Mulhern, interview.

23. Dictionaries

1 Sarah Ogilvie, 'A Nineteenth-Century Garment Throughout: Description, Collaboration, and Thorough Coverage in the *Oxford English Dictionary* (1884–1928)', in *The Whole World in a Book: Dictionaries in the Nineteenth Century,* Sarah Ogilvie, and Gabriella Safran (eds), Oxford University Press, 2020 (online edn, Oxford Academic, 19 December 2019).
2 'Nineteenth-century English – an overview', Oxford English Dictionary, https://www.oed.com/discover/nineteenth-century-english-an-overview/?tl=true

3   Ogilvie, 'A Nineteenth-Century Garment Throughout'.
4   Alison Campsie, 'The Gaelic dictionary from the Highlands funded by slave owners', *Scotsman*. 5 October 2021, https://www.scotsman.com/heritage-and-retro/heritage/the-gaelic-dictionary-from-the-highlands-funded-by-slave-owners-3407047
5   *Human Resources* (podcast), season 2, episode 8, 'Taking the High Ground', 8 March 2022, Broccoli Productions.
6   Sarah Ogilvie, and Gabriella Safran (eds), *The Whole World in a Book: Dictionaries in the Nineteenth Century*, Oxford University Press, 2020.
7   Ibid.
8   Ibid.
9   Lynda Mugglestone, *Dictionaries: A Very Short Introduction*, Oxford University Press, 2011.
10 Christine Whyte, recorded interview, 7 March 2024.
11 Catherine Dille, 'Johnson's Dictionary in the Nineteenth Century: A Legacy in Transition', in *The Age of Johnson*, vol, 16, AMS Press, 2005, p. 21.
12 Ibid.; John S. Considine, 'The Unfinished Business of Eighteenth-Century European Lexicography', in Ogilvie and Safran (eds), *The Whole World in a Book: Dictionaries in the Nineteenth Century*, Oxford University Press, 2020.
13 Whyte, interview.
14 Sarah Ogilvie, and Gabriella Safran (eds), *The Whole World in a Book: Dictionaries in the Nineteenth Century*, Oxford University Press, 2020.
15 Considine, 'The Unfinished Business'.
16 Joan M. Fayer, 'African Interpreters in the Atlantic Slave Trade', *Anthropological Linguistics*, vol. 45, no. 3, 2003, pp. 281–95, http://www.jstor.org/stable/30028896
17 Whyte, interview.
18 Fayer, 'African Interpreters in the Atlantic Slave Trade'.
19 Considine, 'The Unfinished Business'.
20 Whyte, interview; Dille, 'Johnson's Dictionary'.
21 Whyte, interview.
22 Ibid.
23 Listen to Christine Whyte talking about child labour in the British Empire on the *Human Resources* podcast, season 3, episode 12, 'Think of the Children', 21 November 2023, Broccoli Productions.
24 Whyte, interview.
25 Ibid.
26 Whyte, interview; Dille, 'Johnson's Dictionary'.

27 Whyte, interview.
28 Ogilvie and Safran (eds), *The Whole World in a Book*; Considine, 'The Unfinished Business'.
29 Mugglestone, Dictionaries: a very short introduction.
30 Whyte, interview.
31 Ogilvie and Safran (eds), *The Whole World in a Book*.

24. Greene King Brewery

1 Ben Johnson, 'The Great British Pub', Historic UK, https://www.historic-uk.com/CultureUK/The-Great-British-Pub/
2 *Human Resources* (podcast), season 1, episode 7, 'The Pubs Are Open', 23 June 2021, Broccoli Productions.
3 Johnson, 'The Great British Pub'.
4 'Our History', Greene King, https://www.greeneking.co.uk/our-company/our-history
5 Ibid.
6 Centre for the Study of the Legacies of British Slavery, UCL database, https://www.ucl.ac.uk/lbs/person/view/1265637725
7 R. G. Wilson, 'Greene Family', *Oxford Dictionary of National Biography*, 23 September 2004, https://www.oxforddnb.com/display/10.1093/ref:odnb/9780198614128.001.0001/odnb-9780198614128-e-50414
8 Kevin Rawlinson, 'Lloyds of London and Greene King to make slave trade reparations', *Guardian*, 18 June 2020, https://www.theguardian.com/world/2020/jun/18/lloyds-of-london-and-greene-king-to-make-slave-trade-reparations
9 Ibid.
10 'Calling time on Racism', Greene King, https://www.greeneking.co.uk/our-company/calling-time-on-racism
11 Craig Simpson, 'Caribbean nation seeks slavery reparations from British brewer Greene King', 27 January 2024, *Telegraph*, https://www.telegraph.co.uk/news/2024/01/27/caribbean-nation-seeks-reparations-from-uk-brewer/
12 Ben Whitman, 'Radical Resistance? The Opposition to Impressment of British Seamen into the Royal Navy 1770–1779', University of Bristol, 2016, https://www.bristol.ac.uk/media-library/sites/history/documents/dissertations/Ben_Whitman2016.pdf
13 Ibid.
14 Ibid.
15 Ibid.
16 David Emeney, 'Historic Site, The Hole in the Wall Pub', Discovering

Bristol website, 2003, https://discoveringbristol.org.uk/browse/slavery/
historic-site-the-hole-in-the-wall-pub/

25. Pirates

1   Erin Mackie, 'Welcome the Outlaw: Pirates, Maroons, and Caribbean
    Countercultures', *Cultural Critique*, no. 59, 2005, pp. 24–62, http://
    www.jstor.org/stable/4489197

2   Mackie, 'Welcome the Outlaw'; Robert C. Ritchie, 'Government
    Measures against Piracy and Privateering in the Atlantic Area,
    1750–1850', in *Pirates and Privateers: New Perspectives on the War on
    Trade in the Eighteenth and Nineteenth Centuries*, University of Exeter
    Press, 1997, pp. 10–28; Marcus Rediker, *Villains of All Nations:
    Atlantic Pirates in the Golden Age*, Beacon Press, 2004.

3   Martin Mumper, 'Piracy and the Atlantic Slave Trade', *History Is Now
    Magazine*, 29 March 2023, http://www.historyisnowmagazine.com/
    blog/2023/3/29/piracy-and-the-atlantic-slave-trade

4   'Historians Link Pirate Ships and Slave Vessels', NPR, 15 March 2007,
    https://www.npr.org/templates/story/story.php?storyId=8925862

5   Arne Bialuschewski, 'Slaves of the Buccaneers: Mayas in Captivity in
    the Second Half of the Seventeenth Century', *Ethnohistory*, vol. 64, no.
    1, 2017, pp. 41–63.

6   Kris Lane and Arne Bialuschewski (eds), *Piracy in the Early Modern
    Era: An Anthology of Sources*, Hackett Publishing, 2019.

7   Lane and Bialuschewski, *Piracy in the Early Modern Era*; Kevin P.
    McDonald, *Pirates, Merchants, Settlers, and Slaves: Colonial America
    and the Indo-Atlantic World*, University of California Press, 2015;
    Rebecca Simon, *The Pirates' Code: Laws and Life Aboard Ship*,
    Reaktion Books, 2024.

8   McDonald, *Pirates, Merchants, Settlers, and Slaves*.

9   Mackie, 'Welcome the Outlaw'.

10 Simon, *The Pirates' Code*.

11 Arne Bialuschewski, *Raiders and Natives: Cross-Cultural Relations in
    the Age of Buccaneers*, University of Georgia Press, 2022.

12 Ben Johnson, 'Barbary Pirates and English Slaves', Historic UK, 2023,
    https://www.historic-uk.com/HistoryUK/HistoryofEngland/
    Barbary-Pirates-English-Slaves/

13 Bialuschewski, *Raiders and Natives*.

14 Simon, *The Pirates' Code*.

15 Lane and Bialuschewski, *Piracy in the Early Modern Era*.

16 Brooke Keling, 'Pirates and Plantations: Exploring the Relationship
    between Caribbean Piracy and the Plantation Economy during the

Notes

Early Modern Period'. *Tucaksegee Valley Historical Review*, vol. 26, Spring 2020, https://affiliate.wcu.edu/tuckasegeevalleyhistoricalreview/spring-2020/pirates-and-plantations-exploring-the-relationship-between-caribbean-piracy-and-the-plantation-economy-during-the-early-modern-period/.

17 Mumper, 'Piracy and the Atlantic Slave Trade'.
18 Gregory E. O'Malley, 'Black Markets for Black Labor: Pirates, Privateers, and Interlopers in the Origins of the Intercolonial Slave Trade, ca. 1619–1720', in *Final Passages: The Intercolonial Slave Trade of British America, 1619–1807*, North Carolina Scholarship Online, 2015, https://doi.org/10.5149/northcarolina/9781469615349.003.0003; Lane and Bialuschewski, *Piracy in the Early Modern Era*.
19 Bialuschewski, *Raiders and Natives*.
20 Matthew R. Bahar, *Storm of the Sea: Indians and Empires in the Atlantic's Age of Sail*, Oxford University Press, 2018.
21 See chapter 17, 'Mahogany'.
22 Bialuschewski, *Raiders and Natives*.
23 Ibid.; Bialuschewski, 'Slaves of the Buccaneers'.
24 Bialuschewski, *Raiders and Natives*.
25 McDonald, *Pirates, Merchants, Settlers, and Slaves*.
26 McDonald, *Pirates, Merchants, Settlers, and Slaves*; James H. Thomas, 'Merchants and Maritime Marauders: The East India Company and the Problem of Piracy in the Eighteenth Century', *Great Circle*, vol. 36, no. 1, 2014.
27 Arne Bialuschewski, 'Pirates, Slavers, and the Indigenous Population in Madagascar, c.1690–1715', *International Journal of African Historical Studies*, vol. 38, no. 3, 2005, p. 404; Ryan Holroyd, 'Whatever Happened to those Villains of the Indian Seas? The Happy Retirement of the Madagascar Pirates, 1698–1721', *International Journal of Maritime History* 29, no. 4, 2017, pp. 752–70.
28 Bialuschewski, 'Pirates, Slavers, and the Indigenous Population in Madagascar'; see chapter 2, 'Gunpowder'.
29 Thomas, 'Merchants and Maritime Marauders'.
30 Bialuschewski, 'Pirates, Slavers, and the Indigenous Population in Madagascar'.
31 Ibid.
32 McDonald, *Pirates, Merchants, Settlers, and Slaves*. Currency converted on The National Archives Currency Convertor: https://www.nationalarchives.gov.uk/currency-converter/
33 Holroyd, 'Whatever Happened to those Villains of the Indian Seas?'
34 Ibid.

35 Ibid.
36 Max Boot, 'Pirates, Then and Now: How Piracy Was Defeated in the Past and Can Be Again', *Foreign Affairs*, vol. 88, no. 4, 2009, pp. 94–107, *JSTOR*, http://www.jstor.org/stable/20699624.
37 Ibid.
38 Lydia G. Fash, 'S04E03: The Literary Capital of Pirates', *C19* (podcast), SoundCloud, 2021. https://soundcloud.com/c19podcast/s04e03-the-literary-capital-of-pirates
39 Benerson Little, *Pirate Hunting: The Fight Against Pirates, Privateers, and Sea Raiders from Antiquity to the Present*, Potomac Books, 2010.
40 Ibid.
41 Lucy Lazzarus, 'Unsettling Facts About Modern Pirates (and Where in the World You'll Find Them)', *Travel*, 20 April 2020, https://www.thetravel.com/pirates-where-to-find-them/
42 Boot, 'Pirates, Then and Now'; Lazzarus, 'Unsettling Facts About Modern Pirates'.
43 Fash, 'The Literary Capital of Pirates'.

26. Boxing

1   Greg Jenner, *Dead Famous: An Unexpected History of Celebrity from Bronze Age to Silver Screen*, Weidenfeld & Nicolson, 2020.
2   From interview with Greg Jenner, 25 February 2022. Listen to *Physical Capital* (podcast), season 1, episode 2, 'Fighting for Freedom (Round 1)', 15 August 2022, and episode 3, 'Fighting for Freedom (Round 2)', 22 August 2022, Broccoli Productions.
3   Kasia Boddy, *Boxing: A Cultural History*, Reaktion Books, 2009.
4   From interview with Louis Moore, 17 February 2022. Listen to *Physical Capital* (podcast), season 1, episode 2, 'Fighting for Freedom (Round 1)', 15 August 2022, Broccoli Productions.
5   Boddy, *Boxing: A Cultural History*.
6   Ibid.
7   *Narrative of the Life and Adventures of Henry Bibb, An American Slave, Written by Himself*, with an introduction by Lucius C. Matlack, 1849.
8   Louis Moore interview, *Physical Capital* podcast.
9   Ibid.
10 'Tom Molineaux', Virginia Museum of History and Culture, https://virginiahistory.org/learn/tom-molineaux
11 Louis Moore interview, *Physical Capital* podcast.
12 'Bill Richmond (1763–1829): Bare-Knuckle King of the Prize Fight Ring', Sky Sports, 2 October 2020.

Notes

27. Voodoo Dolls

1   Nadia Lee, 'The Appropriation of Magic: How White People Demonised Voodoo', *Brizo Magazine*, 15 June 2020, https://brizomagazine.com/2020/06/15/the-appropriation-of-magic-how-white-people-demonised-voodoo/; Danielle N. Boaz, 'Ten Facts About the Racist History of "Voodoo"', *Anthropology News*, 9 August 2023, https://www.anthropology-news.org/articles/ten-facts-about-the-racist-history-of-voodoo/

2   Ibid.

3   Ibid.; Massoud Hayoun, 'In Voodoo's Survival, a Tale of Black Resilience', Al Jazeera America, 25 February 2015, http://america.aljazeera.com/multimedia/2015/2/voodoos-survival-black-history-resilience.html.

4   Lee, 'The Appropriation of Magic'.

5   Lee, 'The Appropriation of Magic'.

6   'New Orleans Voodoo (a Virtual Tour)', Free Tours by Foot New Orleans, YouTube, 2020. https://www.youtube.com/watch?v=aksVg8mNtPg

7   Natalie Armitage, 'European and African Figural Ritual Magic: The Beginnings of the Voodoo Doll Myth', in *The Materiality of Magic: An Artifactual Investigation into Ritual Practices and Popular Beliefs*, Ceri Houlbrook and Natalie Armitage (eds), Oxbow Books, 2015.

8   Ibid.

9   Diana Paton, *The Cultural Politics of Obeah: Religion, Colonialism and Modernity in the Caribbean World*, Cambridge University Press, 2015.

10 Armitage, 'European and African Figural Ritual Magic'.

11 Shantel George, 'Tracing the Ethnic Origins of Enslaved Africans in Grenada', *Atlantic Studies*, vol. 17, no. 2, 2020, pp. 160–83; Lionel and Patricia Fanthorpe, *Mysteries and Secrets of Voodoo, Santeria, and Obeah*, Dundurn, 2008.

12 Danielle N. Boaz, *Voodoo: The History of a Racial Slur*, Oxford University Press, 2023; Alan Richardson, 'Romantic Voodoo: Obeah and British Culture, 1797–1807', *Studies in Romanticism*, vol. 32, no. 1, 1993, pp. 3–28.

13 Boaz, *Voodoo: The History of a Racial Slur*.

14 Richardson, 'Romantic Voodoo'.

15 Boaz, *Voodoo: The History of a Racial Slur*.

16 Ibid.

17 Alasdair Pettinger, 'From Vaudoux to Voodoo', *Forum for Modern Language Studies*, vol. 40, no. 4, 2004; Richardson, 'Romantic Voodoo'.

18 Richardson, 'Romantic Voodoo'.
19 Paton, *The Cultural Politics of Obeah*; Vincent Brown, *The Reaper's Garden: Death and Power in the World of Atlantic Slavery*, Harvard University Press, 2008.
20 Paton, *The Cultural Politics of Obeah*.
21 Jeffrey Cottrell, 'At the End of the Trade: Obeah and Black Women in the Colonial Imaginary', *Atlantic Studies*, vol.12, no. 2, 2015, pp. 200–18; George, 'Tracing the Ethnic Origins'.
22 Juanita De Barros, 'Dispensers, *Obeah* and Quackery: Medical Rivalries in Post-Slavery British Guiana', *Social History of Medicine*, vol. 20, no. 2, 2007, pp. 243–61.
23 J. Alexandra McGhee, 'Fever Dreams: Obeah, Tropical Disease, and Cultural Contamination in Colonial Jamaica and the Metropole', *Atlantic Studies*, vol. 12, no. 2, 2015, pp. 179–99; Monique Allewaert, *Ariel's Eology: Plantations, Personhood, and Colonialism in the American Tropics*, University of Minnesota Press, 2013; Justine S. Murison, 'Obeah and its Others: Buffered Selves in the Era of Tropical Medicine', *Atlantic Studies*, vol. 12, no. 2, 2015, pp. 144–59.
24 Boaz, *Voodoo: The History of a Racial Slur*.
25 'New Orleans Voodoo (a Virtual Tour)'; 'Vodou: History, Worldview and Rituals', Canadian Museum of History, https://www.historymuseum.ca/vodou/files/2012/12/vodou-reference-leaflet.pdf; Hayoun, 'In Voodoo's Survival'.
26 Paton, *The Cultural Politics of Obeah*.
27 Armitage, 'European and African Figural Ritual Magic'.
28 Paton, *The Cultural Politics of Obeah*.

28. Treadmills

1 James Mirza-Davies, 'A short history of apprenticeships in England: from medieval craft guilds to the twenty-first century', 9 March 2015, https://commonslibrary.parliament.uk/a-short-history-of-apprenticeships-in-england-from-medieval-craft-guilds-to-the-twenty-first-century/
2 Interview with Diana Paton on *Human Resources* (podcast), season 3, episodes 10 and 11, 'Abolition Now' (parts 1 and 2), 7 November 2023 and 14 November 2024, Broccoli Productions.
3 Padraic X. Scanlon, *Slave Empire: How Slavery Built Modern Britain*, Robinson, 2020.
4 Diana Paton, 'Maternal Struggles and the Politics of Childlessness under Pronatalist Caribbean Slavery', *Slavery & Abolition*, vol. 38, no.

2, pp. 251–68, https://www.tandfonline.com/doi/full/10.1080/01440 39X.2017.1316963

5   Interview with Diana Paton on *Human Resources*.
6   Ibid.
7   Ibid.
8   Scanlon, *Slave Empire: How Slavery Built Modern Britain*.
9   Interview with Diana Paton on *Human Resources*.

29. Swing Low, Sweet Chariot

1   W. E. B. Du Bois, *The Souls of Black Folk* (1903), Oxford World's Classics, 2008.
2   Judith Michiner, 'Willis, "Uncle" Wallace and "Aunt" Minerva, *The Encyclopedia of Oklahoma History and Culture*, Oklahoma Historical Society, https://www.okhistory.org/publications/enc/entry?entry=WI018
3   'Swing Low, Sweet Chariot', Hymnology Archive, https://www.hymnologyarchive.com/swing-low-sweet-chariot
4   Ibid.
5   Du Bois, *The Souls of Black Folk*.
6   Luke McLaughlin 'RFU survey reveals racism experienced by players "in every area of elite rugby"', *Guardian*, 4 April 2023, https://www.theguardian.com/sport/2023/apr/04/rfu-survey-racism-experienced-elite-rugby-luther-burrell
7   Dena J. Epstein, 'Slave Music in the United States before 1860: A Survey of Sources (Part I)', *Notes*, vol. 20, no. 2, 1963, pp. 195–212, https://doi.org/10.2307/894726
8   Ibid.
9   Andy Bull, 'Complicated history of Swing Low, Sweet Chariot needs to be taught and honoured', *Guardian*, 2 July 2020, https://www.theguardian.com/sport/2020/jul/02/complicated-history-of-swing-low-sweet-chariot-needs-to-be-taught-and-honoured
10 Ibid.
11 Peter Walker, 'Boris Johnson opposes ban on Swing Low, Sweet Chariot', *Guardian*, 19 June 2020, https://www.theguardian.com/sport/2020/jun/19/boris-johnson-opposes-ban-on-swing-low-sweet-chariot

30. Quilts

1   Floris Bennett Cash, 'Kinship and Quilting: An Examination of African-American Tradition', *Journal of Negro History*, vol. 80, no. 1, 1995, pp. 30–41.
2   Ibid.

3   Sea Stachura, 'The Enduring Story for Underground Railroad Quilts',
    NPR, 3 March 2024, https://www.npr.org/2024/03/03/
    1235158989/the-enduring-story-for-underground-railroad-quilts
4   Ibid.

31. Wisbech Chest
1   Catriona Lewis, tweet, 25 August 2020, https://x.com/catrionalewis/
    status/1298150530418704385
2   Andrew Neil, tweet, 25 August 2020, https://x.com/afneil/
    status/1298364804286078976?lang=en
3   Francoise Le Jeune, 'Thomas Clarkson (1760–1846), A Militant
    Abolitionist', *Manifest*, 26 April 2023, https://www.projectmanifest.eu/
    thomas-clarkson-1760-1846-a-militant-abolitionist-en-fr/
4   Thomas Clarkson, 'An Essay on the Slavery and Commerce of the
    Human Species, particularly the African, translated from a Latin
    Dissertation, which was Honoured with the First Prize, in the
    University of Cambridge, for the Year 1785, with Additions' (London,
    J. Phillips, 1786).
5   Ibid.
6   Ibid.
7   Thomas Clarkson, *The History of the Rise, Progress, and
    Accomplishment of the Abolition of the African Slave-Trade by the
    British Parliament*, 2 vols, London, L. Taylor, 1808, vol. 1.

32. Maps
1   Michele Abee, 'The Spread of the Mercator Projection in Western
    European and United States Cartography', *Cartographica: The
    International Journal for Geographic Information and
    Geovisualization*, vol. 56, no. 2, 2021, pp. 151–65.
2   Abee, 'The Spread of the Mercator Projection'; Kei Miller, *The
    Cartographer Tries to Map a Way to Zion*, Carcanet, 2014.
3   Abee, 'The Spread of the Mercator Projection'.
4   The first iteration of the Gall–Peters projection was described by the
    Scotsman James Gall in 1855 and later published by him in 1885. In
    1967, the German historian Arno Peters created the 'Peters World
    Map'. Arthur H. Robinson was the first to name it the Gall–Peters
    projection in 1986.
5   James R. Akerman (ed.), *The Imperial Map: Cartography and the
    Mastery of Empire*, University of Chicago Press, 2009; Matthew H.
    Edney, *Mapping an Empire: The Geographical Construction of British
    India, 1765–1843*, University of Chicago Press, 1997.

Notes

6   Edward Armston-Sheret, recorded interview, 12 April 2024.
7   Angela Sutton and Charlton W. Yingling, 'Projections of Desire and Design in Early Modern Caribbean Maps', *Historical Journal*, vol. 63, no. 4, 2020, pp. 789–810.
8   Armston-Sheret, interview.
9   Armston-Sheret, interview.
10 Dane Kennedy, *Mungo Park's Ghost: The Haunted Hubris of British Explorers in Nineteenth-century Africa*, Cambridge University Press, 2024.
11 Armston-Sheret, interview.
12 Kennedy, *Mungo Park's Ghost*.
13 David Lambert, '"Taken Captive by the Mystery of the Great River": Towards an Historical Geography of British Geography and Atlantic Slavery', *Journal of Historical Geography*, vol. 35, no. 1, 2009, pp. 44–65.
14 Ibid.
15 Armston-Sheret, interview. See the chapters, 'Wool and Linen', 'Gunpowder' and 'Denim'.
16 Armston-Sheret, interview.
17 Ibid.
18 Ibid.
19 Edney, *Mapping an Empire*.
20 Armston-Sheret, interview.
21 Ibid.
22 Ibid.
23 Ibid.
24 See chapter 23, 'Dictionaries', and Christine Whyte on *Human Resources* (podcast), season 3, episode 12, 'Think of the Children', 21 November 2023, Broccoli Productions for more on child labour.
25 'Hidden Histories of Exploration – RGS', Online Exhibition, RGS-IBG Collections, https://www.rgs.org/our-collections/stories-from-our-collections/online-exhibitions/hidden-histories-of-exploration.
26 Armston-Sheret, interview.
27 'Hidden Histories of Exploration', Royal Geographical Society, with IBG, https://www.rgs.org/our-collections/stories-from-our-collections/online-exhibitions/hidden-histories-of-exploration
28 Kennedy, *Mungo Park's Ghost*.
29 'Hidden Histories of Exploration'; Kennedy, *Mungo Park's Ghost*.
30 Armston-Sheret, interview.
31 Ibid.

32 David Lambert, 'Afterword: Critical Geographies of Slavery', *Historical Geography*, vol. 39, no. 1, 2011, pp. 174–81.
33 Abee, 'The Spread of the Mercator Projection'; Edney, *Mapping an Empire*.

33. The *Guardian*

1   Dr Aida Al-Kaisy, 'Structural Racism in UK Newsrooms', Ethical Journalism Network, 2023.
2   Ibid.
3   Cassandra Gooptar, 'The Scott Trust Legacies of Enslavement Report: Part 1 The Taylor Report', 11 December 2020, https://coilink. org/20.500.12592/zqprfr
4   'Peterloo, 1819', Changing Britain, History, BBC Bitesize, https://www. bbc.co.uk/bitesize/guides/z6c6cqt/revision/2
5   Gooptar, 'The Scott Trust Legacies of Enslavement Report: Part 1 The Taylor Report'.
6   Ibid.
7   Ibid.
8   Ibid.
9   Ibid.
10 Ibid.
11 Ibid.
12 Centre for the Study of the Legacies of British Slavery, UCL database, https://www.ucl.ac.uk/lbs/person/view/16791
13 Gooptar, 'The Scott Trust Legacies of Enslavement Report: Part 1 The Taylor Report'.
14 Ibid.

34. Peabody Trust

1   'What Housing Associations Do', National Housing Federation, https://www.housing.org.uk/about-housing-associations/ what-housing-associations-do/
2   'Our History', Peabody, https://www.peabodygroup.org.uk/about-us/ our-history/
3   Ibid.
4   Cassandra Gooptar, 'The Scott Trust Legacies of Enslavement Report: Part 1 The Taylor Report', 11 December 2020, https://coilink. org/20.500.12592/zqprfr
5   Anne-Marie Angelo, 'George Peabody and Slavery', Commissioned by the Peabody Institute, Johns Hopkins University, October 2023.
6   Ibid.

7 Ibid.
8 Ibid.
9 Ibid.
10 Ibid.
11 Ibid.
12 Ibid.
13 Ibid.
14 Ibid.
15 Ibid.
16 David Christy, *Cotton is King*, Moore, Wilstach, Keys & Co., 1855, https://archive.org/details/cottoniskingorcuo1chri
17 Anne-Marie Angelo, 'George Peabody and Slavery', Commissioned by the Peabody Institute, Johns Hopkins University, October 2023.
18 Ibid.
19 David Teather, 'Bank admits it owned slaves', *Guardian*, 22 January 2005, https://www.theguardian.com/world/2005/jan/22/usa.davidteather
20 Our History', Peabody, https://www.peabodygroup.org.uk/about-us/our-history/
21 Abraham Lincoln Online, https://www.abrahamlincolnonline.org/lincoln/art/london.htm
22 'Refurbish don't demolish: the fight for the future of themesmead', Corporate Watch, 10 April 2024, https://corporatewatch.org/residents-fight-to-refurbish-homes-and-save-them-from-being-demolished/

35. The Metropolitan Police and the Conservative Party

1 'Crime and Punishment: Robert Peel – How was law enforcement changed by Sir Robert Peel's new Metropolitan Police Force?', Key Stages 4 & 5, Empire and Industry 1750–1850 Resource Pack, the National Archives, https://www.nationalarchives.gov.uk/education/resources/crime-and-punishment-robert-peel/
2 Ibid.
3 Interview with Sami Pinarbasi, *Human Resources* (podcast), season 1, episode 3, 'Lords of the Manor', 26 May 2021, Broccoli Productions., Broccoli Productions 2021.
4 Ibid.
5 Ibid.
6 Ibid.
7 Ibid.
8 Ibid.
9 Ibid.
10 'Crime and Punishment: Robert Peel', the National Archives.

11 Ben Bowling, Shruti Iyer, Robert Reiner and James Sheptycki, 'Policing: Past, Present, and Future', in Roger Matthews (ed.) *What is to Be Done About Crime and Punishment? Towards a 'Public Criminology'*, Palgrave Macmillan, 2016, pp. 123–58.

12 Ibid.

13 Ibid.

14 'Sir Robert Peel's Policing Principles', The Law Enforcement Action Partnership, https://lawenforcementactionpartnership.org/peel-policing-principles/

15 Ibid.

16 Ibid.

17 Interview with Sami Pinarbasi, *Human Resources* podcast.

18 Clive Emsley, 'Policing the Empire, Policing the Metropole: Some Thoughts on Models and Types', *Crime, Histoire & Sociétés/Crime, History & Societies*, vol. 18, no. 2, 2014, pp. 5–25, http://www.jstor.org/stable/24570700

19 Faith Ridler, 'Kemi Badenoch claims she "became working class" after securing a job at McDonald's as a teenager', Sky News, 18 September 2024, https://news.sky.com/story/kemi-badenoch-claims-she-became-working-class-after-securing-a-job-at-mcdonalds-as-a-teenager-13217266

36. Athletics

1 Matthew W. Hughey, 'Survival of the Fastest?' *Contexts*, vol. 23, no. 4, 2014, pp. 56–58.

2 Matthew W. Hughey and Devon R. Goss, 'A Level Playing Field? Media Constructions of Athletics, Genetics, and Race', *Annals of the American Academy of Political and Social Science*, vol. 661, no. 1, 2015, pp. 182–211.

3 Ibid.

4 Ibid.

5 Hughey, 'Survival of the Fastest'?

6 Ibid.

7 Ben Carrington, *Race, Sport and Politics: The Sporting Black Diaspora*, Sage Publications Ltd, 2010.

8 Hughey and Goss, 'A Level Playing Field?'

9 'Michael Johnson: Survival of the Fastest', Channel 4, 28 June 2012, https://www.youtube.com/watch?v=MIvTNXdIaBo.

10 Vinay Harpalani, 'The Athletic Dominance of African Americans – Is There a Genetic Basis?', in *African Americans in Sports*, Gary A. Sailes (ed.), Routledge, 2017, pp. 103–20.; Gary A. Sailes, 'The Myth of Black

Notes

Sports Supremacy', *Journal of Black Studies*, vol. 21, no. 4, 1991, pp. 480–87.

11 John Naish, 'Why the progeny of slaves will strike gold at the Olympics', MailOnline, 3 July 2012, https://www.dailymail.co.uk/news/article-216796/Why-progeny-slaves-strike-gold-Olympics.html.

12 Hughey and Goss, 'A Level Playing Field?'

13 Carrington, *Race, Sport and Politics*.

14 Hughey and Goss, A level playing field?

15 Jay J. Coakley, 'Sports and Politics: Can They be Kept Separate?', in *Sport in Society: Issues and Controversies*, Jay J. Coakley (ed.), fifth edition, Mosby, 1994, pp. 358–85.

16 Earl Smith, 'The Self Fulfilling Prophecy: Genetically Superior African American Athletes', *Humboldt Journal of Social Relations*, vol. 21, no. 2, 1995, pp. 139–64.

17 Ibid.

18 Orlando Patterson, *The Confounding Island: Jamaica and the Postcolonial Predicament*, Belknap Press, 2019.

19 Ibid.

20 Ibid.

21 John N. Gnida, 'Teaching "Nature" Versus "Nurture": The Case of African-American Athletic Success', *Teaching Sociology*, vol. 23, no. 4, October 1995, pp. 389–95.

22 Naish, 'Why the progeny of slaves will strike gold at the Olympics'; Sailes, 'The Myth of Black Sports Supremacy'.

23 Harpalani, 'The Athletic Dominance of African Americans'.

24 Carrington, *Race, Sport and Politics*.

25 James L. Conyers Jr, (ed.), *Race in American Sports: Essays*, McFarland, 2014.

26 Aaron Morrison, 'Serena's example: Tennis icon's impact felt in Black America', Associated Press, 26 August 2022, https://apnews.com/article/serena-williams-legacy-tennis-ee13cdc0dfaebf9d8afe51c2935622f4; Brooke Newman, 'The long history behind the racist attacks on Serena Williams', 11 September 2018, https://www.washingtonpost.com/outlook/2018/09/11/long-history-behind-racist-attacks-serena-williams/; Jenée Desmond-Harris, 'Serena Williams is constantly the target of disgusting racist an sexist attacks, https://www.vox.com/2015/3/11/8189679/serena-williams-indian-wells-racism

27 Carrington, *Race, Sport and Politics*.

28 'The impact of racism on the mental health of athletes', Accelerate Sport, https://accelerate.sport/blog-post/the-impact-of-racism-on-the-mental-health-of-athletes/; Spencer K. Myler, 'Media Exploitation of

Black Athletes: Challenges, Consequences, and Empowerment', Student Publications, 2023, https://cupola.gettysburg.edu/cgi/viewcontent. cgi?article=2166&context=student_scholarship

29 Timothy Davis, 'Racism in Athletics: Subtle Yet Persistent', *University of Arkansas at Little Rock Law Review*, vol. 21, no. 4, 1999, https:// lawrepository.ualr.edu/cgi/viewcontent. cgi?article=1594&context=lawreview

30 Hughey and Goss, 'A Level Playing Field?'

31 Hughey, 'Survival of the Fastest?'

32 Patterson, *The Confounding Island.*

37. Trains

1 Interview with Oliver Betts, *Human Resources* (podcast), season 2, episode 4, 'All Aboard', 1 February 2022, Broccoli Productions.

2 Gareth Dennis, 'Slavery and the Railways, Part 1: Acknowledging the Past', 11 September 2020, London Reconnections, https://www. londonreconnections.com/2020/ slavery-and-the-railways-part-1-acknowledging-the-past/

3 Ibid.

4 Centre for the Study of the Legacies of British Slavery, UCL database, https://www.ucl.ac.uk/lbs/commercial/view/63547350

5 Ibid.

6 Ibid.

7 Gareth Dennis, 'Slavery and the Railways, Part 1'.

8 Leigh Shaw-Taylor and Xuesheng You, 'The Development of the Railway Network in Britain 1825–1911,' 2018, https://www.campop. geog.cam.ac.uk/research/projects/transport/onlineatlas/railways.pdf

9 Ibid.

10 Ibid.

11 Ibid.

12 Interview with Oliver Betts, *Human Resources* podcast.

13 Ibid.

14 Ibid.

38. Surnames

1 Rowan Walker, 'From Ian to Kwame – why slavery made me change my name', *Guardian*, 25 March 2007, https://www.theguardian.com/ uk/2007/mar/25/humanrights.britishidentity

2 Sojourner Ahébée, 'For African Americans, DNA tests offer some answers beyond the "wall of slavery"', WHYY, https://whyy.org/ segments/tracing-your-ancestry-through-dna/

Notes

3   Walker, 'From Ian to Kwame – why slavery made me change my name'.
4   Trevor Burnard, 'Slave Naming Patterns: Onomastics and the Taxonomy of Race in Eighteenth-Century Jamaica', *Journal of Interdisciplinary History*, vol. 31, no. 3, 2001, pp. 325–46, http://www.jstor.org/stable/207085
5   Ibid.
6   'Afro-American (Slavery Era) submitted names', Behind the Name, https://www.behindthename.com/submit/names/usage/afro-american-slavery-era
7   Burnard, 'Slave Naming Patterns'.
8   Walker, 'From Ian to Kwame – why slavery made me change my name'.
9   Liz Mineo, 'How Dating Sites Automate Racism', 4 April 2024, *Harvard Gazette*, https://news.harvard.edu/gazette/story/2024/04/how-dating-sites-automate-sexual-racism/
10 Niketan Sharma, 'Dating App Statistics for 2024: Users, Revenue, Apps, & More', 4 January 2024, Nimble App Genie, https://www.nimbleappgenie.com/blogs/dating-app-statistics/
11 Burnard, 'Slave Naming Patterns: Onomastics and the Taxonomy of Race in Eighteenth-Century Jamaica.'
12 Ibid.

39. Holiday Resorts
1   Sundance Villa, The Tryall Club in Jamaica, https://sundancejamaica.com/the-tryall-club-in-jamaica/#:~:text=A%20former%20sugar%20cane%20plantation,a%20rich%20and%20colorful%20history.
2   'The Tryall Club: Villas of Distinction', *Business View Caribbean*, 24 July 2017, https://businessviewcaribbean.com/the-tryall-club-villas-of-distinction/
3   'The Great House, Antigua, https://www.thehotelguru.com/hotel/the-great-house-antigua-antigua; James Henderson, 'The Caribbean hotels giving a fresh perspective on the past', *Telegraph*, 5 November 2020, https://www.telegraph.co.uk/travel/destinations/caribbean/articles/antigua-barbados-plantation-hotels/
4   Ann Abel, 'The hottest new-old resort in the Caribbean: Sugar Beach in St. Lucia', *Forbes*, 15 April 2013, https://www.forbes.com/sites/annabel/2013/04/15/the-hottest-new-old-resort-in-the-caribbean-sugar-beach-in-st-lucia/
5   Jill Fergus, 'Colonial Caribbean: a step back in time', NBC News, 10 March 2009, https://www.nbcnews.com/id/wbna29471992
6   'Montpelier History' Montpelier Nevis, https://montpeliernevis.com/montpelier-history/

7 Robert C. Ritchie, *The Lure of the Beach: A Global History*, University of California Press, 2023.
8 Ibid.
9 Ibid.
10 Ibid.
11 Krista A. Thompson, *An Eye for the Tropics: Tourism, Photography, and Framing the Caribbean Picturesque*, Duke University Press, 2006.
12 Ibid. See also chapter 27, 'Voodoo Dolls', and listen to the following *Human Resources* episodes on health and medicine: season 3, episode 1, 'Inventing Race', 4 September 2023; season 3, episode 2, 'Hippocrits', 11 September 2023; and season 3, episode 3, 'The Dis-carded', 18 September 2023, Broccoli Productions.
13 Ibid.
14 Renée Landell, 'Why we need to stop thinking of the Caribbean as a tourist "paradise"', *Conversation*, 11 August 2021, https://theconversation.com/why-we-need-to-stop-thinking-of-the-caribbean-as-a-tourist-paradise-162978
15 Thompson, *An Eye for the Tropics*.
16 Ibid.
17 Michael J. Hawkins, 'Tourism and Place in Treasure Beach, Jamaica: Imagining Paradise and the Alternative', Louisiana State University and Agricultural & Mechanical College, 1999, https://repository.lsu.edu/gradschool_disstheses/7044/
18 See also chapter 17, 'Mahogany'.
19 Thompson, *An Eye for the Tropics*.
20 Hawkins, 'Tourism and Place in Treasure Beach'.
21 'Caribbean Tourism Experiences Strong Growth in 2023, Recovery to Continue into 2024', Caribbean. Tourism Organization, https://www.onecaribbean.org/caribbean-tourism-experiences-strong-growth-in-2023-recovery-to-continue-into-2024/#:~:text=%E2%80%9CBased%20on%20preliminary%20data%20provided,a%20continuous%20growth%20trend%20over
22 Wendy Sealy, 'From Colonialism to Transnationalism: The Neo-colonial Structure of Caribbean Tourism', *Journal on Tourism and Sustainability*, vol. 1, no. 2, 2018, pp. 81–92.
23 Sealy, 'From Colonialism to Transnationalism'; Polly Pattullo, *Last Resorts: The Cost of Tourism in the Caribbean*, New York University Press, 2005; Mimi Sheller, *Consuming the Caribbean: From Arawaks to Zombies*, Routledge, 2003.
24 Sealy, 'From Colonialism to Transnationalism'.

Notes

25 Gavan Titley, 'Global Theory and Touristic Encounters', *Irish Communications Review*, vol. 8, no. 1, 2000.

26 Sealy, 'From Colonialism to Transnationalism'; Polly Pattullo, *Last Resorts*.

27 Sealy, 'From Colonialism to Transnationalism'; Sheller, *Consuming the Caribbean*.

28 Ritchie, *The Lure of the Beach*; Sheller, *Consuming the Caribbean*; Landell, 'Why we need to stop thinking of the Caribbean as a tourist "paradise"'.

29 Henrice Altink, 'Out of Place: Race and Color in Jamaican Hotels, 1962–2020', *New West Indian Guide/Nieuwe West-Indische Gids*, vol. 95, no. 3–4, 2021, pp. 254–87.

30 Titley, 'Global Theory and Touristic Encounters'.

31 Sealy, 'From Colonialism to Transnationalism'.

32 Ibid.

33 Ibid.

34 Sheller, *Consuming the Caribbean*; Ysabel Muñoz Martínez, 'Swimming with trash in the Caribbean', *Edge Effects*, 19 May 2022, https://edgeeffects.net/caribbean-wastescapes/

35 Sheller, *Consuming the Caribbean*.

36 Titley, 'Global Theory and Touristic Encounters'; Karen Wilkes, *Whiteness, Weddings, and Tourism in the Caribbean: Paradise for Sale*, Palgrave Macmillan, 2016.

37 Pattullo, *Last Resorts*; Wilkes, *Whiteness, Weddings, and Tourism*.

38 Landell, 'Why we need to stop thinking of the Caribbean as a tourist "paradise"'

39 Sheller, *Consuming the Caribbean*.

40 Kenneth G. Kelly, 'Sugar Plantations in the French West Indies: Archaeological Perspectives from Guadeloupe and Martinique' in *Archaeological Perspectives on the French in the New World*, Elizabeth M. Scott (ed.), University Press of Florida, 2017.

Select Bibliography

Akerman, James R. (ed.), *The Imperial Map: Cartography and the Mastery of Empire*, University of Chicago Press, 2009.

Alford, B. W. E., *W. D. and H. O. Wills and the Development of the UK Tobacco Industry 1786–1965*, Routledge, 1973.

Allewaert, Monique, *Ariel's Eology: Plantations, Personhood, and Colonialism in the American Tropics*, University of Minnesota Press, 2013.

Anderson, Jennifer L., *Mahogany: The Costs of Luxury in Early America*, Harvard University Press, 2012.

Annapoorani, S. G., 'Introduction to Denim', in *Sustainability in Denim*, Subramanian Senthilkannan Muthu (ed.), Woodhead Publishing, 2017.

Arabindan-Kesson, Anna, *Black Bodies, White Gold: Art, Cotton, and Commerce in the Atlantic World*, Duke University Press, 2021.

Armitage, Natalie, 'European and African Figural Ritual Magic: The Beginnings of the Voodoo Doll Myth', in *The Materiality of Magic: An Artifactual Investigation into Ritual Practices and Popular Beliefs*, Ceri Houlbrook and Natalie Armitage (eds), Oxbow Books, 2015.

Ashby, Jack, *Black Atlantic: Power, People, Resistance*, Jake Subryan Richards and Victoria Avery (eds), Bloomsbury (exhibition catalogue), 2023.

Bagneris, Mia L., *Colouring the Caribbean: Race and the Art of Agostino Brunias*, Manchester University Press, 2018.

Bahar, Matthew R., *Storm of the Sea: Indians and Empires in the Atlantic's Age of Sail*, Oxford University Press, 2018.

Ball, Philip, *Bright Earth: The Invention of Colour*, Vintage, 2008.

Bédat, Maxine, *Unraveled: The Life and Death of a Garment*, Portfolio, 2021.

Select Bibliography

Bialuschewski, Arne, *Raiders and Natives: Cross-Cultural Relations in the Age of Buccaneers*, University of Georgia Press, 2022.

Bibb, Henry, *Narrative of the Life and Adventures of Henry Bibb, An American Slave, Written by Himself*, with an introduction by Lucius C. Matlack, 1849.

Boaz, Danielle N., *Voodoo: The History of a Racial Slur*, Oxford University Press, 2023.

Boddy, Kasia, *Boxing: A Cultural History*, Reaktion Books, 2009.

Bond, Emma, and Michael Morris (eds), *Scotland's Transnational Heritage: Legacies of Empire and Slavery*, Edinburgh University Press, 2023.

Bosma, Ulbe, *The World of Sugar: How the Sweet Stuff Transformed our Politics, Health and Environment over 2,000 Years*, Belknap Press, 2023.

Brown, Vincent, *The Reaper's Garden: Death and Power in the World of Atlantic Slavery*, Harvard University Press, 2008.

Buckridge, Steeve, *The Language of Dress: Resistance and Accommodation in Jamaica, 1750–1890*, University of West Indies Press, 2004.

Carney, Judith, *In the Shadow of Slavery: Africa's Botanical Legacy in the Atlantic World*, University of California Press, 2010.

Carrington, Ben, *Race, Sport and Politics: The Sporting Black Diaspora*, Sage Publications Ltd, 2010.

Chakrabarti, Pratik, 'Medical Botany in Jamaican Plantations', in *Materials and Medicine: Trade, Conquest and Therapeutics in the Eighteenth Century'*, Manchester University Press, 2017.

Chirimuuta, Mazviita, *Outside Color: Perceptual Science and the Puzzle of Color in Philosophy*, The MIT Press, 2016.

Clarkson, Thomas, *The History of the Rise, Progress, and Accomplishment of the Abolition of the African Slave-Trade by the British Parliament*, 2 vols, London, L. Taylor, 1808, vol. 1.

Coakley, Jay J., 'Sports and Politics: Can They be Kept Separate?', in *Sport in Society: Issues and Controversies*, Jay J. Coakley (ed.), fifth edition, Mosby, 1994.

Coe, Sophie D., and Michael D. Coe, *The True History of Chocolate*, Thames and Hudson, 1996.

Collins, Tony, *How Football Began: A Global History of How the World's Football Codes were Born*, Routledge, 2018.

Considine, John, *Academy Dictionaries 1600–1800*, Cambridge University Press, 2014.

Considine, John, 'The Unfinished Business of Eighteenth-Century European Lexicography', in Sarah Oglivie and Gabriella Safran (eds), *The Whole World in a Book: Dictionaries in the Nineteenth Century*, Oxford University Press, 2020.

Conyers Jr, James L., (ed.), *Race in American Sports: Essays*, McFarland, 2014.

Deetz, Kelley Fanto, 'Stolen Bodies, Edible Memories: The Influence and Function of West African Foodways in the Early British Atlantic,' in *The Routledge History of Food*, Carol Helstosky (ed.), Routledge, 2014.

Dew, Nicholas, 'Vers la ligne: Circulating Measurements Around the French Atlantic', in *Science and Empire in the Atlantic World*, James Delbourgo and Nicholas Dew (eds), Routledge, 2008.

Drummond, Barb, *The Midas of Manumission: The Orphan Samuel Gist and his Virginian Slaves*, Barb Drummond, 2018.

Du Bois, W. E. B., *The Souls of Black Folk* (1903), Oxford World's Classics, 2008.

Eaton, Natasha, *Colour, Art and Empire: Visual Culture and the Nomadism of Representation*, I. B. Tauris, 2013.

Edney, Matthew H., *Mapping an Empire: The Geographical Construction of British India, 1765–1843*, University of Chicago Press, 1997.

Equiano, Olaudah, *The Interesting Narrative of the Life of Olaudah Equiano or Gustava Vassa, The African by Himself* (1789).

Evans, Chris, *Slave Wales: The Welsh and Atlantic Slavery, 1660–1850*, University of Wales Press, 2010.

Fanthorpe, Lionel and Patricia, *Mysteries and Secrets of Voodoo, Santeria, and Obeah*, Dundurn, 2008.

Fend, Mechthild, 'Introduction', in *Fleshing Out Surfaces: Skin in French Art and Medicine, 1650–1850*, Manchester University Press, 2016.

Fenner, Thomas P., (ed.) *Religious Folk Songs of the Negro as Sung on the Plantations*, Hampton, 1909.

Fox, James, *The World According to Colour: A Cultural History*, Penguin Books, 2023.

Freedgood, Elaine, 'Souvenirs of Sadism: Mahogany Furniture, Deforestation, and Slavery in Jane Eyre', in *The Ideas in Things: Fugitive Meaning in the Victorian Novel*, University of Chicago Press, 2006.

Green, Toby, *A Fistful of Shells: West Africa from the Rise of the Slave Trade to the Age of Revolution*, Penguin, 2019.

Grivetti, Louis Evan, and Howard-Yana Shapiro (eds), *Chocolate: History, Culture and Heritage*, John Wiley & Sons, 2009.

Herschthal, Eric, *The Science of Abolition: How Slaveholders Became the Enemies of Progress*, Yale University Press, 2021.

Jablonski, Nina G., *Living Color: The Biological and Social Meaning of Skin Color*, University of California Press, 2014.

Select Bibliography

Jenner, Greg, *Dead Famous: An Unexpected History of Celebrity from Bronze Age to Silver Screen*, Weidenfeld & Nicolson, 2020.

Karras, Alan L., 'The Caribbean Region: Crucible for Modern World History', Cambridge University Press (published online, May 2015, DOI:10.1017/CBO9781139194594.017).

Kennedy, Dane, *Mungo Park's Ghost: The Haunted Hubris of British Explorers in Nineteenth-century Africa*, Cambridge University Press, 2024.

Kennedy, David, *A Social and Political History of Everton and Liverpool Football Clubs*, Routledge, 2019.

Kennedy, David, *The Man Who Created Merseyside Football: John Houlding, Founding Father of Liverpool and Everton*, Rowman & Littlefield, 2020.

King, Tiffany Lethabo, *The Black Shoals: Offshore Formations of Black and Native Studies*, Duke University Press, 2019.

Knight, Frederick. 'In an Ocean of Blue: West African Indigo Workers in the Atlantic World to 1800', in *Diasporic Africa: A Reader*, Michael A. Gomez (ed.), New York University Press, 2006.

Kuhn, Mary, *The Garden Politic: Global Plants and Botanical Nationalism in Nineteenth-Century America*, New York University Press, 2023.

Kumar, Prakash, *Indigo Plantations and Science in Colonial India*, Cambridge University Press, 2012.

Lane, Kris, and Arne Bialuschewski (eds), *Piracy in the Early Modern Era: An Anthology of Sources*, Hackett Publishing, 2019.

Little, Benerson, *Pirate Hunting: The Fight Against Pirates, Privateers, and Sea Raiders from Antiquity to the Present*, Potomac Books, 2010.

Matthews, Roger (ed.), *What is to Be Done About Crime and Punishment? Towards a 'Public Criminology'*, Palgrave Macmillan, 2016.

McDonald, Kevin P., *Pirates, Merchants, Settlers, and Slaves: Colonial America and the Indo-Atlantic World*, University of California Press, 2015.

McDougall, Alan, *Contested Fields: A Global History of Modern Football*, University of Toronto Press, 2020.

Miller, Kei, *The Cartographer Tries to Map a Way to Zion*, Carcanet, 2014.

Millman, Liz, in *Woven Histories of Welsh Wool and Slavery*, Charlotte Hammond and Laura Moseley (eds), trans. Elin Meek, Common Threads Press, E-book, 2023.

Mintz, Sidney W., *Sweetness and Power: The Place of Sugar in Modern History*, Penguin Books, 1986.

Moody, Jessica, *The Persistence of Memory: Remembering Slavery in*

Liverpool, 'Slaving Capital of the World', Liverpool University Press, 2020.

Moore, Louis, *I Fight for a Living: Boxing and the Battle for Black Manhood 1880–1915*, University of Illinois Press, illustrated edition, 2017.

Mugglestone, Lynda, *Dictionaries: A Very Short Introduction*, Oxford University Press, 2011.

Murray, Donald S., *Herring Tales: How the Silver Darlings Shaped Human Taste And History*, Bloomsbury Publishing, 2016.

Newman, Brooke, *A Dark Inheritance: Blood, Race, and Sex in Colonial Jamaica*, Yale University Press, 2018.

Ogilvie, Sarah, and Gabriella Safran (eds), *The Whole World in a Book: Dictionaries in the Nineteenth Century*, Oxford University Press, 2019.

Owens, Deirdre Cooper, *Medical Bondage: Race, Gender, and the Origins of American Gynecology*, University of Georgia Press, 2017.

Paton, Diana (ed.), *A Narrative of Events, since the First of August, 1834, by James Williams, an Apprenticed Labourer in Jamaica*, Duke University Press, 2001.

Paton, Diana, *The Cultural Politics of Obeah: Religion, Colonialism and Modernity in the Caribbean World*, Cambridge University Press, 2015.

Patterson, Orlando, *The Confounding Island: Jamaica and the Postcolonial Predicament*, Belknap Press, 2019.

Pattullo, Polly, *Last Resorts: The Cost of Tourism in the Caribbean*, New York University Press, 2005.

Perry, Victoria. *A Bittersweet Heritage: Slavery, Architecture and the British Landscape*, Hurst Publishers, 2022.

Poskett, James, *Horizons: A Global History of Science*, Penguin Books, 2022.

Priya, Satia, *Empire of Guns: The Violent Making of the Industrial Revolution*, Prelude Books, 2018.

Rediker, Marcus, *Villains of All Nations: Atlantic Pirates in the Golden Age*, Beacon Press, 2004.

Ribeyrol, Charlotte, Matthew Winterbottom and Madeline Hewitson (eds), *Colour Revolution: Victorian Art, Fashion & Design*, Ashmolean Museum, 2023.

Rice, Tony, *Voyages of Discovery: Three Centuries of Natural History Exploration*, Clarkson Potter, 1999.

Rice, Tony, *Voyages of Discovery: A Visual Celebration of Ten of the Greatest Natural History Expeditions*, Natural History Museum, 2017.

Richardson, David, Anthony Tibbles and Suzanne Schwarz (eds), *Liverpool and Transatlantic Slavery*, Liverpool University Press, 2007.

Select Bibliography

Riello, Giorgio, *Cotton: The Fabric that Made the Modern World*, Cambridge University Press, 2013.

Ritchie, Robert C., *The Lure of the Beach: A Global History*, University of California Press, 2023.

Ritchie, Robert C., 'Government Measures against Piracy and Privateering in the Atlantic Area, 1750–1850', in *Pirates and Privateers: New Perspectives on the War on Trade in the Eighteenth and Nineteenth Centuries*, University of Exeter Press, 1997

Rosenthal, Caitlin, *Accounting for Slavery: Masters and Management*, Harvard University Press, 2018.

Scanlon, Padraic X., *Slave Empire: How Slavery Built Modern Britain*, Robinson, 2020.

Sailes, Gary A. (ed.), *African Americans in Sports*, Routledge, 2017.

St Clair, Kassia, *The Secret Lives of Colour*, John Murray, 2017.

Schaffer, Simon, 'Golden Means: Assay Instruments and the Geography of Precision in the Guinea Trade', in *Instruments, Travel and Science: Itineraries of Precision from the Seventeenth to the Twentieth Century*, Marie-Noëlle Bourguet, Christian Licoppe and H. Otto Sibum (eds), Routledge, 2002.

Schaffer, Simon, Lissa Roberts, Kapil Raj and James Delbourgo (eds), *The Brokered World: Go-Betweens and Global Intelligence, 1770–1820*, Science History Publications, 2009.

van Schendel, Willem, 'The Social Locations of Colonial Knowledge: Indigo in Bengal, Java and Senegal', in *Across Colonial Lines*, Devyani Gupta and Purba Hossain (eds), Bloomsbury Publishing, 2023.

Schiebinger, Londa L., *Plants and Empire: Colonial Bioprospecting in the Atlantic World*, Harvard University Press, E-book, 2004.

Sheller, Mimi, *Consuming the Caribbean: From Arawaks to Zombies*, Routledge, 2003.

Scott, Elizabeth M., (ed.), *Archaeological Perspectives on the French in the New World*, University Press of Florida, 2017.

Simon, Rebecca, *The Pirates' Code: Laws and Life Aboard Ship*, Reaktion Books, 2024.

Taussig, Michael T., *What Color Is the Sacred?*, University of Chicago Press, 2009.

Thompson, Krista A., *An Eye for the Tropics: Tourism, Photography, and Framing the Caribbean Picturesque*, Duke University Press, 2006.

Vargas, Jonas, 'Charque and Tasajo (Salt-Cured Beef) as an Atlantic Commodity in the 18th and 19th Centuries', Oxford University Press (published online October 2023, Oxford Research Encyclopedias, Latin American History, doi.org/10.1093/acrefore/9780199366439.013.1089).

Walker, Rowan, 'From Ian to Kwame – why slavery made me change my name', *Guardian*, 25 March 2007.

Walvin, James, *Slavery in Small Things: Slavery and Modern Cultural Habits*, John Wiley & Sons, 2017.

Welsh, Sarah Lawson, *Food, Text and Culture in the Anglophone Caribbean*, Rowman & Littlefield, 2019.

Wharton, David, Carole Patricia Biggam et al. (eds), *A Cultural History of Color*, vols 1 to 6, Bloomsbury Academic, 2021.

Wheeler, Roxann, *The Complexion of Race: Categories of Difference in Eighteenth-Century British Culture*, Philadelphia: University of Pennsylvania Press, 2010.

Wilkes, Karen. *Whiteness, Weddings, and Tourism in the Caribbean: Paradise for Sale*, New York: Palgrave Macmillan, 2016.

Whyte, Iain, *Scotland and the Abolition of Black Slavery, 1756–1838*, Edinburgh University Press, 2006.

Acknowledgements

When I first started working on the Human Resources podcast, I knew a book had to be part of this project. To make the history accessible, we had to give people different mediums to access it. Without the podcast, this book would not exist and for that reason I would like to thank all those who were part of bringing the podcast to life, including every guest who was so willing to give us their time and knowledge. I must shout out to Tony Phillips for developing the idea with me, my book co-writer Arisa Loomba and Dr Alison Bennett for their tireless research and care in bringing underused voices to the forefront. Rory Boyle who was our production assistant on all three seasons. Benjamin Yellowitz for trying something new and experimenting with our sound design, Lucy Carr and Cassandra Greenberg for providing additional production support and, of course, Moya Lothian-McLean whose voice and words helped spring the podcast to life.

Without Caleh Singleton and Cecily Gayford I would never have been brave enough to tackle a history book. Jon Petre for helping my words make sense and giving the pep when needed and truly enjoying working with us. Everyone at Profile Books has been a dream and made this process exciting and challenging, in all the right ways. I'd also like to thank Alex Bewley and Matilda Forbes Watson from WME, both made the impossible possible and their belief in my company, Broccoli Productions and me opened many doors I didn't think was possible. Danielle 'Berry' Sykes and Twila Dang for the group chat hype and just knowing that I could do this before I even knew I could. Lauren Eisen, you were a gift and helped me in the early stages of book research and uncovering excellent people to interview. The academics who I interviewed for this book, I'm so grateful for your time and warm conversation.

Most importantly, the belief I have that I can do anything, including

313

co-writing this book, comes from my mother, without her instilling delusion within me I have no idea where I would be now. And finally, thanks to my stepdad Simon for always having a good, supportive chat with me whenever I have a crazy idea. I hope this book is tangible evidence for my girls that anything is possible.

RR

I would like to thank Dr Alison Bennett for being the most wonderful research partner for three seasons of the podcast. I loved our team of two. Working with you was an honour and a privilege, and I enjoyed every moment of it. Thank you for your continued support and cheerleading ever since. I would not have been able to finish researching and writing this book without the unwavering support and encouragement of my parents and my sister, who is an extension of myself. Helena, your ceaseless care and patience, putting up with the nightmare I could be during the months of writing and greeting me at the other end, was what kept me going. I am thankful for friends and family whose excitement motivated me, to all the teachers of history over the years who have ignited my imagination, and to Oana, without whom I would have had no idea how to do this. Lastly, I am so grateful to all the academics we spoke to in the process of making both the podcast and the book (there are far too many to name them all). For their willingness and enthusiasm to share their innovative and exciting research with us, the readers and listeners, and to join us on our pursuit to share knowledge with a wider audience.

AL

Index

Index

Index

Index

Newfoundland 126
Newgate prison, London 107
Newton, Isaac 41, 92–7, 155
Nicaragua 75, 168
Niger river 209–10
Nîmes, France 47
nkisi nkondi 179–80
Northwestern University 198
Nott, Josiah 101–2
Nottingham Castle,
    Nottinghamshire 112
Nova Scotia 118, 126
Novar Estate, Demerara 154

O

Oakden, Benjamin 217
Obeah 180, 181–3
Observer 219
Offiah, Martin 195
Oglethorpe, James 106
Ohio, United States 64
OkCupid 250
Olmec people 75
Olympic Games
    1936 Berlin 234
    2012 London 233
    2024 Paris 102
Omani Empire (1696–1856) 210, 211
orchids 79–80
Osbourne, George 55
Osnaburg 51
Oswald family 119–20
Owens, Jesse 234
Oxford English Dictionary 153

P

Pacific Islanders 148
palm oil 24, 149
palo wood 41
Paltrow, Gwyneth 254
Panama 169

Paris Olympics (2024) 102
Park, Mungo 209–10, 212
Paton, Diana 185–8
Patterson, Orlando 237–8
Paul, Helen 32, 34
Peabody, George 220–26
Peel, Robert 227–32
Pemberton Valley estate, Jamaica
    119–20
Penistone cloth 50
pepperpot 127
Perkin, William Henry 40
Peru 89, 115, 148
Peter, Daniel 78
Peterloo Massacre (1819) 216
Petiver, James 84, 89–90
Pew Research Center 102–3
philanthropy 220–21, 225
Philip II, King of Spain 111–12
Philippines 115
Philips, George 218
Philips, Robert 217, 218
physical abuse 17
Pinarbasi, Sami 228, 230
Plantation Union 131
policing 8, 32, 144, 227–32
polio 99
polygenesis theory 102
Portugal 2–3, 21, 76, 78, 167
Potter, Richard 218
Potter, Thomas 218
Powys, Wales 132
press gangs 163–4
Principia (Newton) 92–3, 95
privateers 167
pubs 160–64
Puerto Rico 139
Pullein, Samuel 218

Q

Quakers 11, 188

Index

Slave Trade Act (1807) 10, 128, 170, 205

Slavery Abolition Act (1833) 10, 46, 71, 205
  apprenticeships and 184, 187
  compensation and 70, 119, 136–7, 145, 161
  sugar industry and 59–60
  Underground Railroad and 198

Slavery Compensation Act (1837) 70, 119, 136–7, 145, 161

Sloane Square, Chelsea 90

Sloane, Hans 84, 87–91, 94, 254

Smeathman, Henry 85

Society for the Promotion of Christian Knowledge 106

Soft Drinks Industry Levy 55

'Sold Off to Georgy' 192

Somalia 170

Souls of Black Folk, The (Du Bois) 191

South Carolina Colony (1629–1776) 39–40, 108

South China Sea 171

South Sea Company 15, 30, 32–3, 35, 69–70, 94

Sowemimo, Annabel 100–101, 103

Spain 3–4, 30, 32–3, 70, 75, 78, 167

Spanish Town, Jamaica 93

Speke, John 210, 212

spirituals 190–95

Sport England 137

St Croix 145

St Domingo's FC 146

St Kitts and Nevis 4, 149, 162, 164

St Lucia 129, 183, 254

St Petersburg, Russia 132

St Vincent 82–3, 129, 139

Storer, Arthur 95

Strauss, Levi 47

Stuart dynasty 27–30, 32

Sturge, Joseph 188

Sugar Beach Resort, St Lucia 254

Suriname 79–80, 131, 145, 156

Survival of the Fastest (2012 documentary) 233, 235

Swim England 137

T

tabernae 160

Tacky's Revolt (1760) 181

Tahiti 83, 96

Tain, Highland 128

Taino people 112

Tamworth Manifesto (1834) 228

tartan 53

Taylor, John Edward 216–19

Tembo, George 212

textiles 45, 50

Thames River Police 229

Thamesmead Estate, London 225

Thistlewood, Thomas 84

Thornton, Henry 71

Thornton, Samuel 71–2

Times, The 216

tobacco 119–20

Tobago 114, 129, 183

Tony's Chocolonely 134

torture 181, 186–7, 203–4

tourism 253–60

Treaty of Utrecht (1713) 33

Triangular Trade 4, 130

Trinidad 12, 77, 129, 183

Tryall Club, Jamaica 253

Turnbull, Ivor 195

23andMe 247

Tyley, John 83

Tyrian purple 41

U

Underground Railroad 198–9

undocumented workers 17